The Muncy Historical Society

Presents

The retrospective art work
of

Bruce Storm

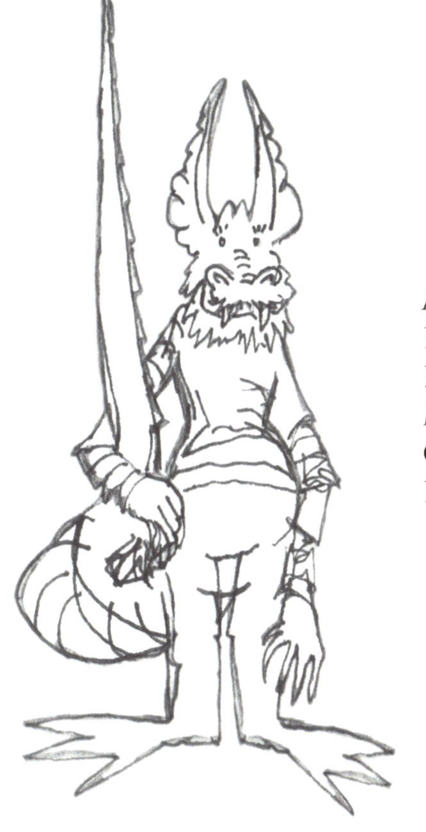

As it preserves our heritage through his unique imagination, humor and elegant complex style. Storm epitomizes the Muncy Historical Society's goal of shaping the present by interpreting the past.

Front Cover image:

Suppertime

The temperature begins to drop as the sky darkens slightly--the aroma of "Dragon Chow" fills his every thought. Off in the distance a familiar voice calls, "Suppertime!"

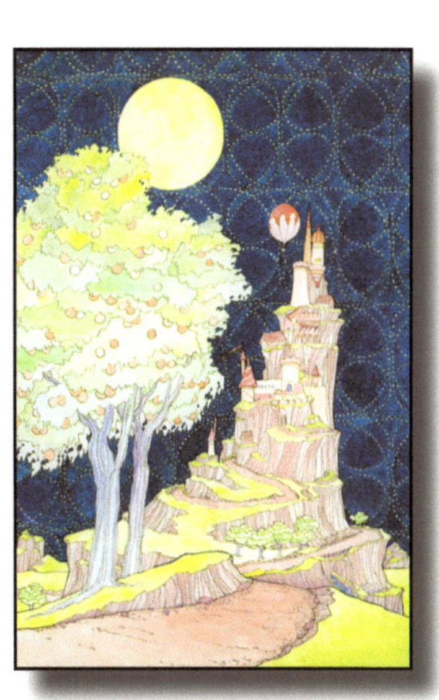

Preparing to Launch

DEDICATION

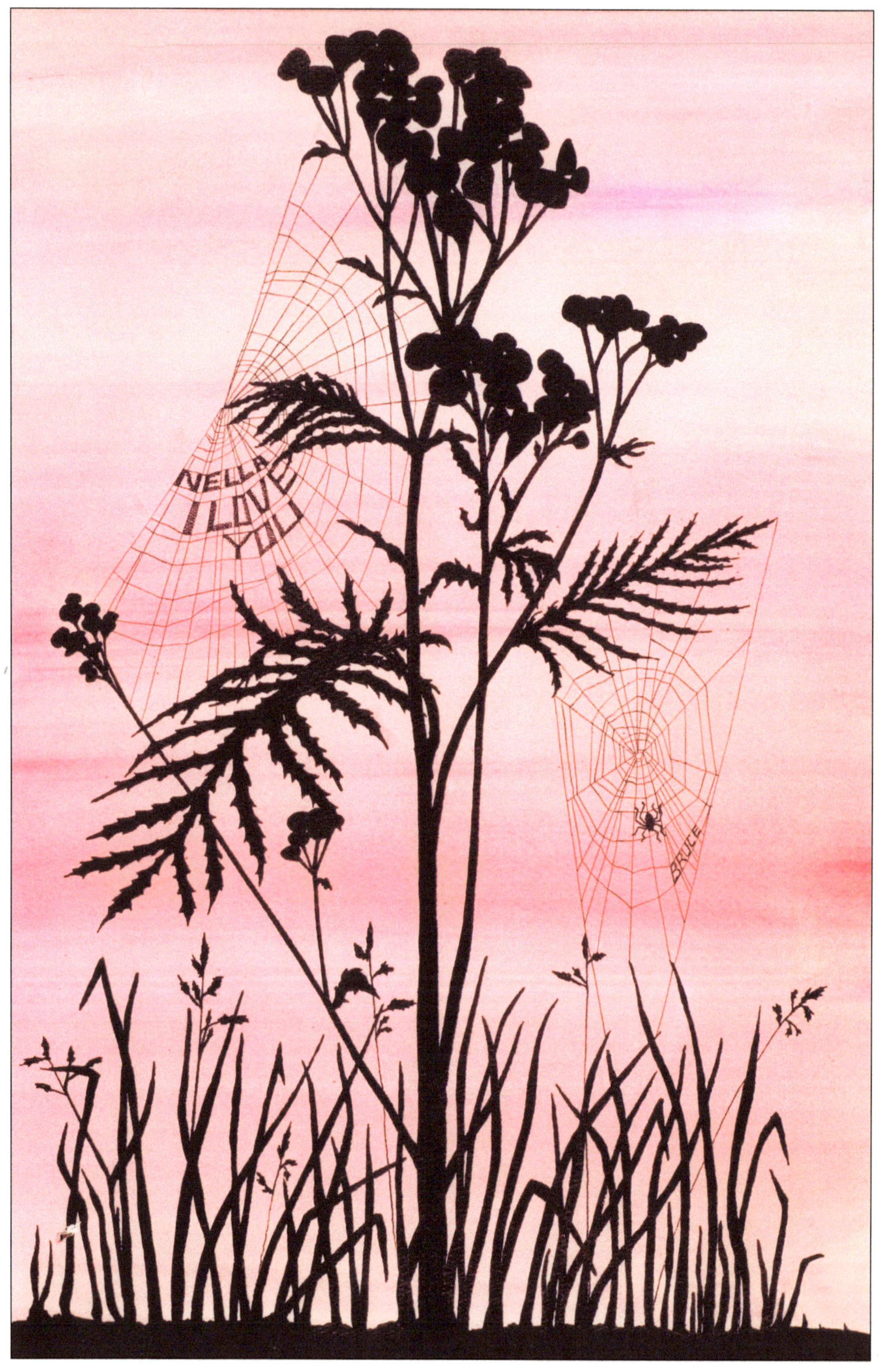

FOR NELLA,
WHOSE BOUNDLESS PATIENCE AND UNDERSTANDING MADE THIS PROJECT POSSIBLE. YOU ARE MY CONSTANT COMPANION, INSPIRATION AND CHAMPION. WITH MY UNENDING LOVE, BRUCE

Bruce James Storm was born in Palmerton, Pa., the second of five children. Working as a paper boy to help support the family, Storm's most constant companion on those 5:00 A.M. long walks was his active imagination. It was not until Bruce graduated from Penn State University after studying commercial art and art education, that he began to find his voice, or perhaps some might say his dragon voice. Working as a cartoonist for Werner films Storm still felt that his images were too atypical for the gallery market. He feared that people might assume that his work was drug inspired. He was not at all involved in the drug scene, so he rarely showed his drawings or paintings even to friends. When Bruce returned to Pennsylvania after three years in California, he brought back with him a uniquely inspired sense of color and love for bold patterns. This combined with his Pa. Dutch heritage recalled those images his Mother created in her quilt making. Eventually these meshed and became the complex skies that so often mesmerize the viewers in Storm's work.

Intensely private Bruce draws inspiration from landscapes and cityscapes. Bucks Co., PA., where Storm lived in Center Bridge, a community just up river from New Hope, and the farm of friends Claire and David in Pineville have remained inspirational. Perhaps the greatest source for his art are the hills and farms that surround Muncy, Pa., where the artist and his wife Nella have lived for more than thirty years. Yearly treks to the tiny island of Campobello, N. B., Canada, and Lubec, Maine, produce much of the work featuring ships and bold coasts of Quoddy Head State Park. Using only Arches 100% rag paper Storm personally selects each hand made sheet in Paris. Drawing on location during trips to China, France, England, Germany, and other exotic spots, Bruce says that the magic begins long before paint ever hits the paper. Settings inspire visions of the unseen world; the world that eludes those who hurry past or speed down the interstates. A world where the benevolent dragons disguise themselves so they can gain ever closer access to castles only for the pleasure of hearing children laugh or sing; this world of the sandman, brilliant cats, skateboarding dragons, and of sleeping soldiers who, like so many of us, miss the wondrous events that transpire. These are but a part of Storm's aesthetic reality that often takes place as a huge moon, Storm's symbol for himself, smiles from above. His students, brothers and sisters, his wife Nella Godbey Storm, their dogs, neighbors, and friends inspire or simply appear reincarnated in his art. Lycoming and Bucks County residents serve as inspiration in paintings that read on three levels: first artistic, then humor, then philosophical. Pattern, color, craftsmanship, and imagination combined with strong symbolic compositions are integral parts of Storm's painting. Working in acrylic washes he applies paint often ten layers until the spectacular effects are achieved.

Bruce Storm has shown his work in Long Beach Island, New Jersey, New Hope, State College, Williamsport, the Penn State University at Altoona, Pittsburgh, Flourtown, and the Philadelphia areas of Pennsylvania. Bruce Storm has Illustrated text books, and he has worked in clay, and various sculptural materials, but the vast body of his work is in watercolor and acrylic wash. Now 65, Bruce resides with his wife and dogs in their home which was featured in Colonial Homes magazine. There he maintains his studio surrounded by his vast garden where he feeds the birds, squirrels, chipmunks, and the occasional dragon.

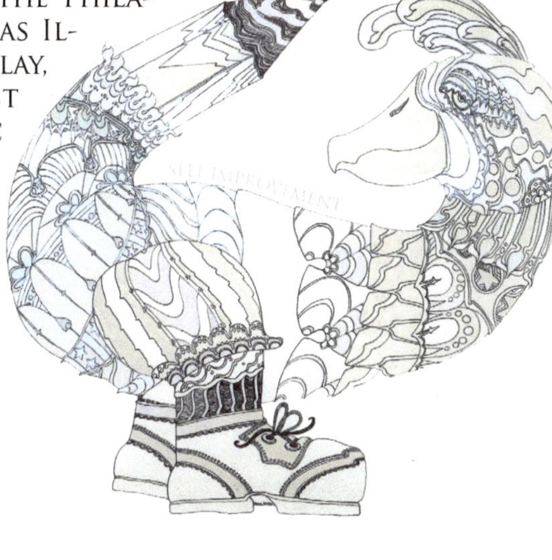

HERE YOU ENTER MY WORLD OF LOVING DRAGONS, MAGICAL SKIES AND INFINITE POSSIBILITIES....

BRUCE STORM

Night View

Everyone thought his imagination most keen, his detail superb, his fantasy unique. They did not bother to come down to the water for the night view!

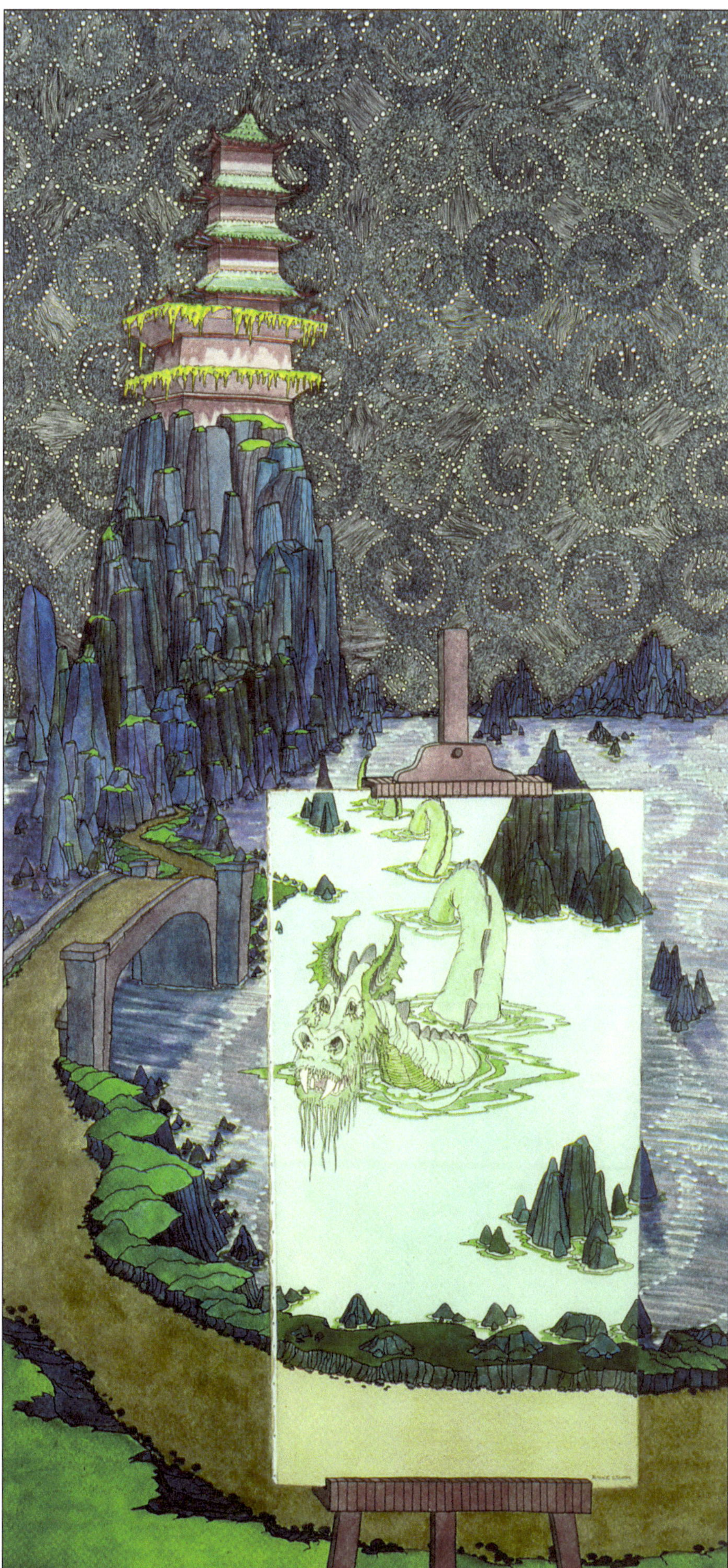

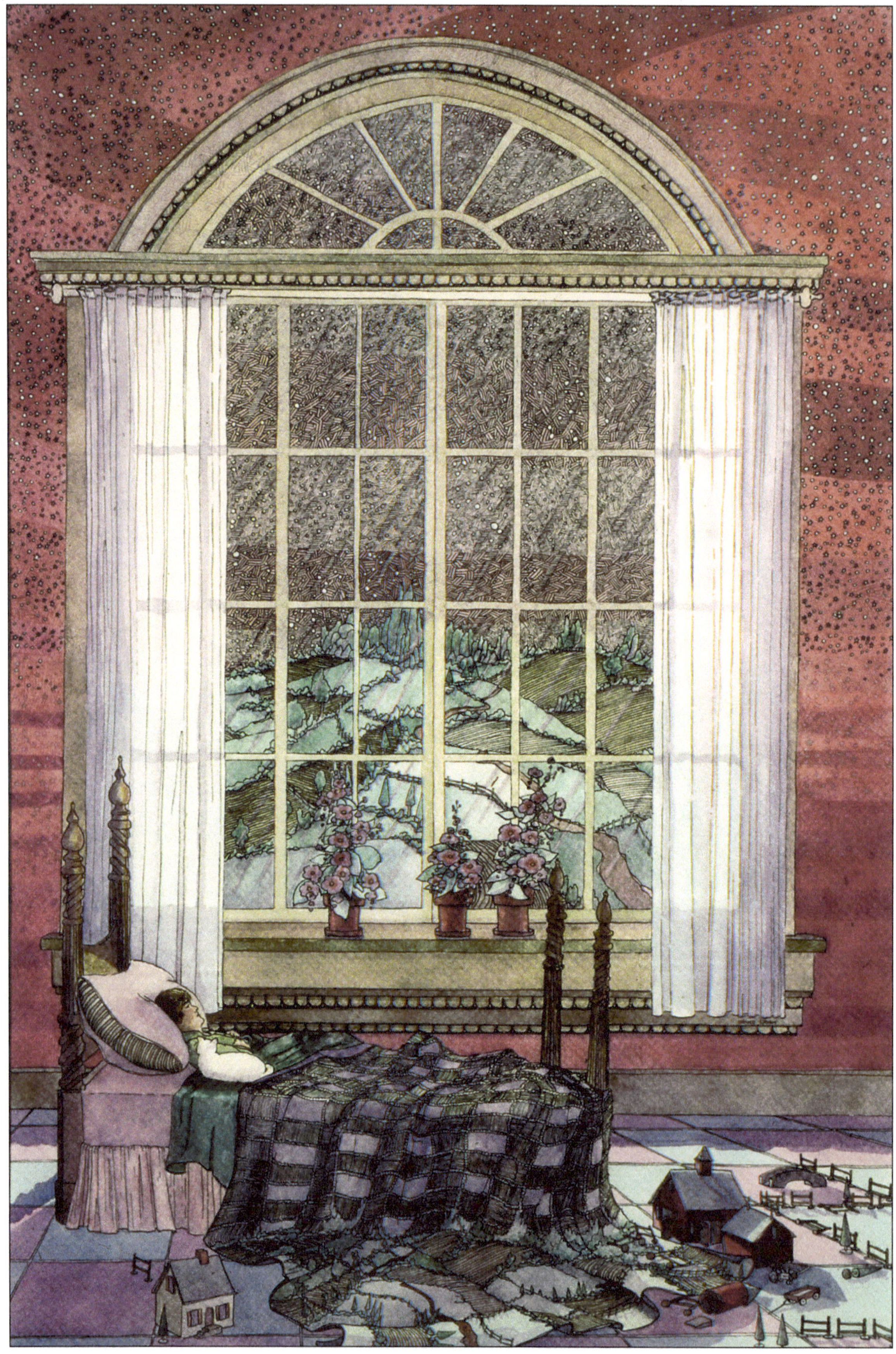

Dream Quilt

Warm and comfortable in their bed, the boy and cat are unaware that the toys he has been playing with are becoming the landscape outside his window. Even as they dream, his play becomes reality.

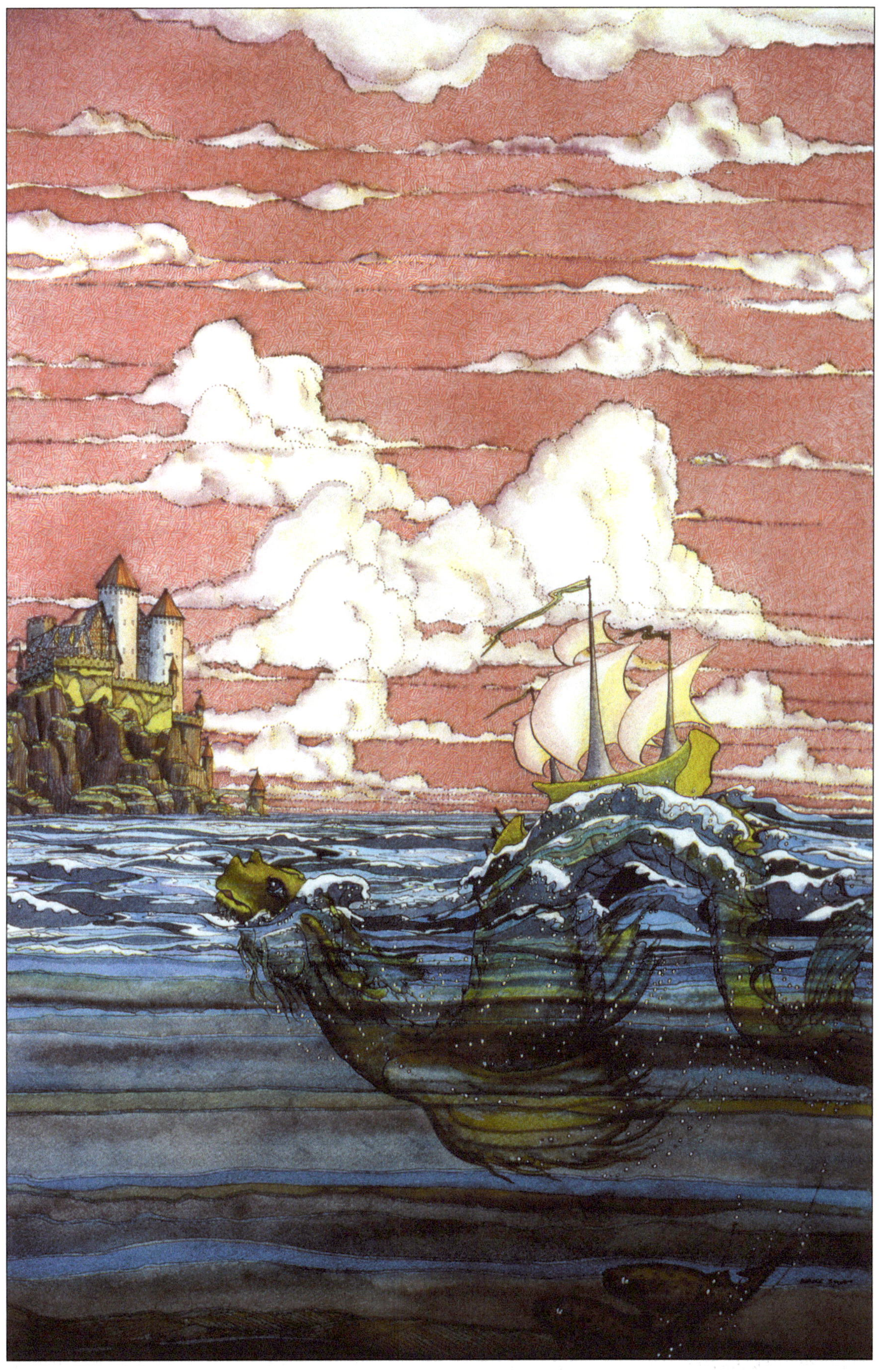

Sea Dragon

She loved to hear the children's laughter. The waltzes and witty conversation drifted over the balconies and parapets. A brief metamorphosis and she could be close without alarming those lovely creatures. She wondered how many other ships were dragons, too.

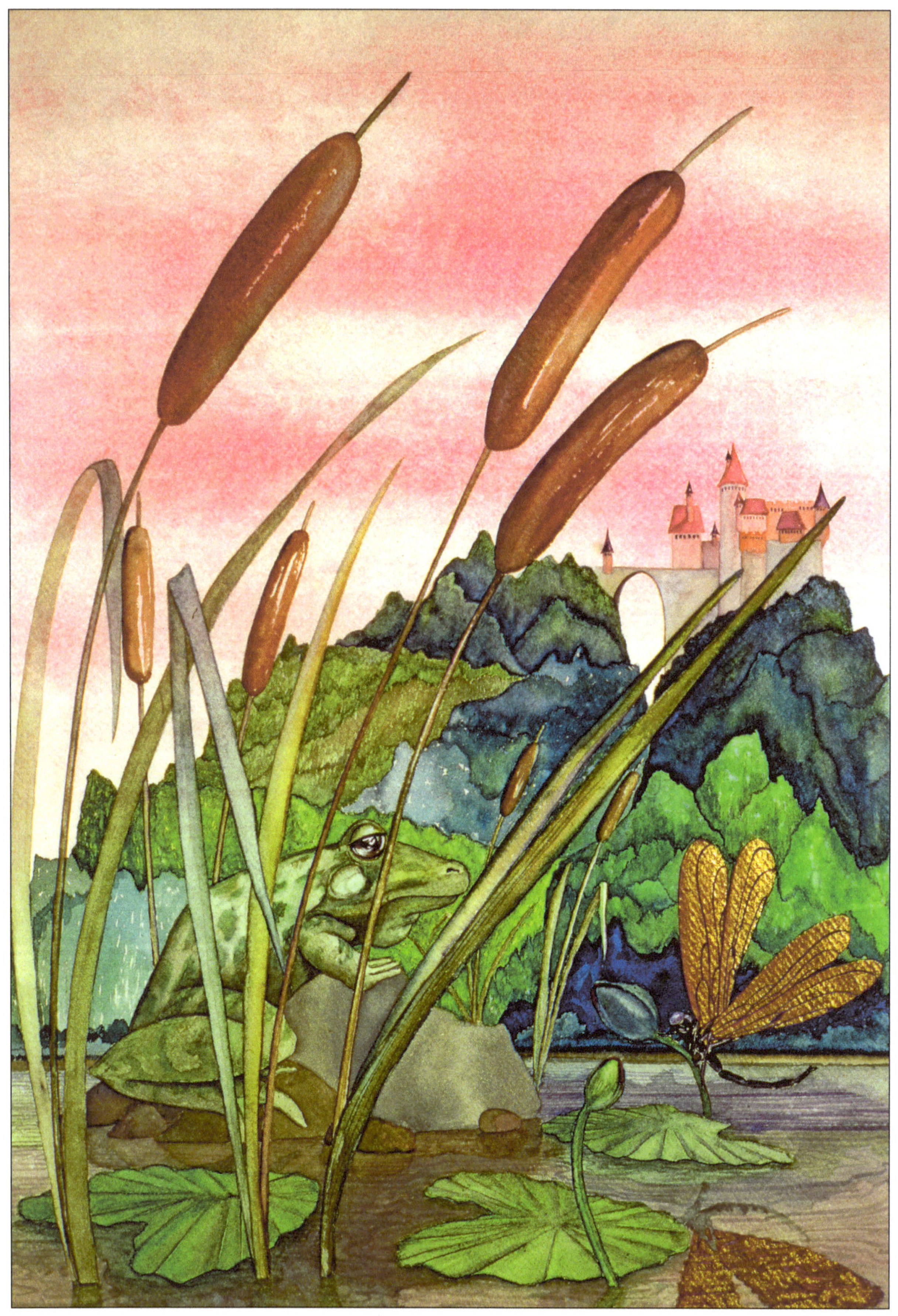

Almost Enchanted

Trusted messenger the dragonfly brought word to "Morton" from his true love. This seemed a truly peaceful moment in their often hectic days. Everything seemed almost enchanted; The world felt warm, The future filled with hope.

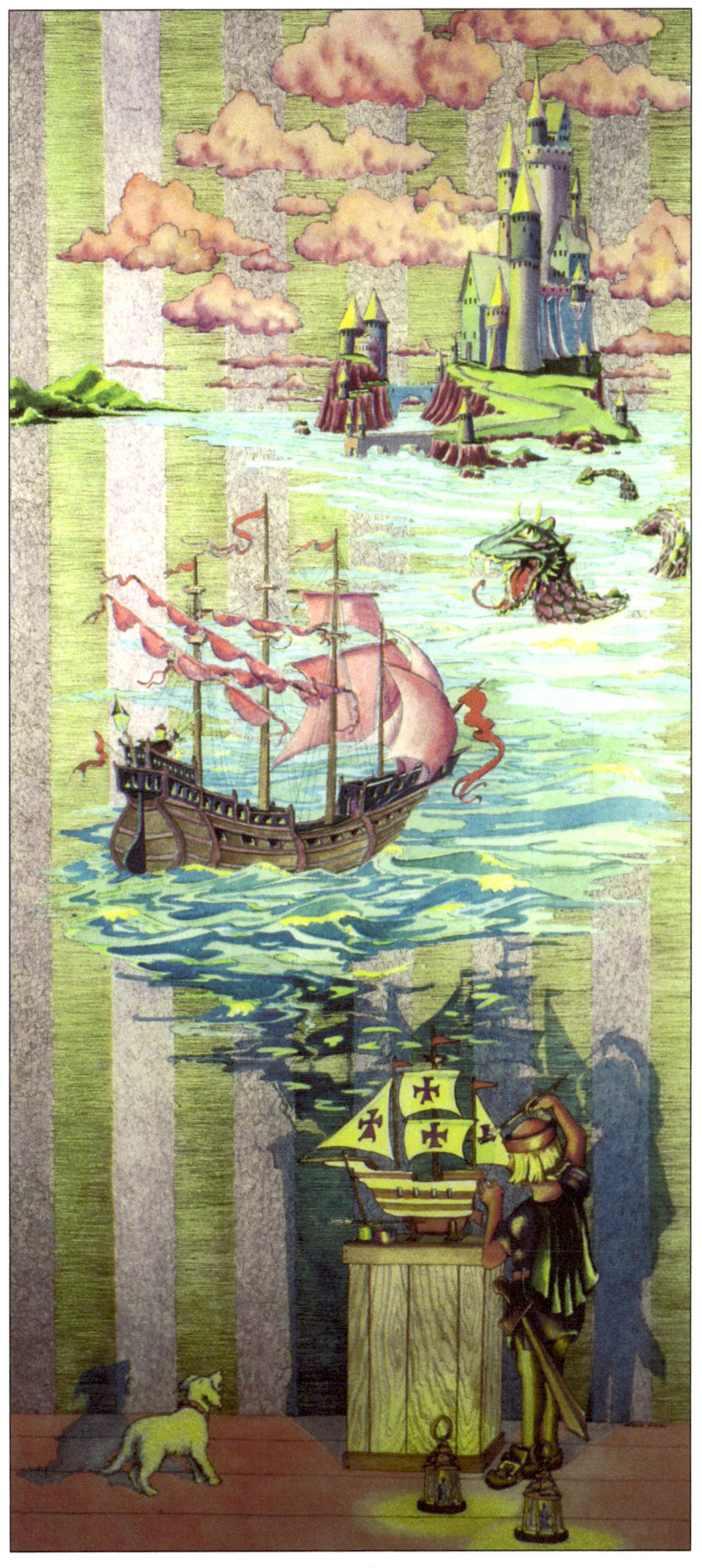

Young Chris

What if there were fierce dragons in those distant waters, Chris pondered. Nevertheless he and his pup would take them on. You're never really afraid when you got your pup.

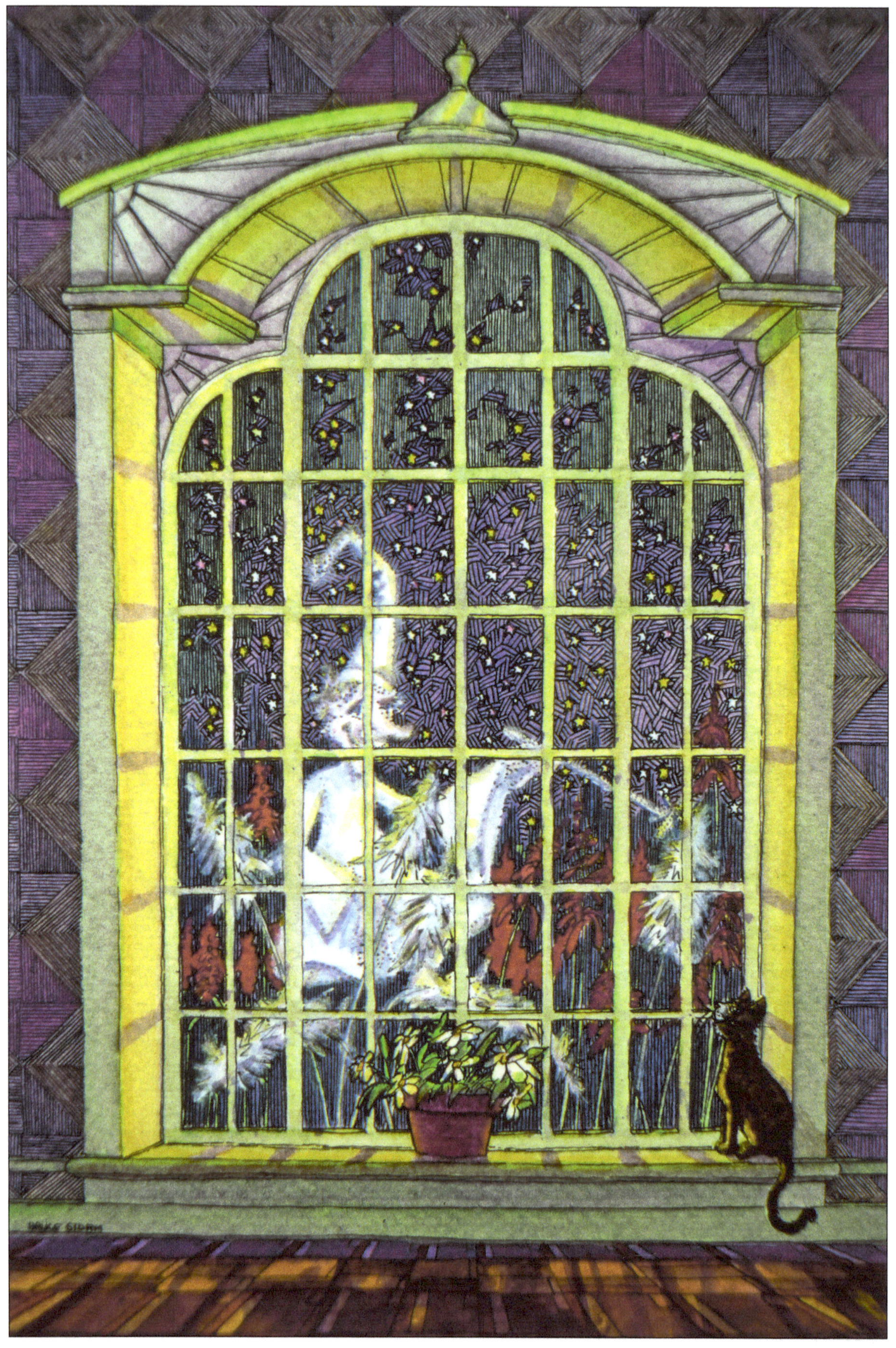

Jack Frost 2nd Observation

She watched with fascination as each flower turned to crystal. He seemed so pleased. How did he do it? She wondered.

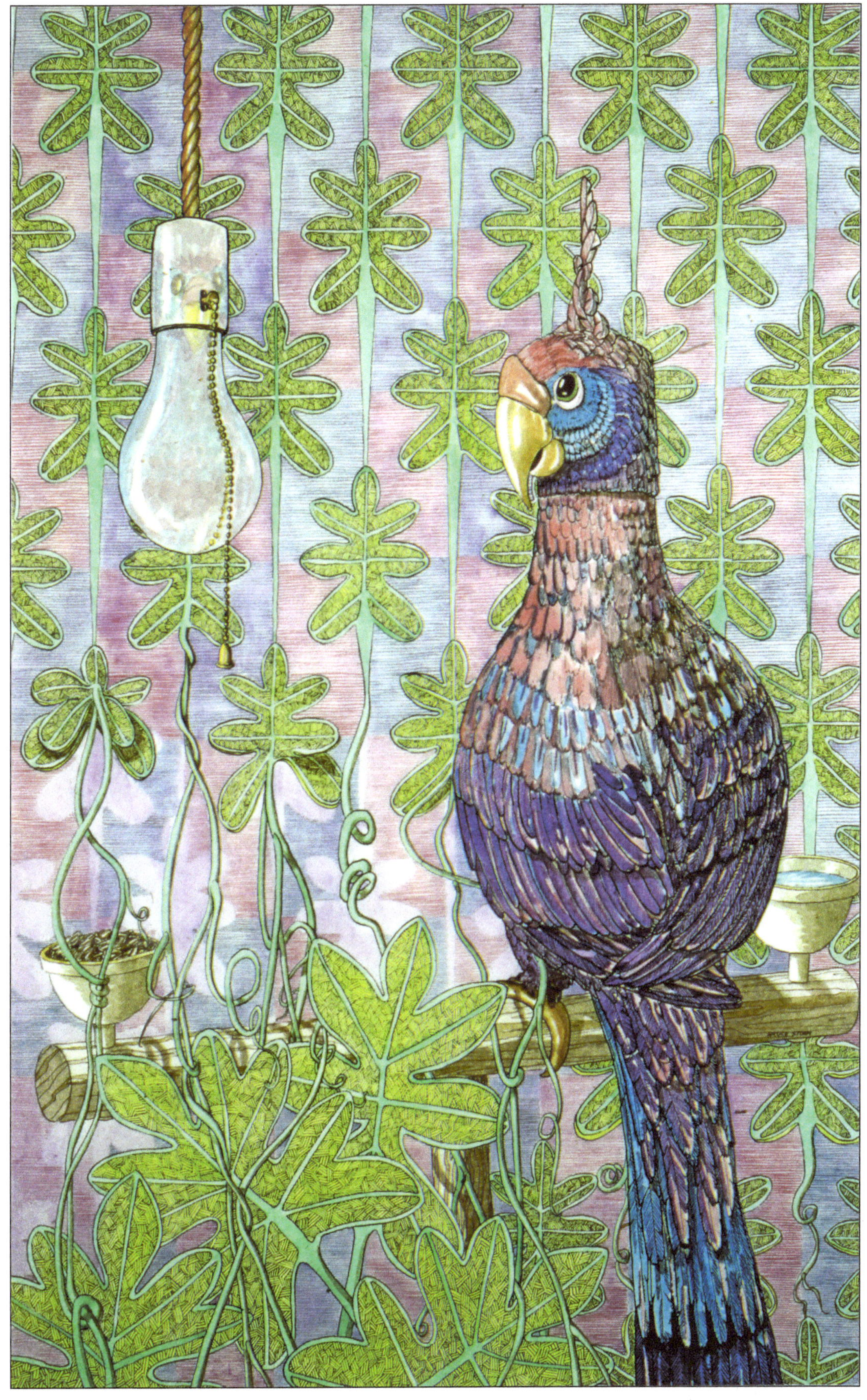

Narcissus

After months of captivity, the parrot noticed a reflection in the light bulb. Sadly the bird in the bulb gave no response to his amorous cries and exhaustive preening. Almost in desperation he struck upon the answer-he must make himself look like the other bird to win its attention.

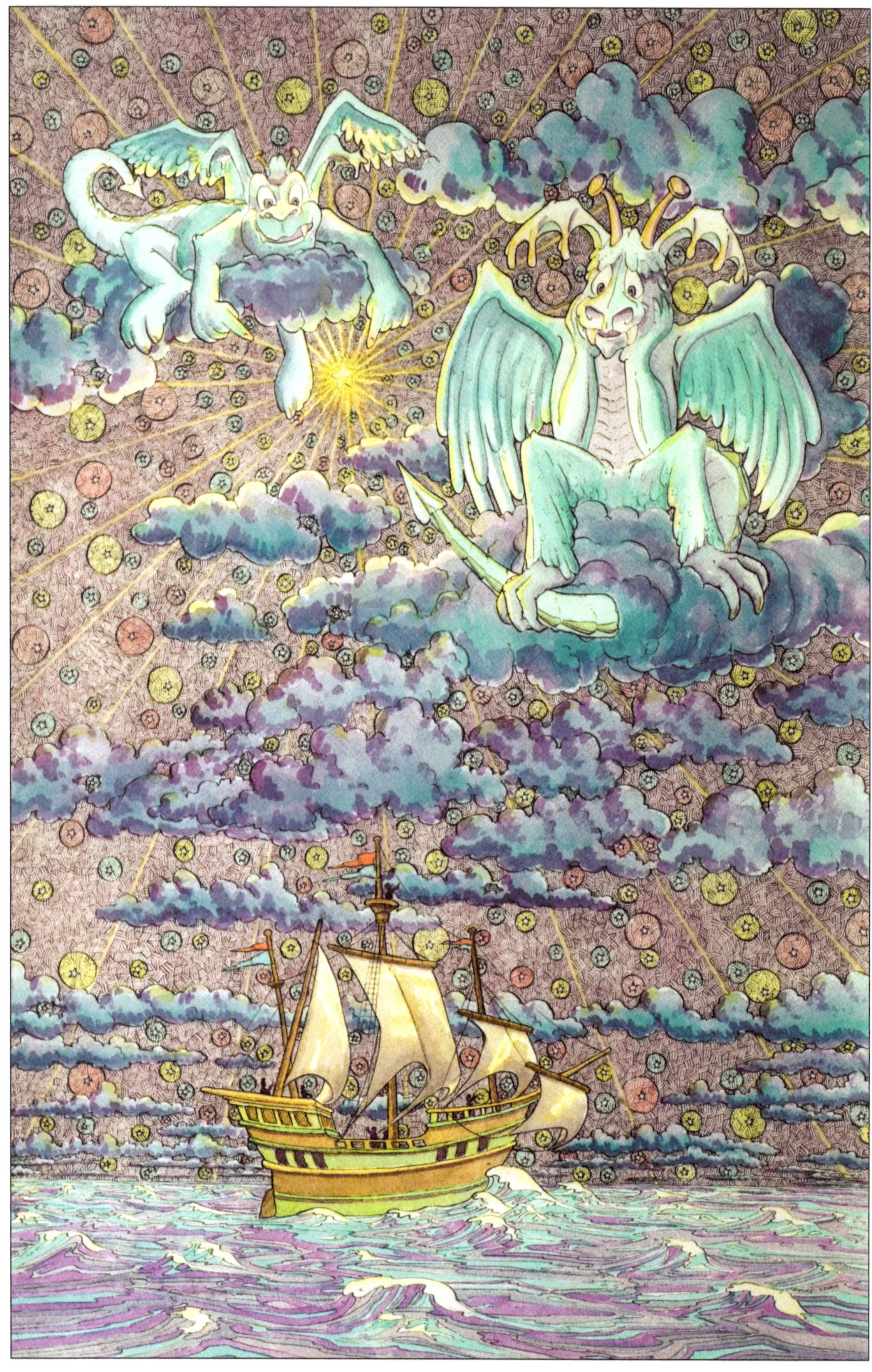

North Star

We all need a friend from time to time; someone to help us steer in the right direction. The navigator's friends did all they could to keep the North Star sparkling bright and clear of clouds. How they worried about the poor little humans in their fragile little boats.

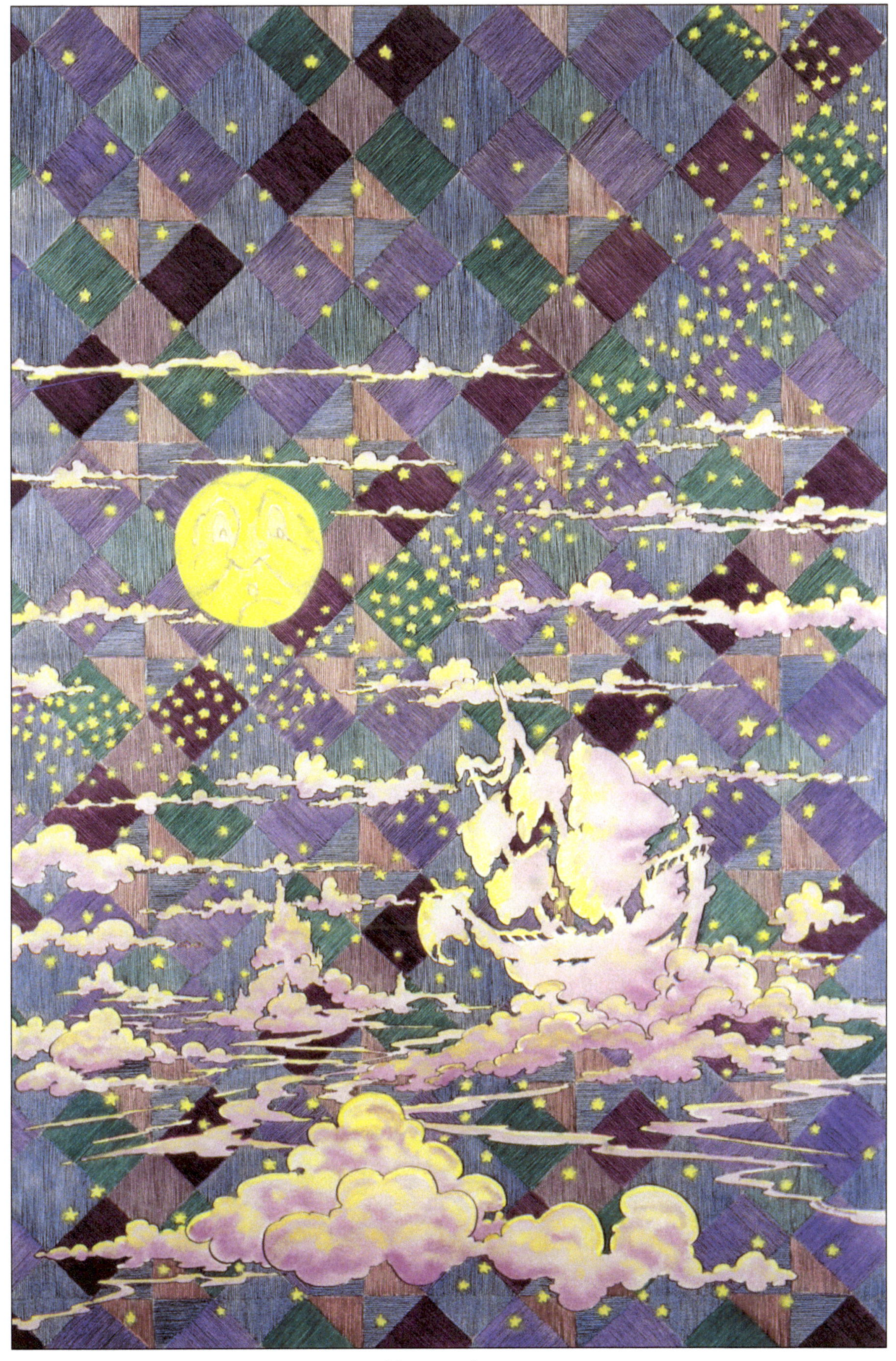

Misted Ship

What the old moon saw most missed, Few remembered, and only the little stars understood.

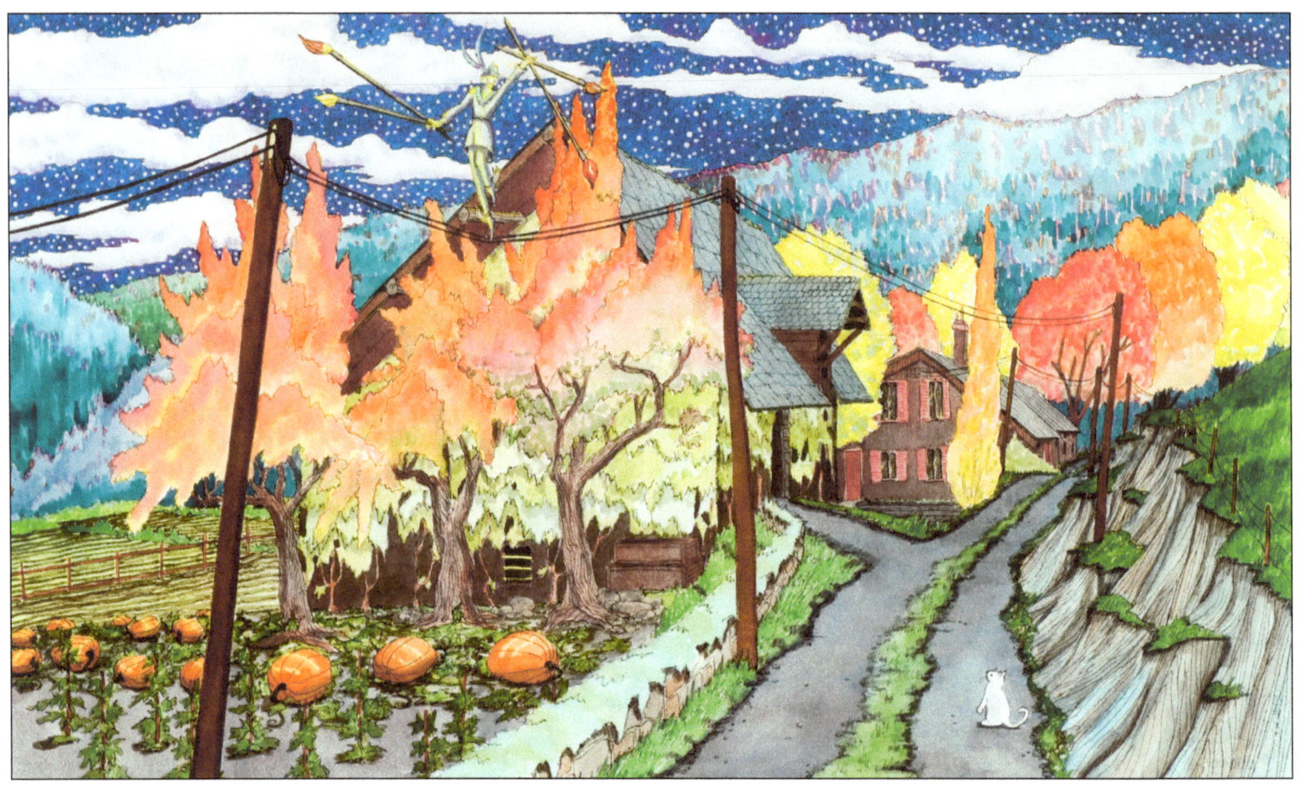

Light Frost

Last night the frost danced among the trees - splashing her reds and golds while all slept except the cat who missed very little.

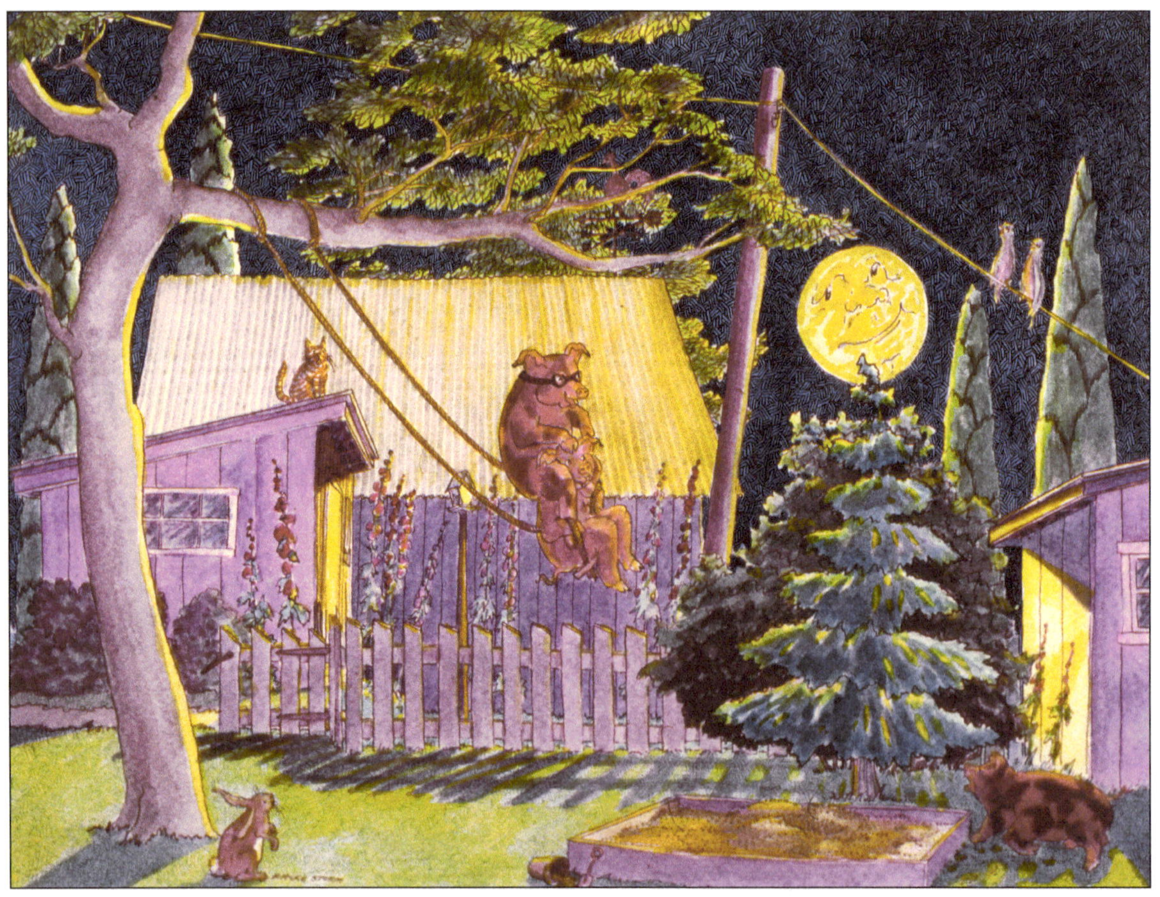

When Pigs Fly

Tales of the Flying Wallendas and Evil Knievel had fortified their hopes. The sandbox was perfectly placed in case of an unsuccessful launch. The brothers were ready for lift off.

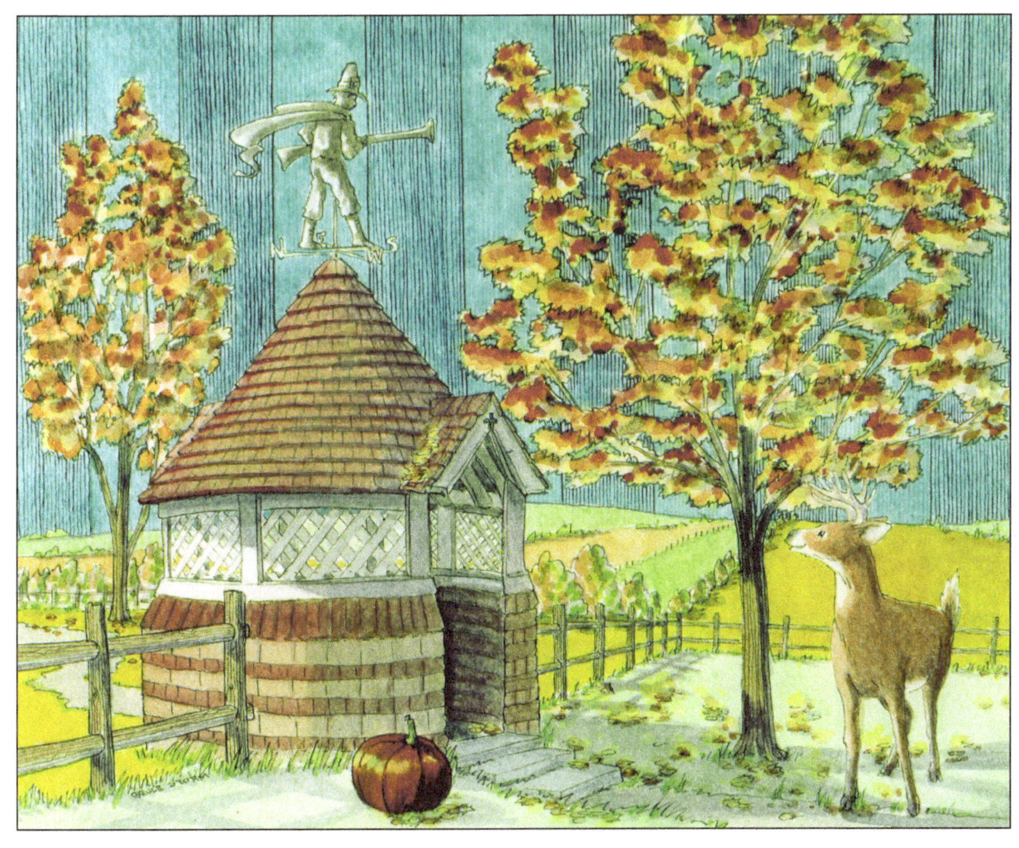

Fall News

An Autumn Breeze, crisp and cool, swung the old blunderbuss toteing pilgrim around. Time to get to the posted forest thought Harold

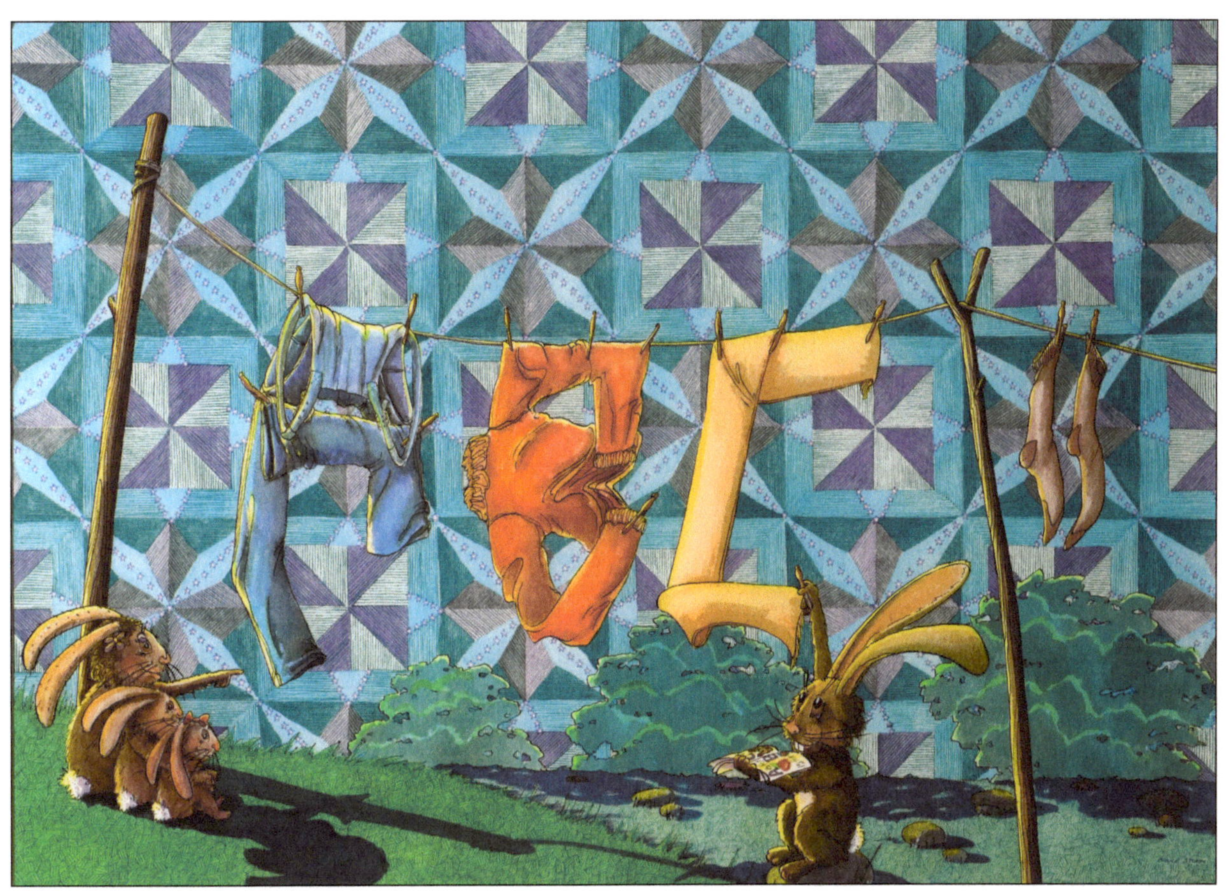

Alphabet Lesson

Papa was clever with visual aids. They made such lasting impressions.

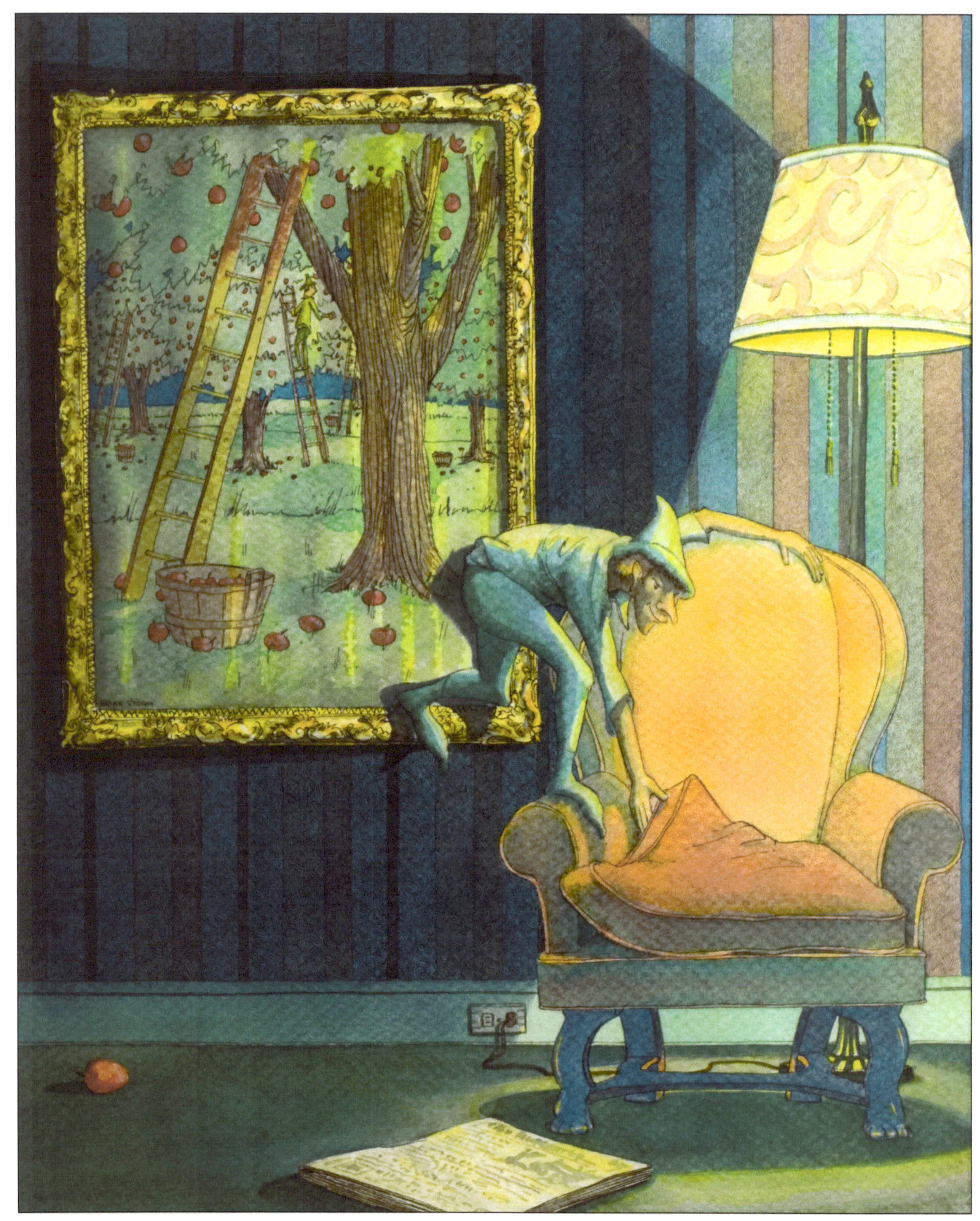

Lost Coins

The company had left. The hour was late. Gently he stepped from the apple orchard onto the frame to search through the cushions for lost coins.

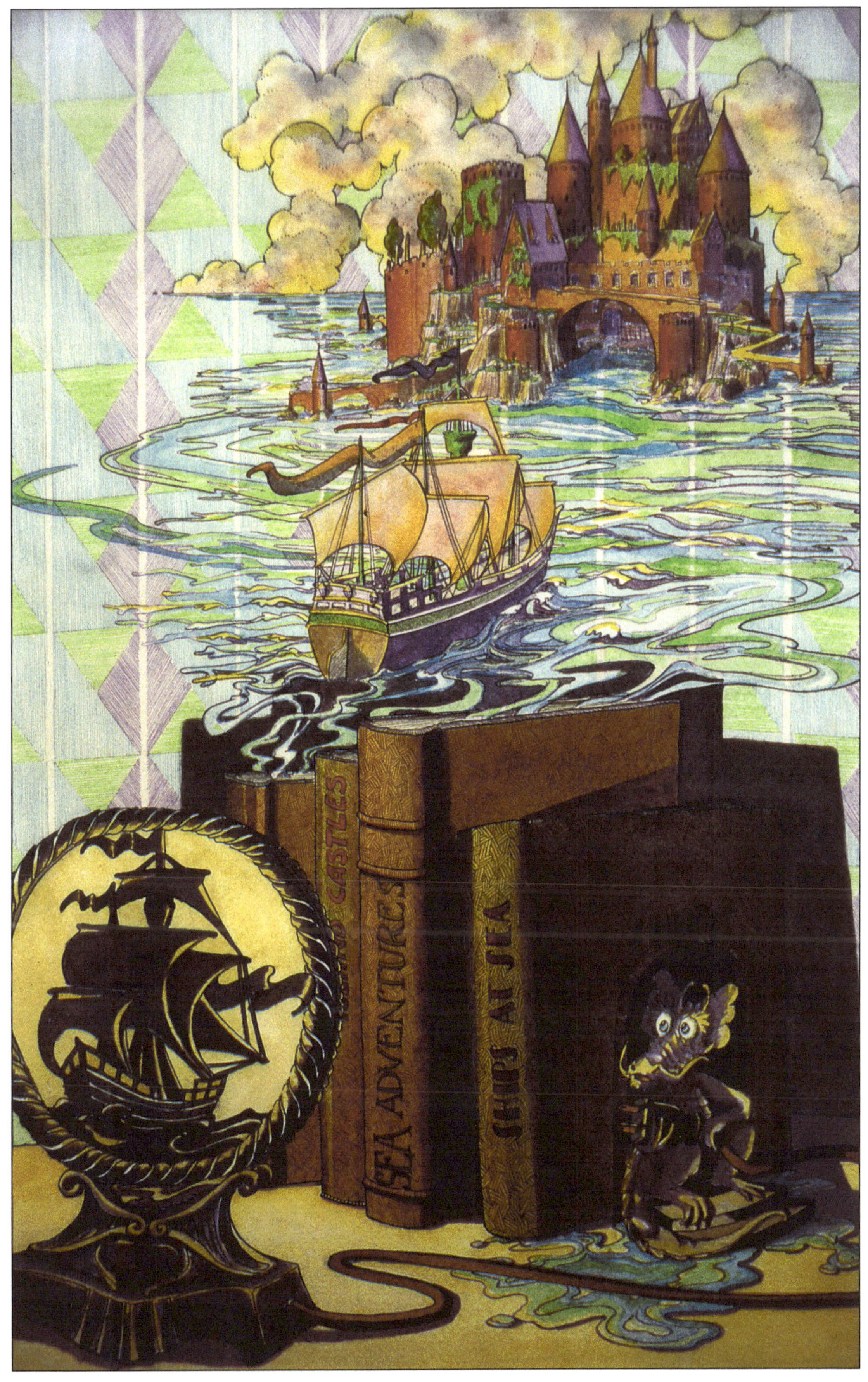

The Night Light

The little dragon had hidden on the bookend for ever so long. The mystic glow of the night light hindered his escape. Unaware of its real source of power he pulled the plug, and then strange things began to happen....

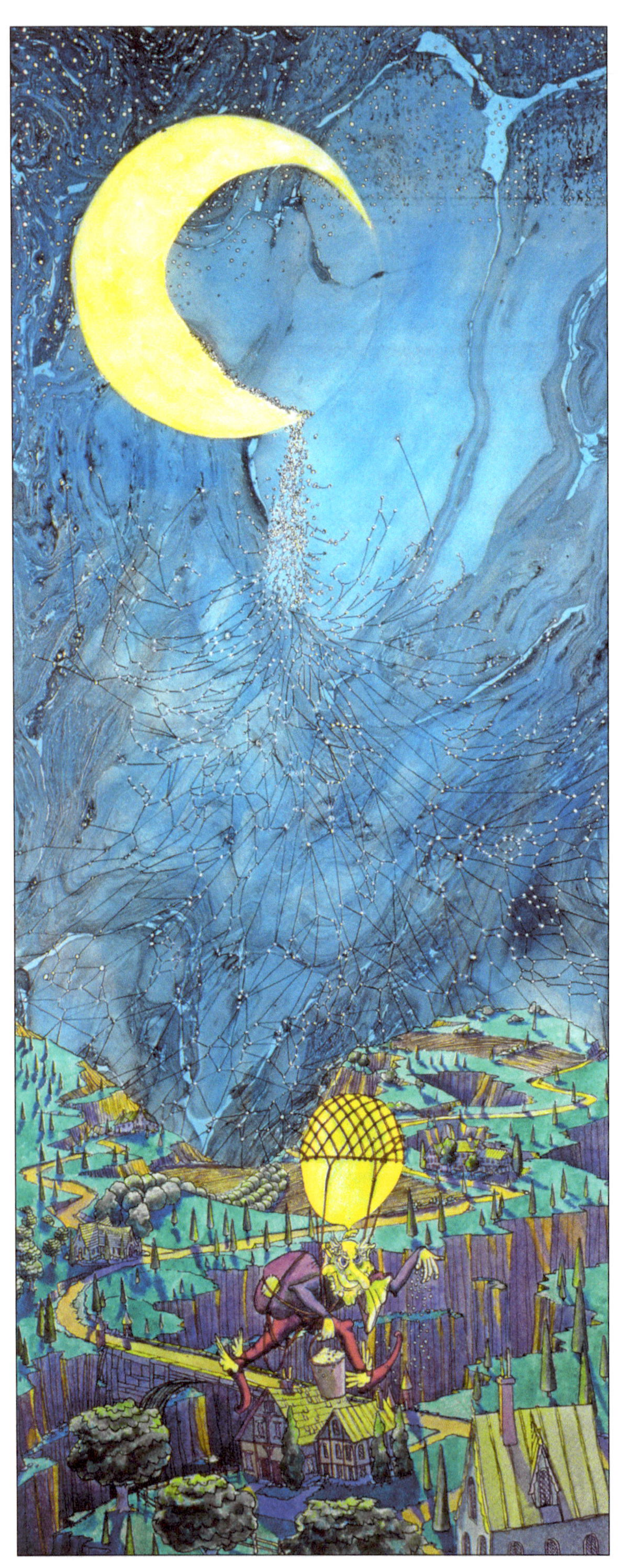

Sandman

Every evening he gathers the star sand that spills from the growing moon. He glides through balmy nights sprinkling sand gently into the eyes of sleepy little ones.

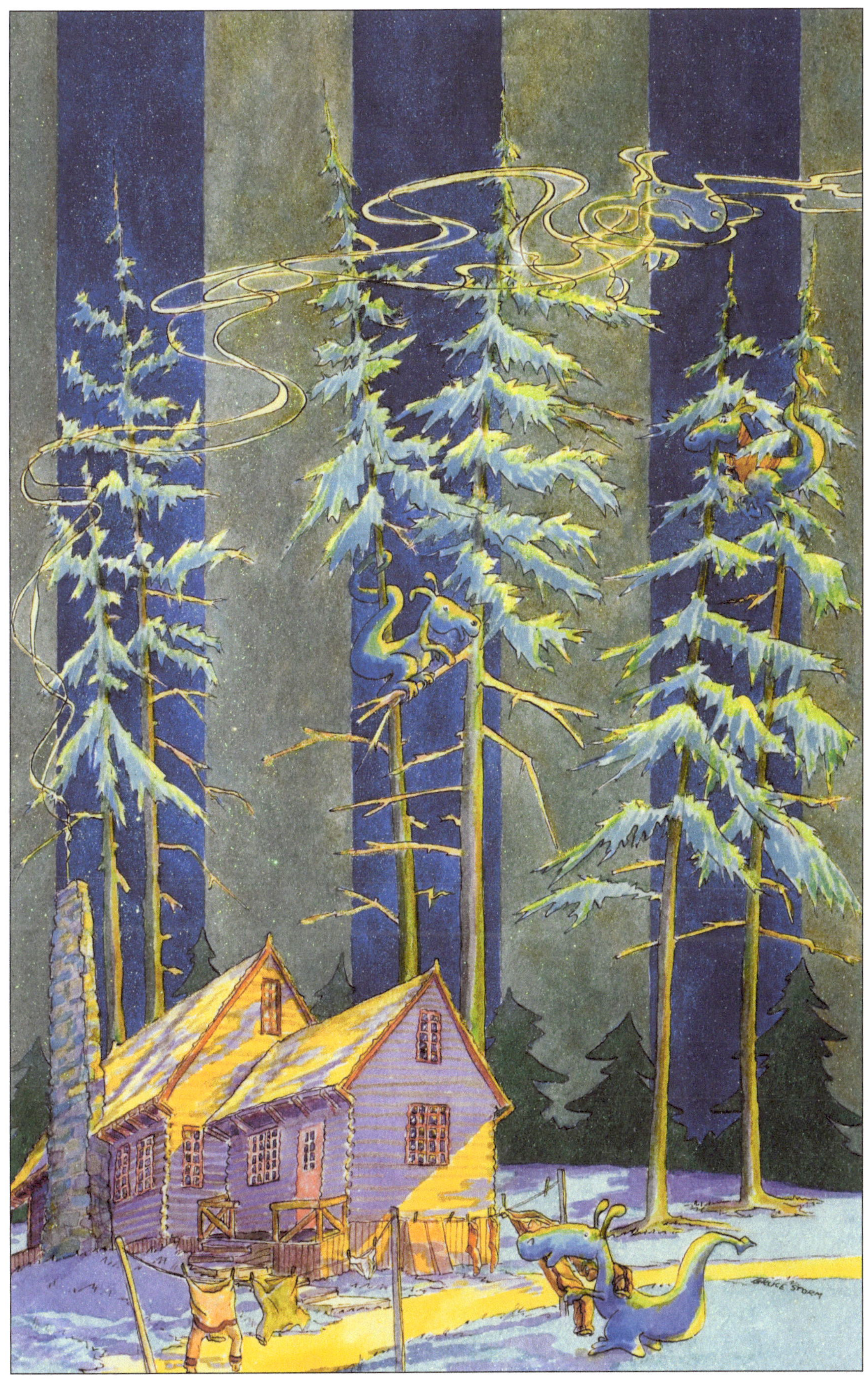

Night Sweats

When nights turned nippy the dragon fledglings glided down to the washline. Borrowing sweat pants or shirts they stayed cozy until dawn. The wash returns by sunrise, no one the wiser.

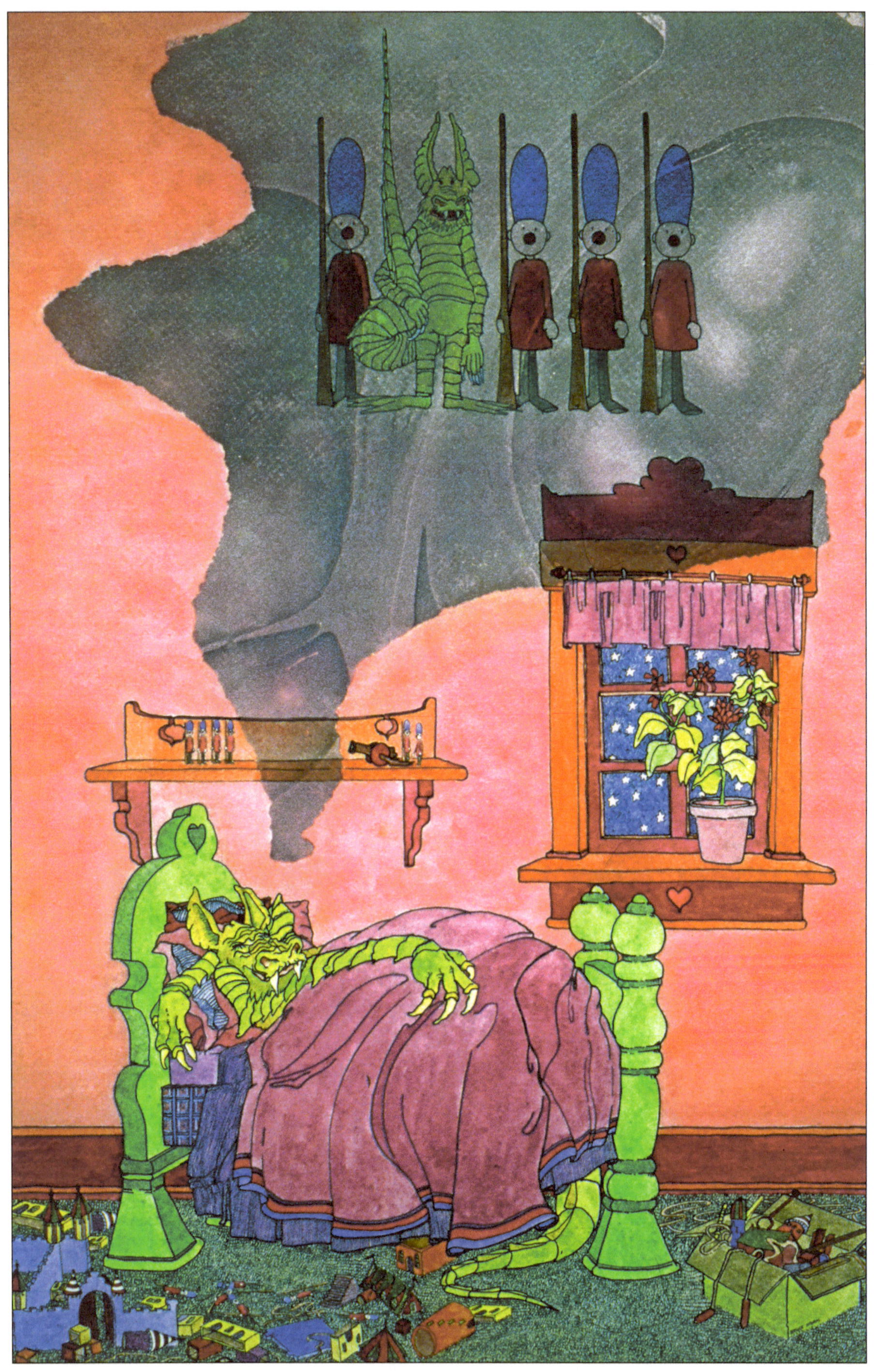

ACCEPTANCE

THE LITTLE DRAGON, QUITE EXHAUSTED FROM HOURS OF PLAY WITH HIS BELOVED TOY SOLDIERS, IS TUCKED IN BED ONLY TO DREAM OF BEING ACCEPTED AS ONE OF THEM - LOVED JUST AS HE IS.

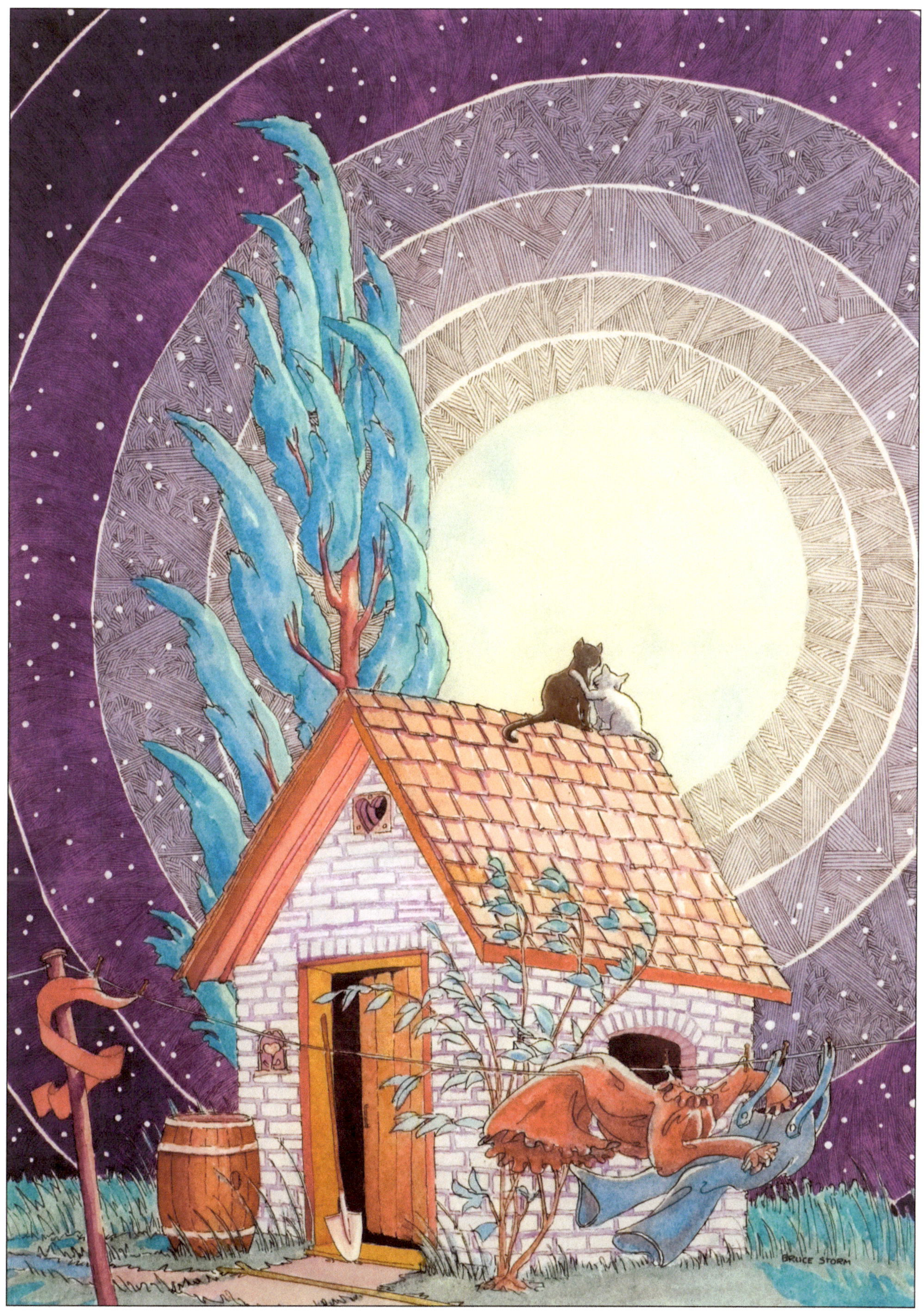

Love Spell

When love casts its spell who will not dance the clothesline waltz or warble to the stars with alley cat exhuberance?

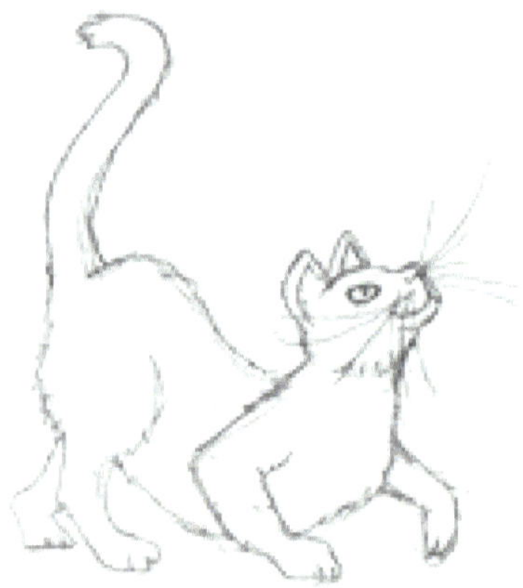

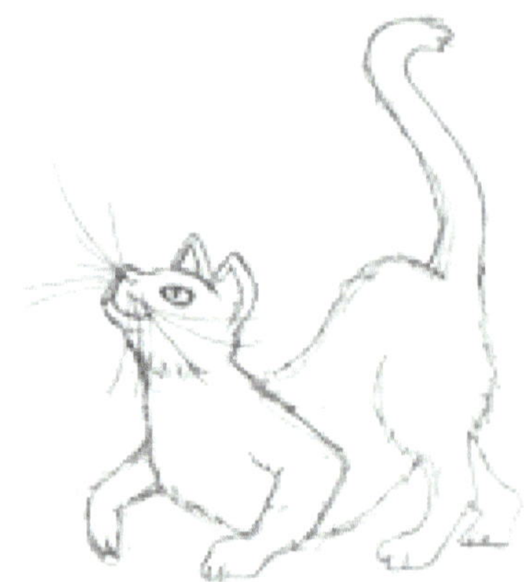

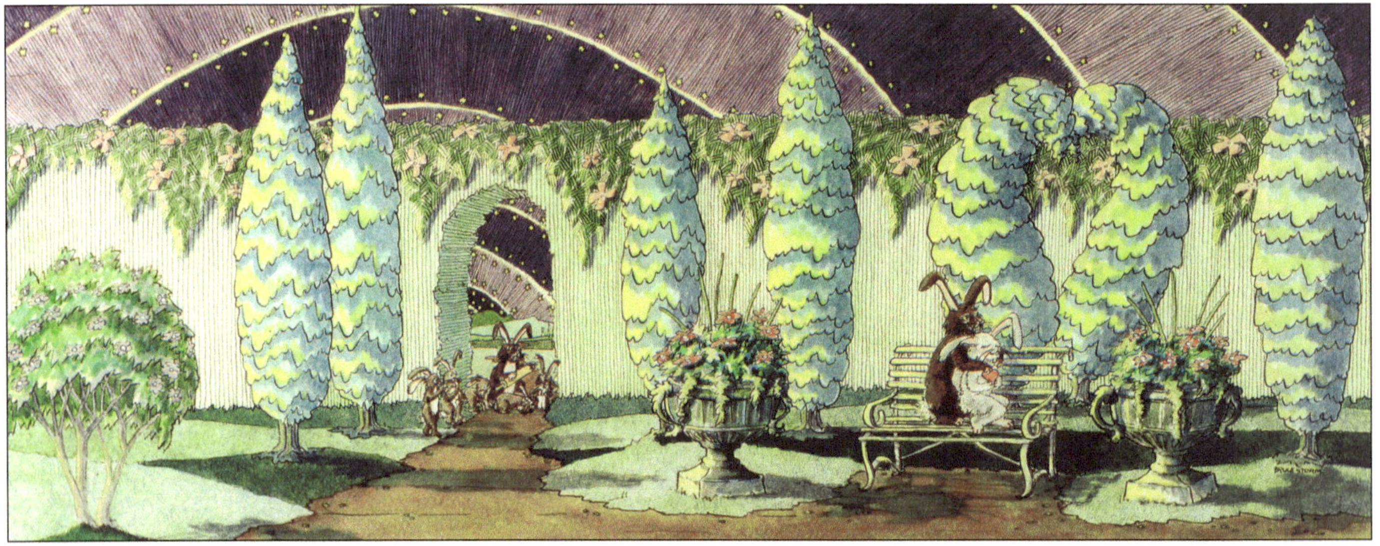

Rabbit Expose'

Everyone knows the habits of rabbits.

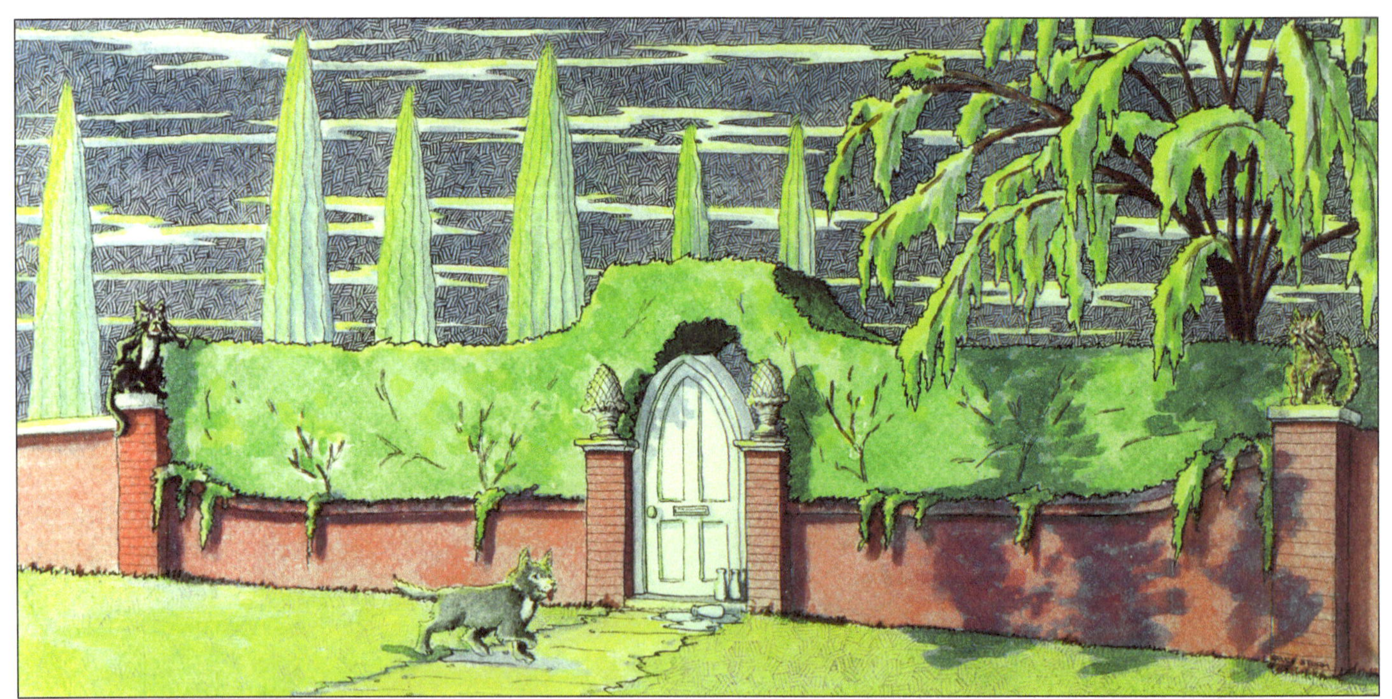

Playing Statue

Sparky, the great defender of the milk bottles, was no match for Itsa and Bitsa who seemed to vanish after their early morning raids.

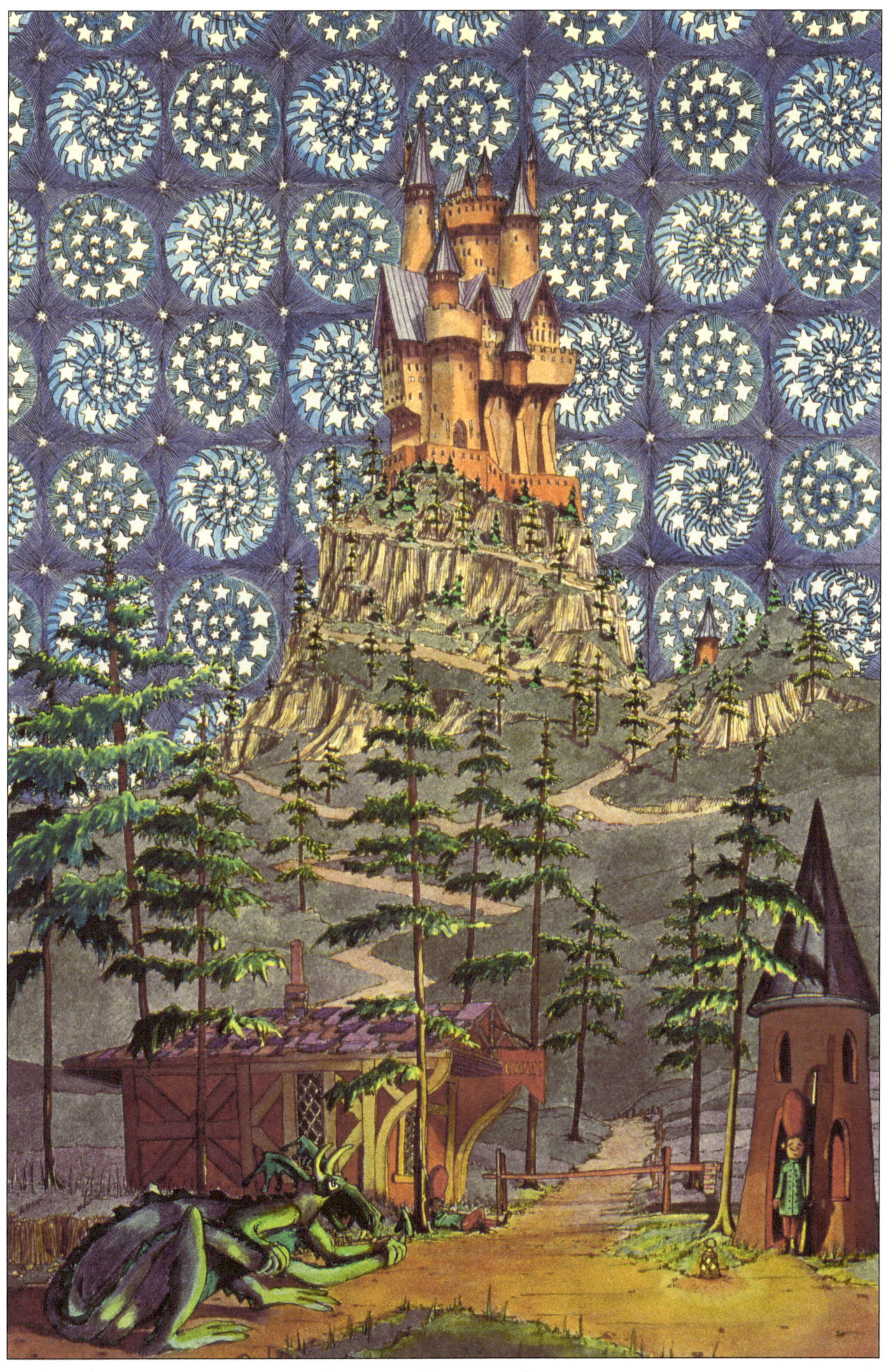

Tale of a Dragon Tail

Absolutely he hadn't intended to arrive home so late, but attempting not to wake the gate keepers, Cuddles decided to carry his tail which normally would make an horrendous racket on the roadway. Just a few more miles and he'd be curled up in his warm basket.

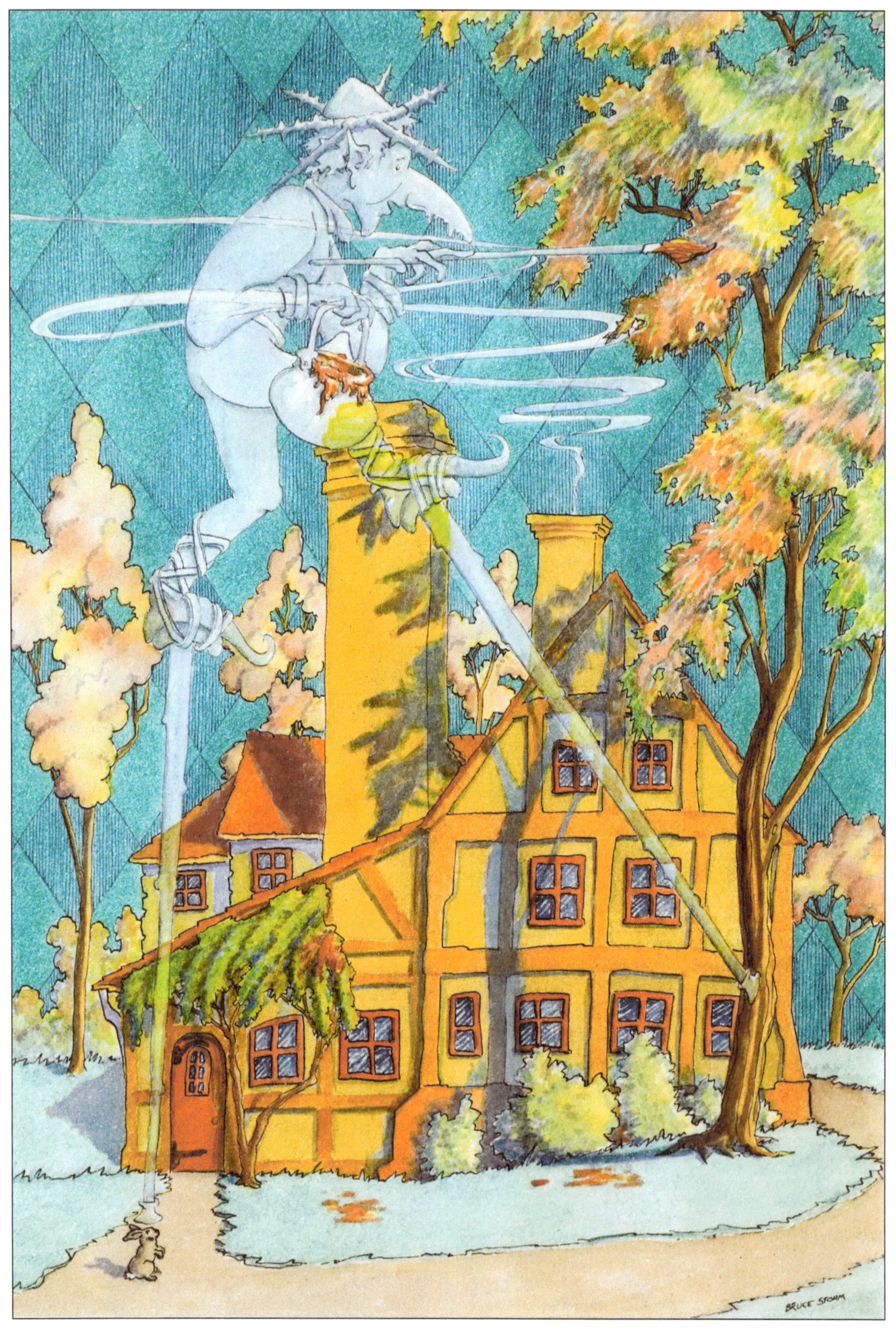

Jack's Back

Few saw his nimble brush; fewer still noticed the artistic fellow on his ice stilts transforming the world to Autumn's magic.

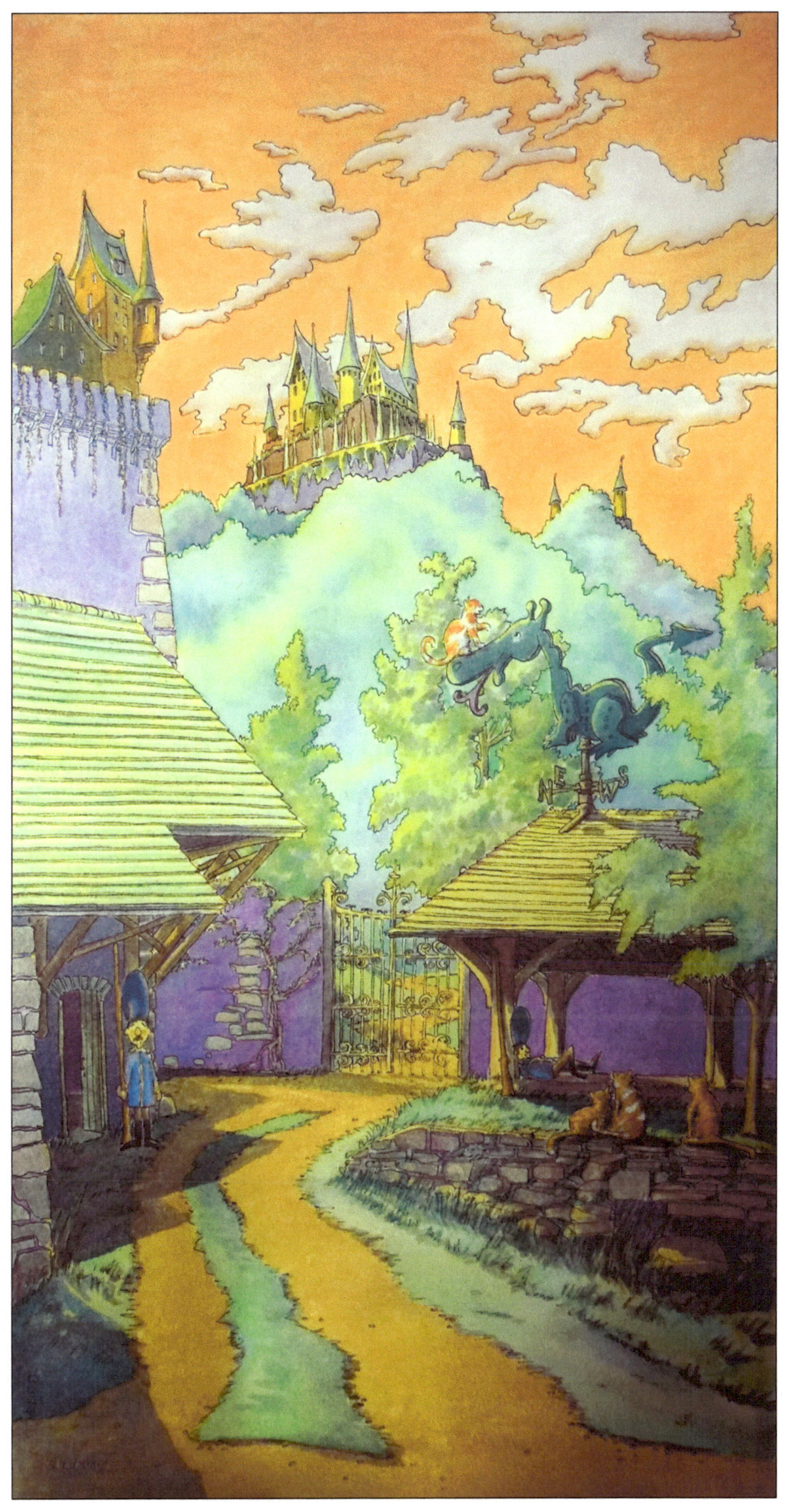

Keeping watch over all

The chorus of cats purred their lullaby. "Not much longer and you can fly away," consoled Pussums. The baby dragon held his breath and waited.

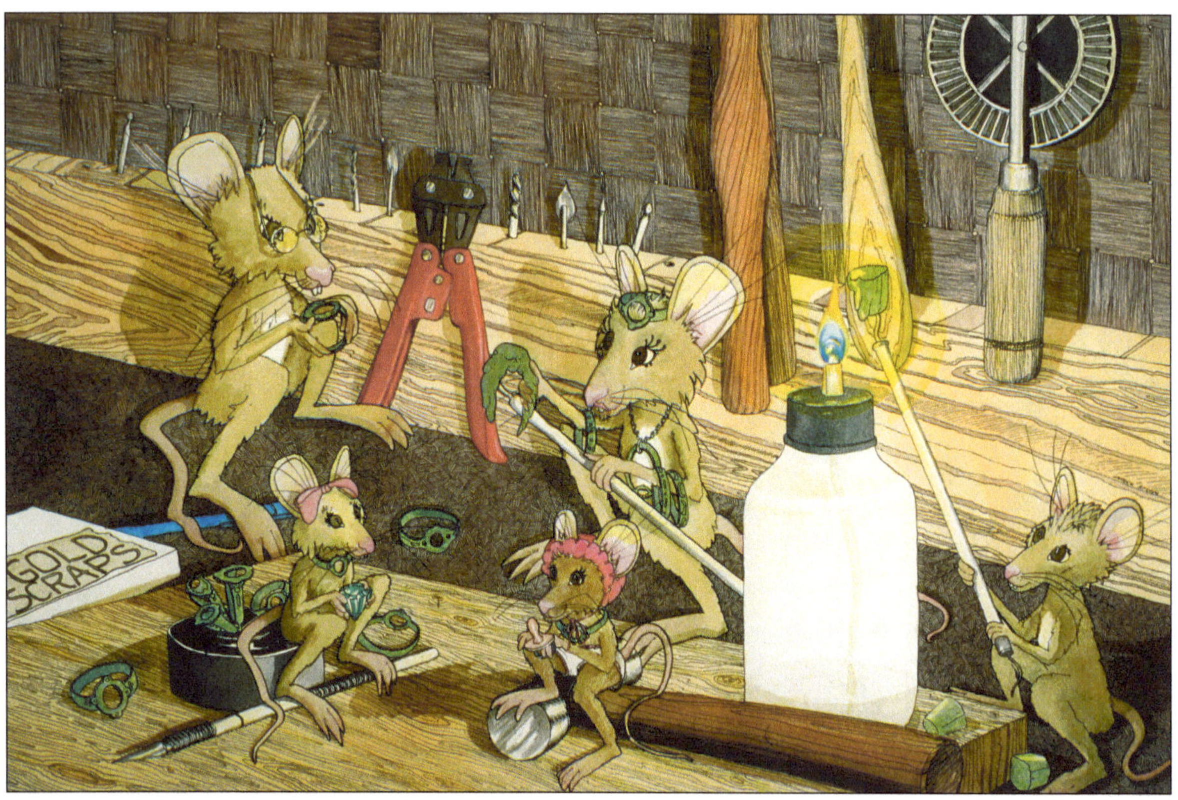

MICE CRAFTSMEN

FREQUENTLY RICK DID NOT HAVE TIME TO DO THE ENTIRE GOLDSMITHING PROCESS HIMSELF, SO HE ACQUIRED THE ASSISTANCE OF THE SMALLER RESIDENTS OF CLINTON AVE. IN NO TIME AT ALL THEY WERE SPRUING THE WAX AND HELPING WITH THE FINE TECHNICAL WORK.

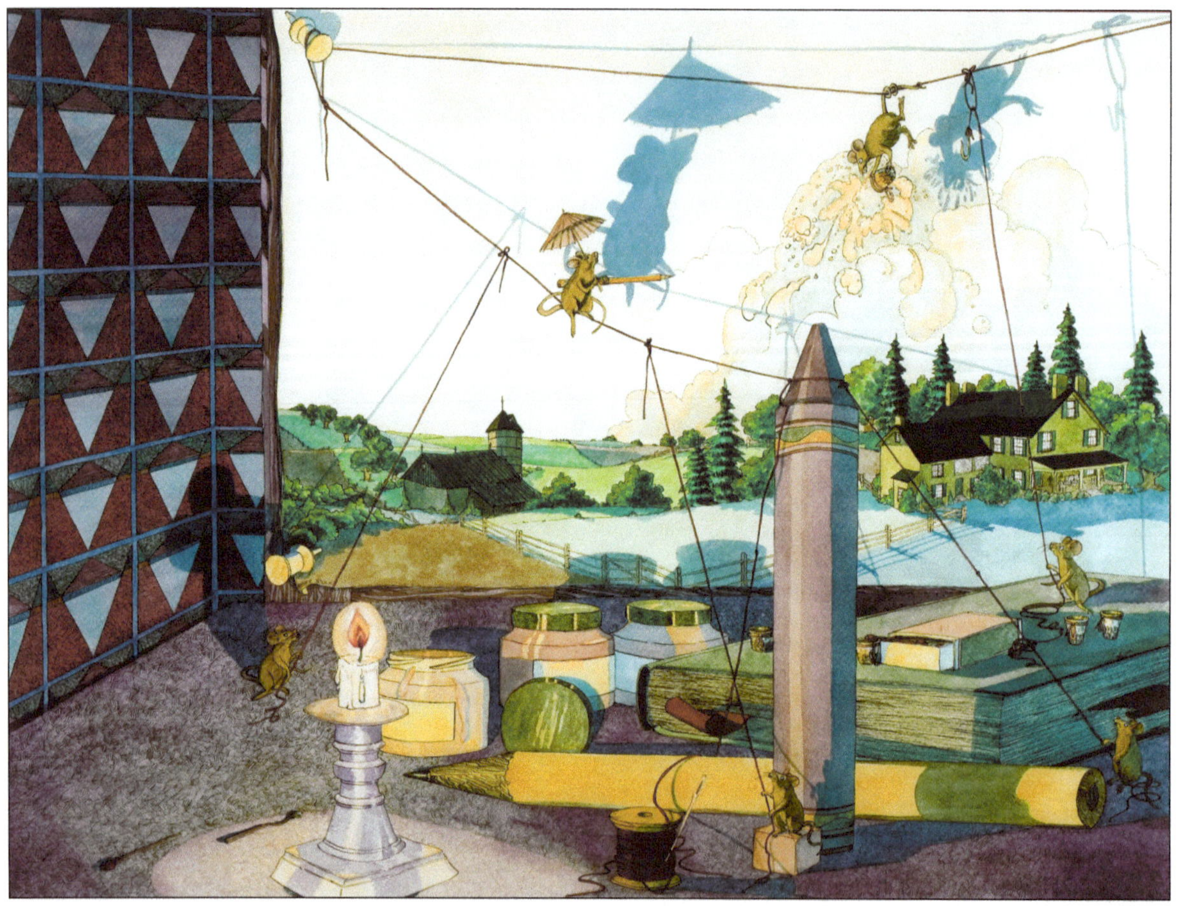

ART DIRECTOR

IMPECCABLE--SIMPLY RIGHT. HE HAD FLAIR. EVERYONE KNEW IT. THOSE COLORS! IT WAS REALLY A PITY THAT THE HUMANS ALWAYS GOT THE CREDIT--BUT STILL ART FOR ARTS' SAKE.

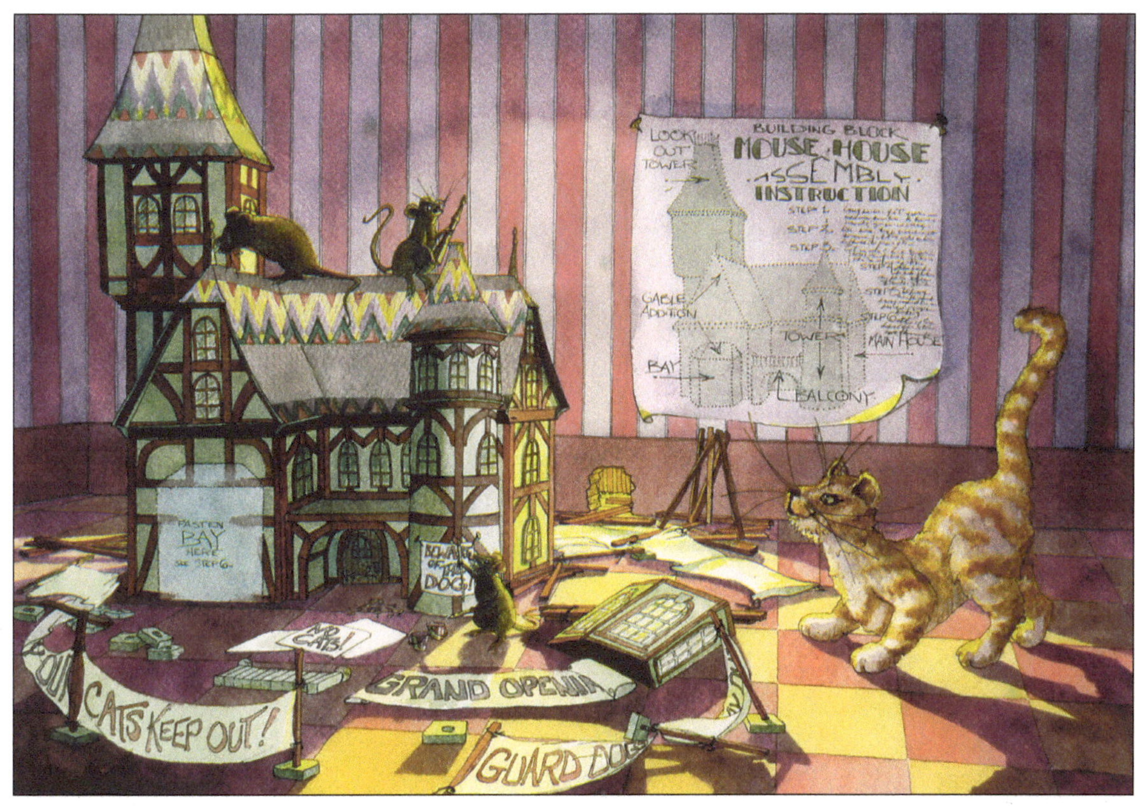

MOUSE HOUSE

ALL THIS TAB "A" INTO SLOT "B" HAD THEM REALLY EXHAUSTED, SO THEY WERE UNAWARE THAT THE HALF GROWN KITTEN HAD COME TO INVESTIGATE WHO WAS MAKING ALL THOSE SQUEAKS.

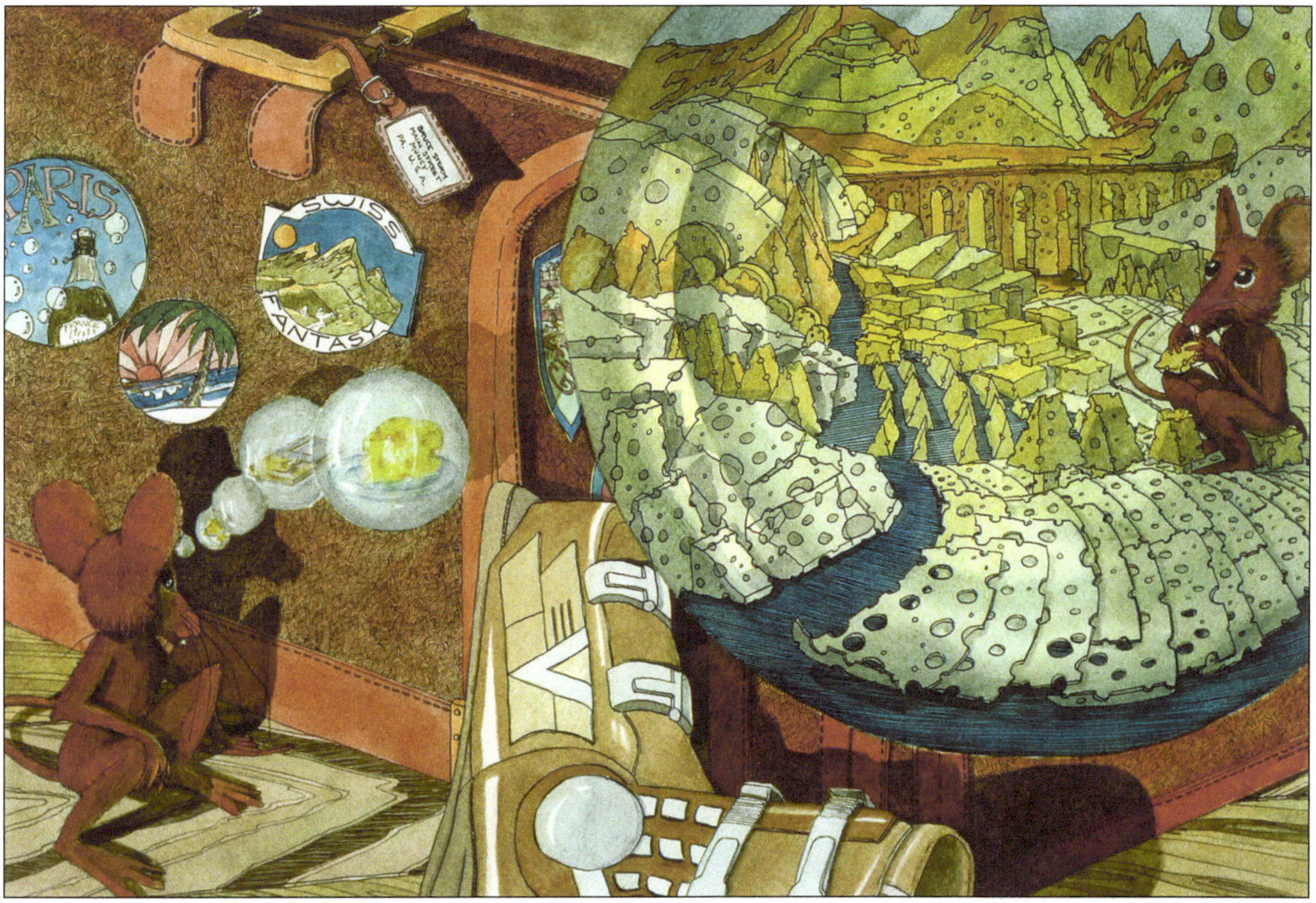

SWISS FANTASY

WHILE EXPLORING THE STORAGE CLOSET, "HERBERT" IS AMAZED BY THE STICKERS ON THE OLD LEATHER SUIT CASE...SWISS FANTASY, WHAT DOES IT MEAN..?

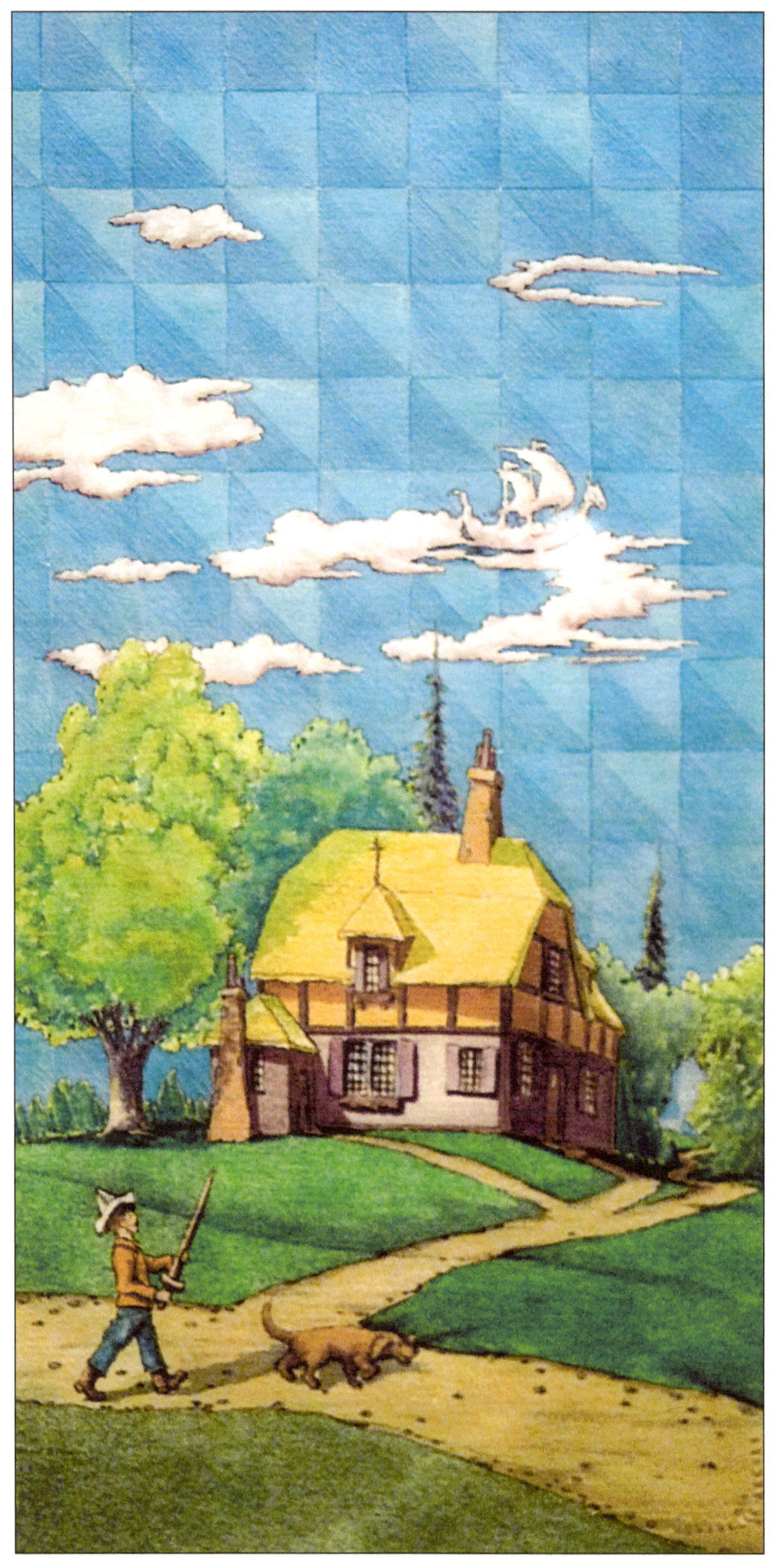

Hi Ho Off We Go

Dragons in the sky; A sword of wood; my doggies good; The smell of baking pie.

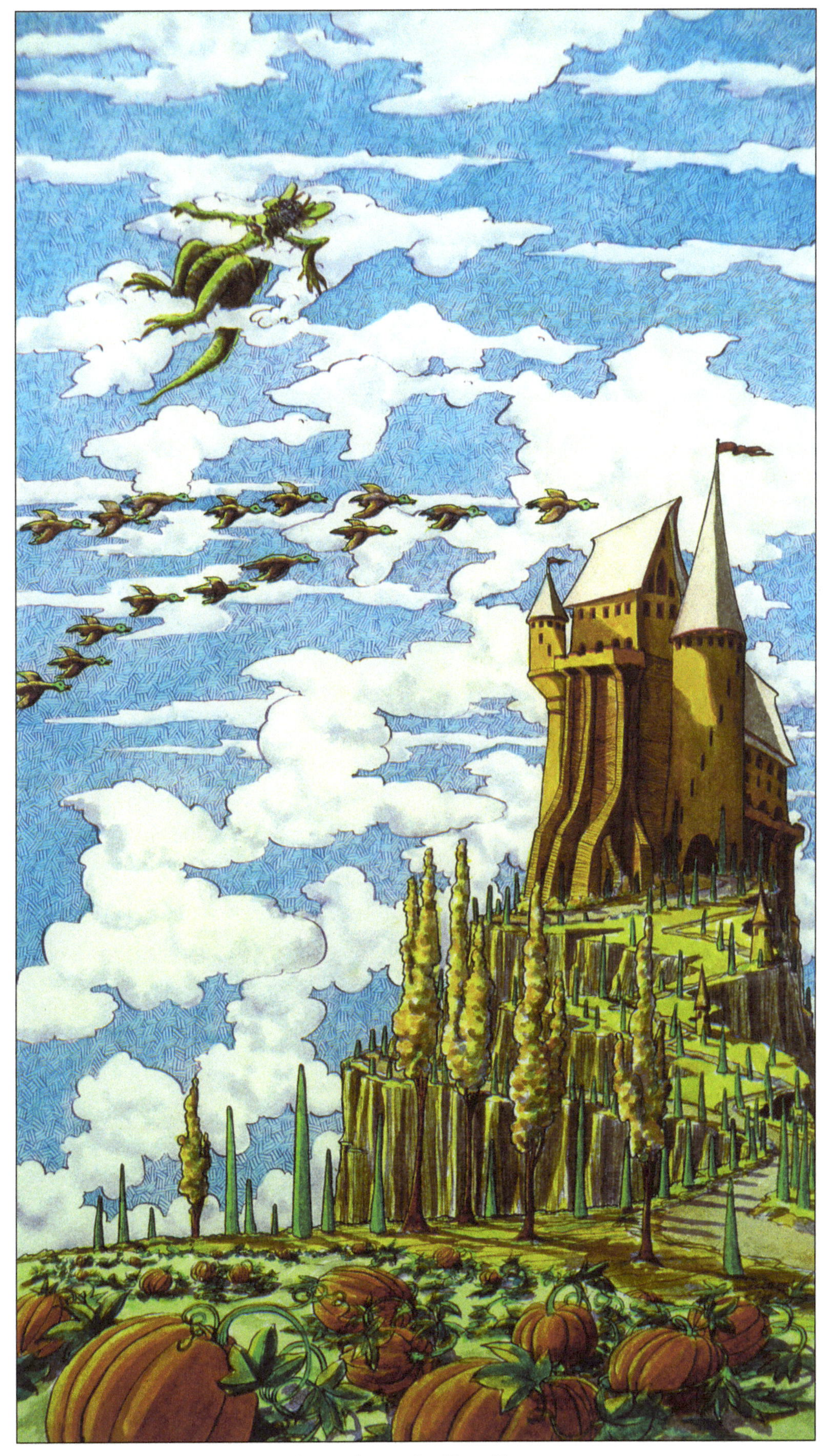

Sure Sign Of The Fall

The aroma of the burning leaves, pumpkins in the patch, ducks flying south, fat dragons in the clouds... sure signs of the fall.

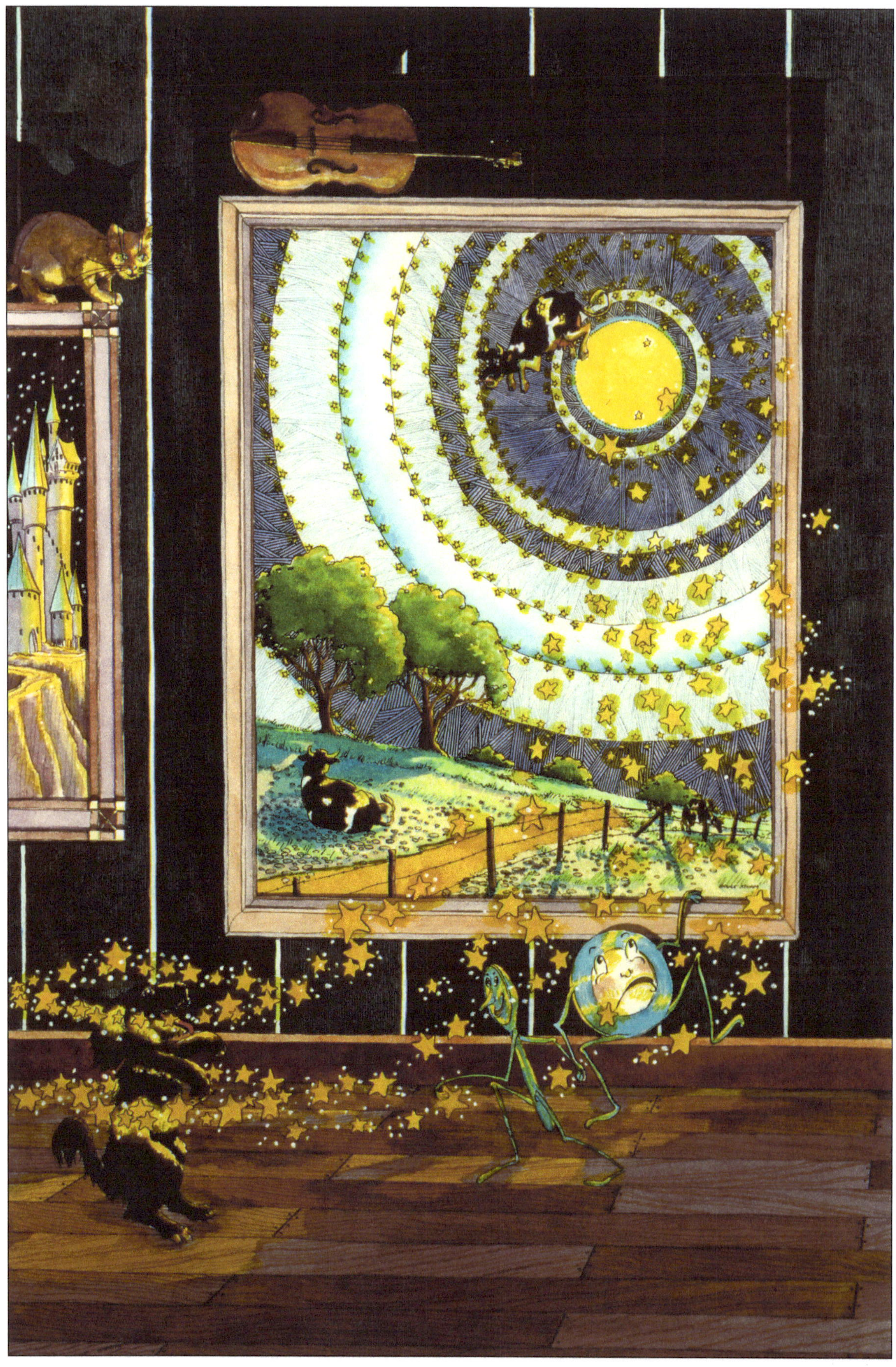

AFTER HOURS

SPOONY AND MISS PLATE HAD CHOSEN FOR THEIR ELOPEMENT THE SAME MOMENT THAT LAURETTA HAD PUT HER NEW VAULTING TECHNIQUE INTO PLAY. EVERYONE IN THE GALLERY WATCHED WITH CURIOSITY AND DELIGHT AS THE STARS ZIPPED AROUND THE EXHIBIT IN UTTER SILENCE.

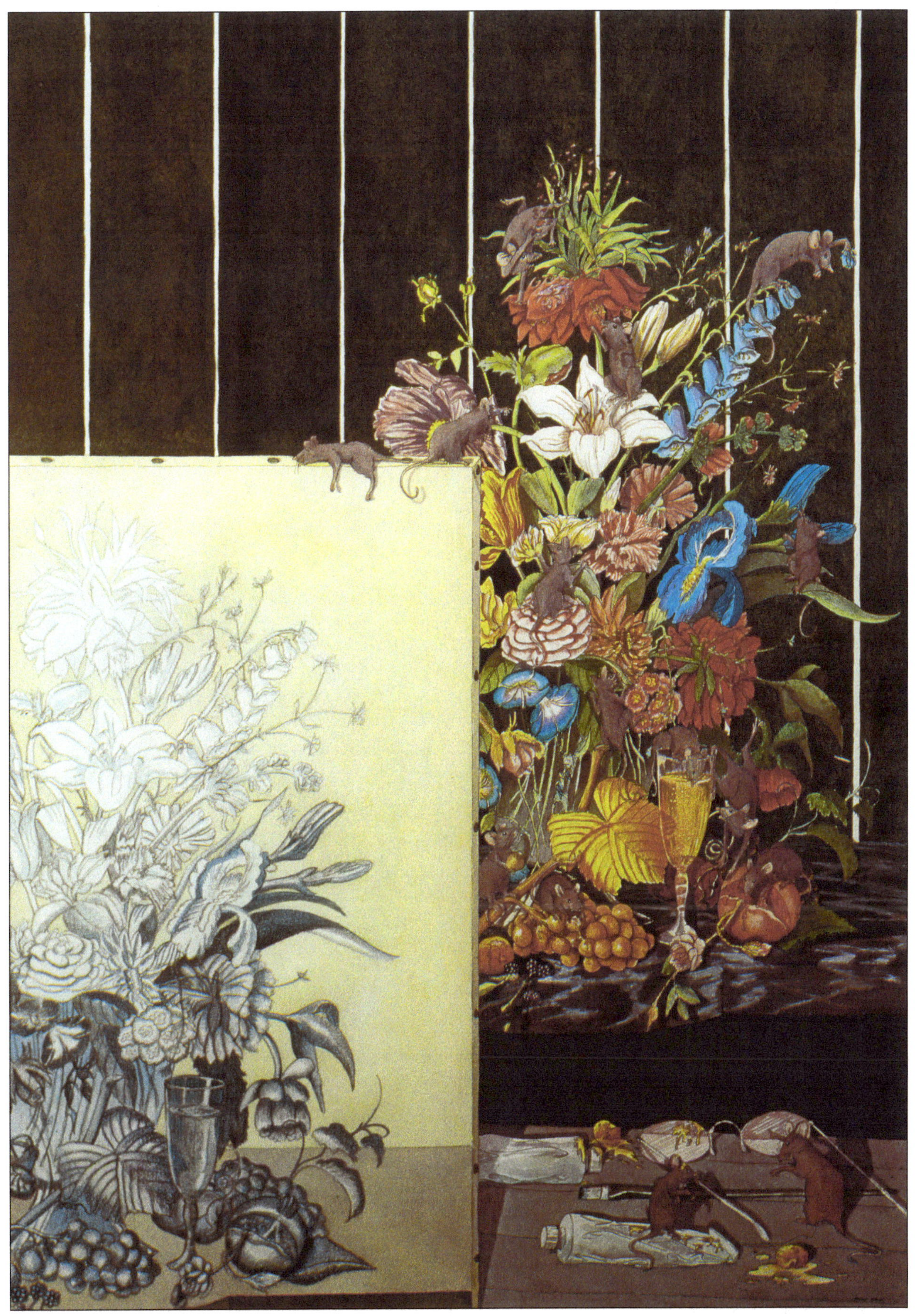

Through Roesen Colored Glasses

Staring through the Roesen colored glasses Otto saw a different world. Peaceful and glowing, each blossom seemed a unique marvel, the grapes perfection, the glass always full. His frolicking friends disappeared along with the smashed grapes. Through the old artist's glasses Otto saw a quiet classic harmony. He beckoned for Beatrix to look, too.

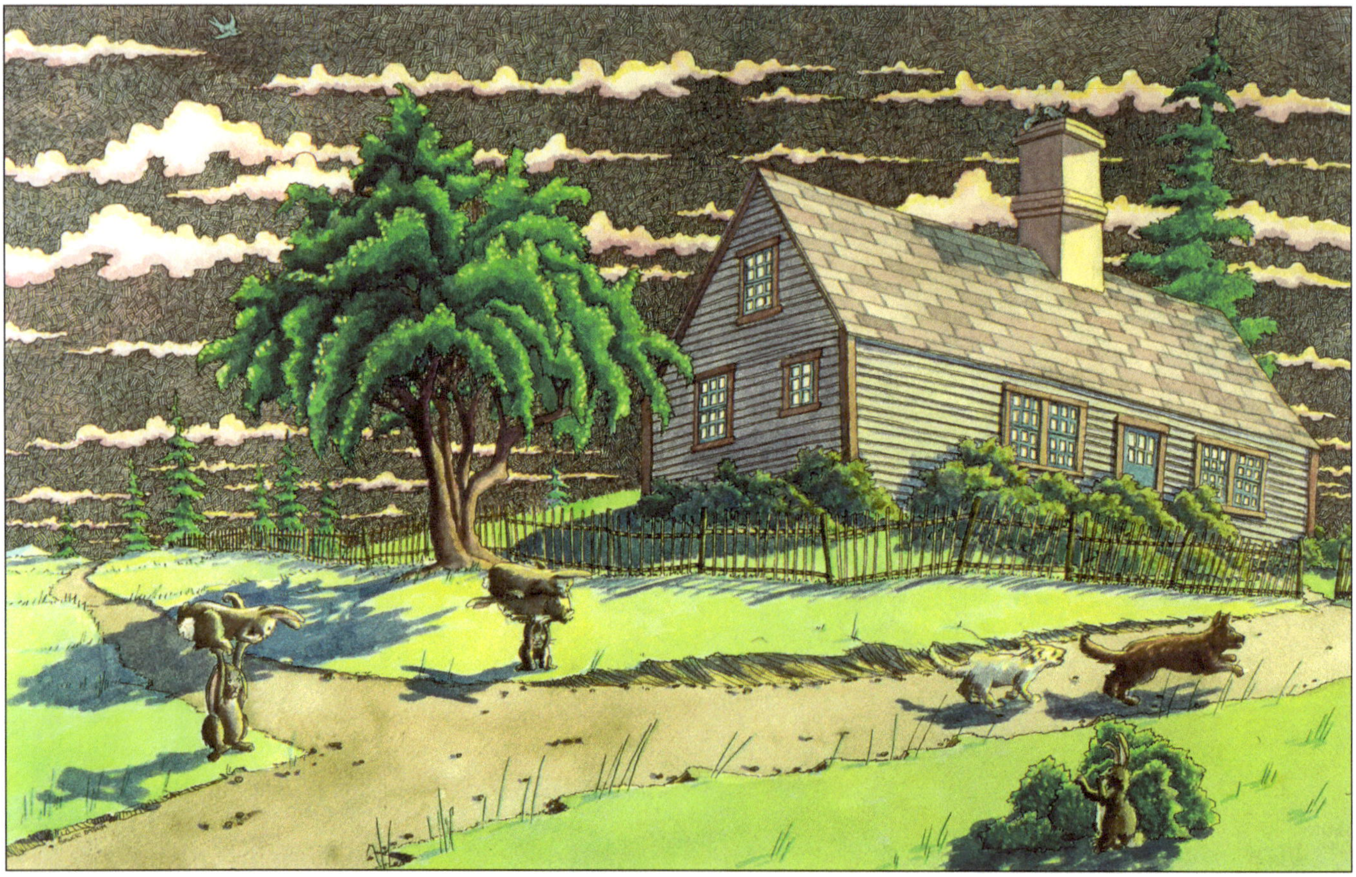

Faux Mailbox

Posing as directional signs and mailboxes were only a few of the tricks in the rabbit family's extensive repertoire when put to the challenge of pups in hot pursuit.

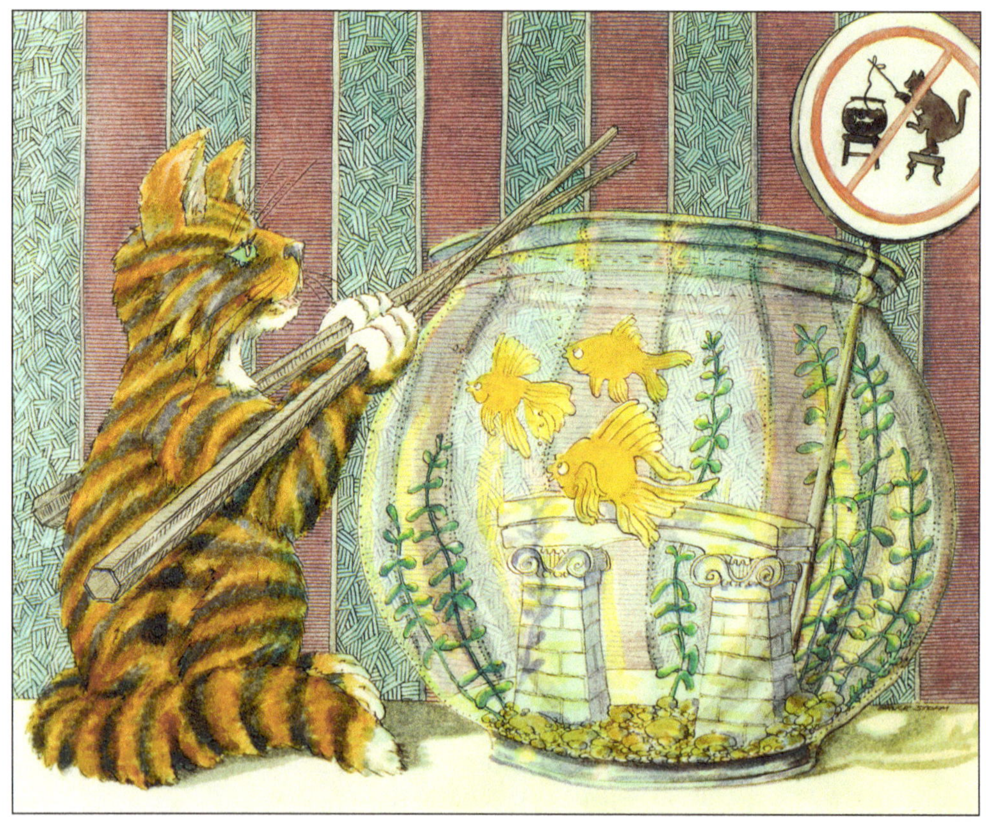

Sushi

A Japanese delicacy of rawfish...Fluffy loved the whole concept. As for the sign, well, he wasn't using a pole or a line. Just how do those things work, anyway?

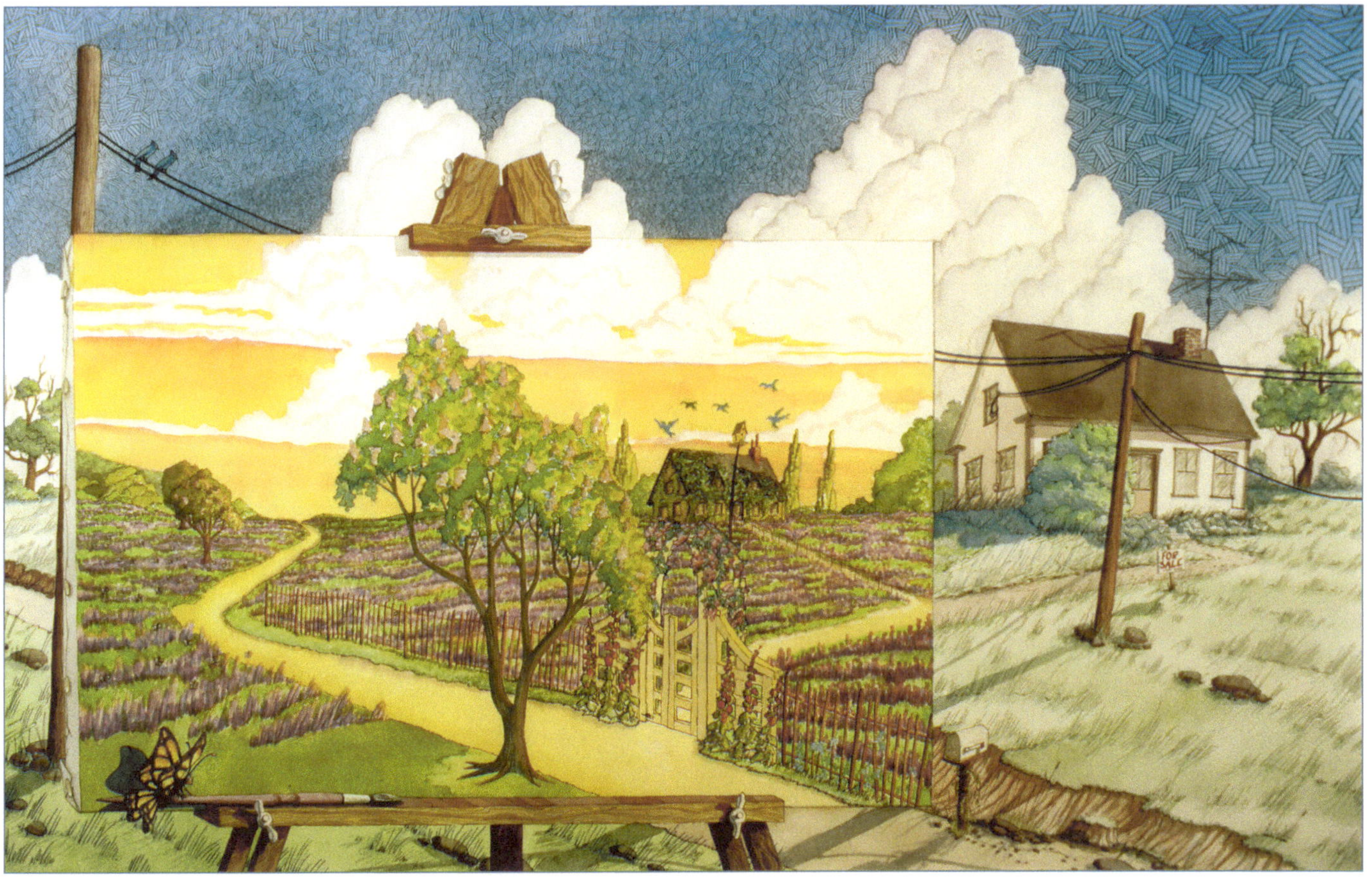

For Sale

He painted what could be or should be, thought The butterfly as she longed to find a way into the painted fields of flowers.

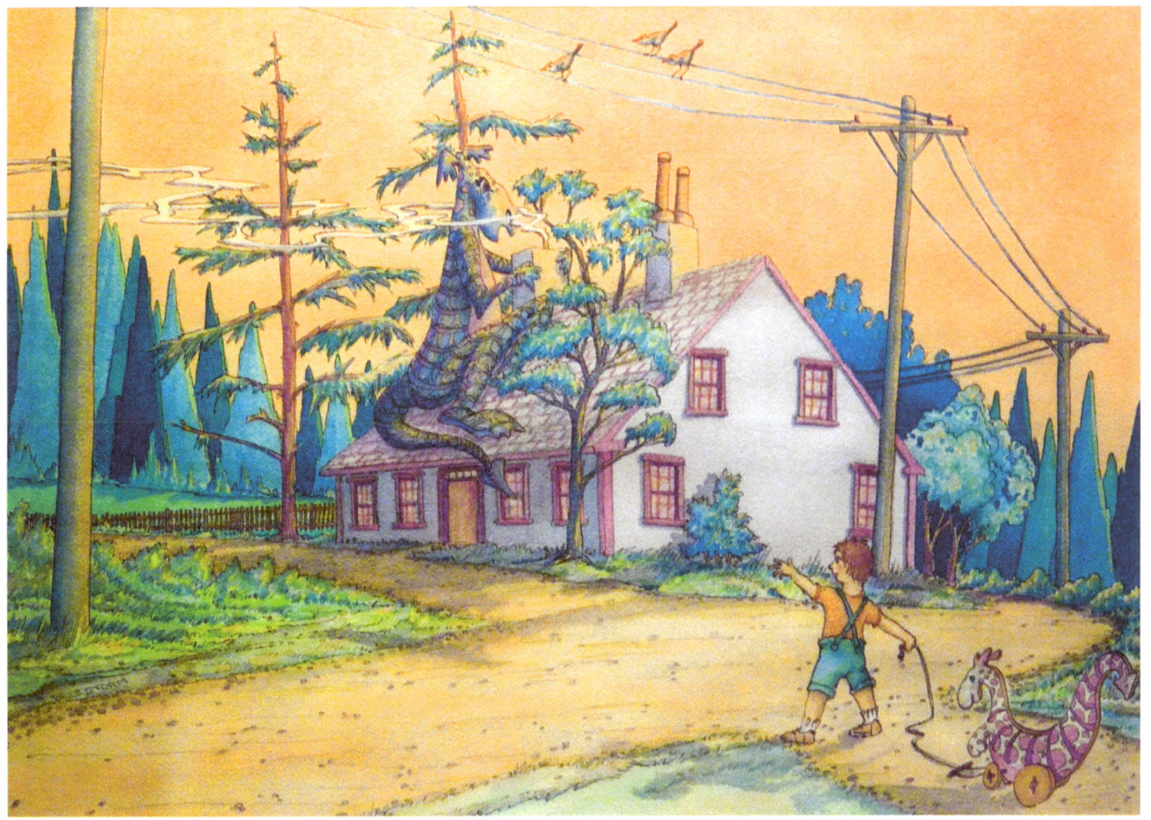

The Smell of Home Cooking

How can you know me - we just met, the dragon protested! Can one only see dragons through a child's eyes?

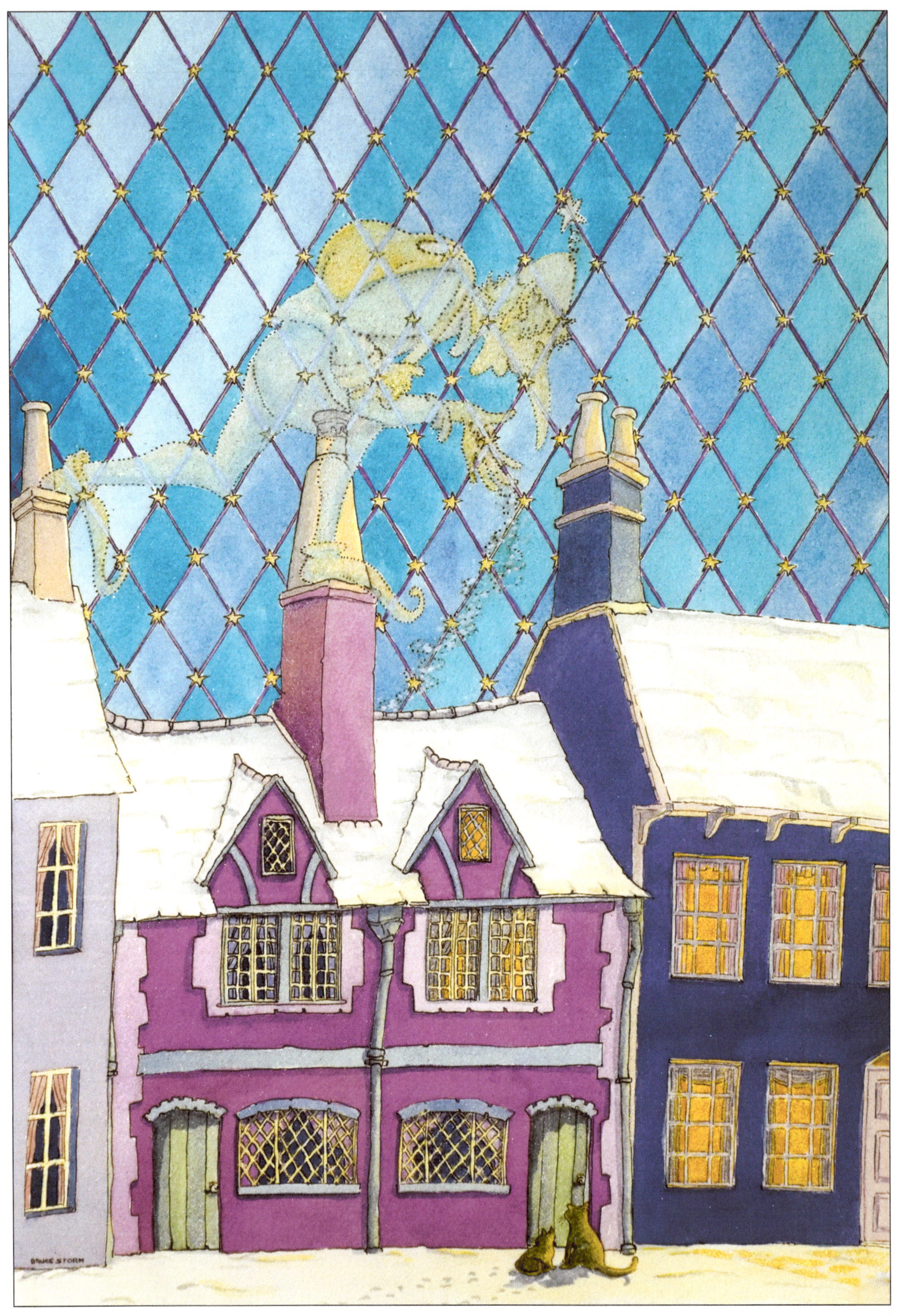

Sandman Country Town

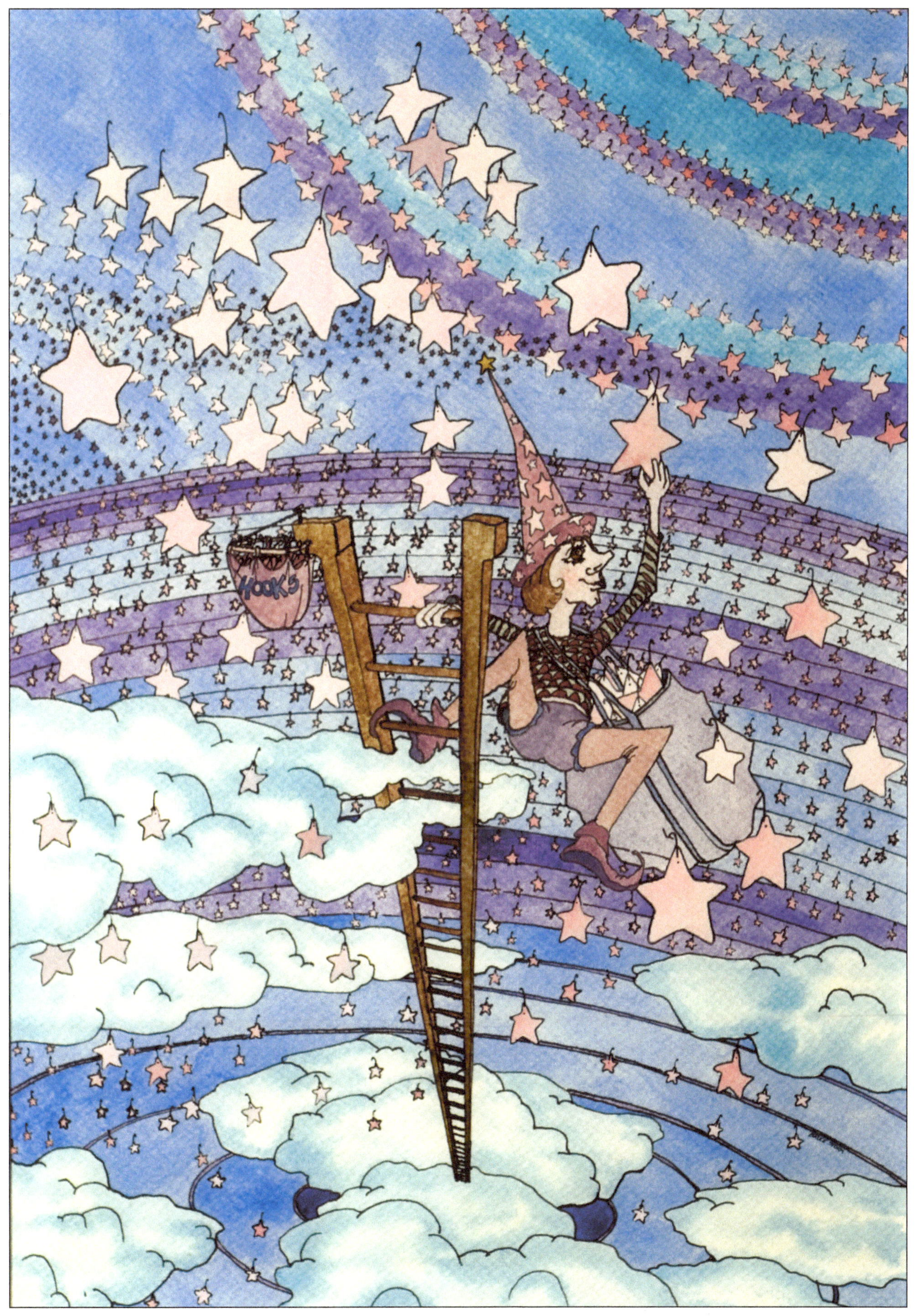

Star Hanger

Among the clouds in rows of sheer perfection, He festooned the heavens with starry splendor.

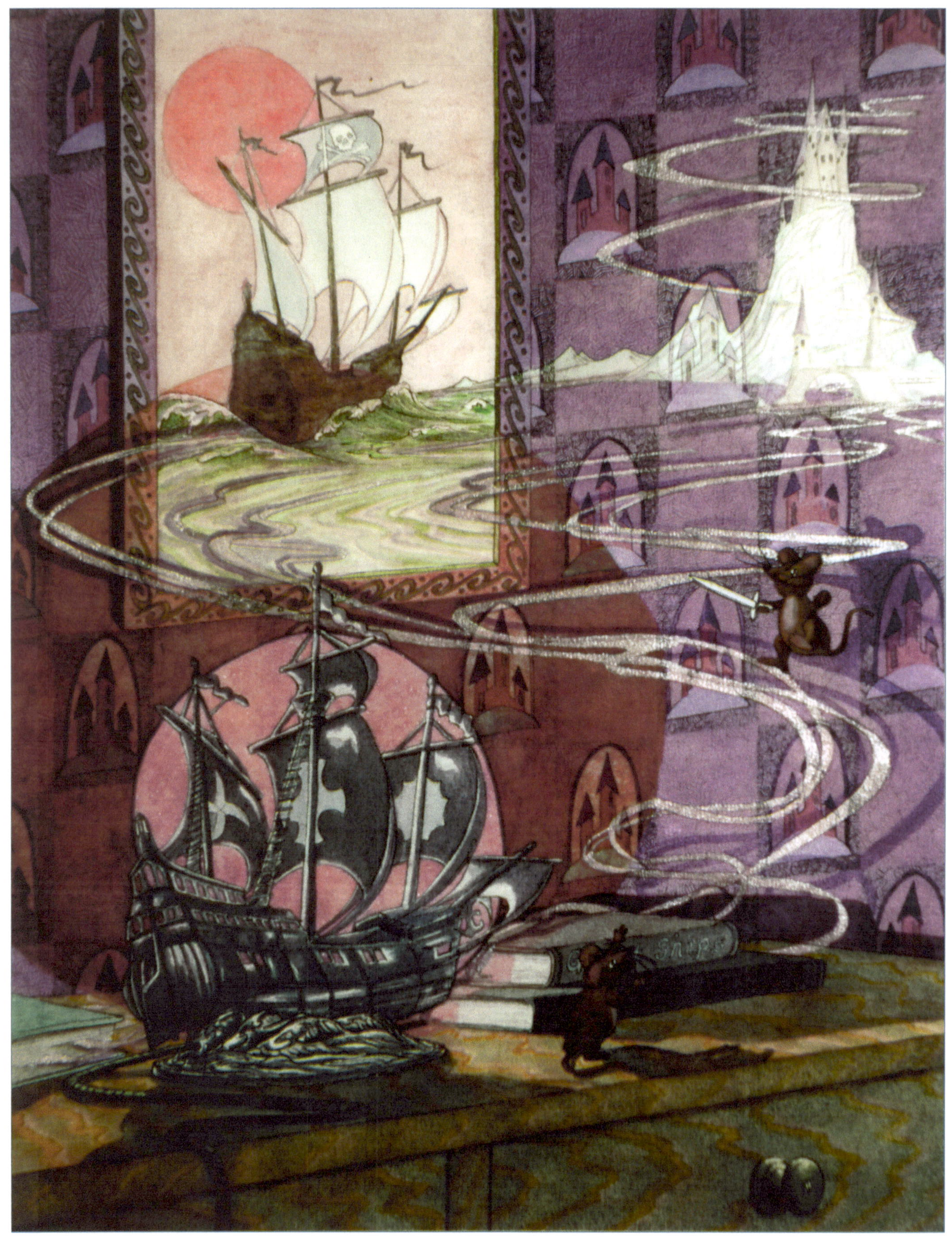

Night Light Adventure

They were devotees of Flynn's Films. The Drama - the adventure. Now the night light's rosey glow illuminated what seemed to be a castle. A wisp of cloud lifted Topher, toy sword in hand. He was ready for action while Binz watched, puzzled and mesmerized.

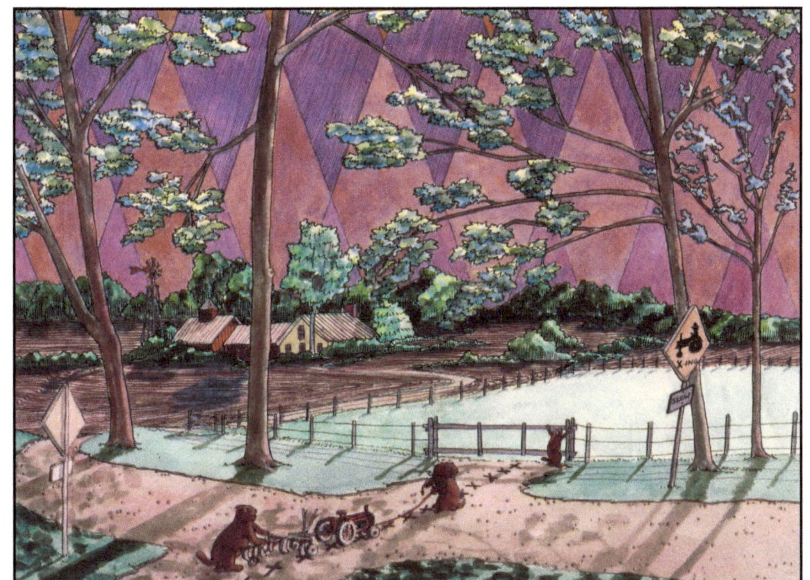

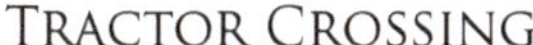

Tractor Crossing

Iggy and Grace were sticklers for crossing in properly marked areas.

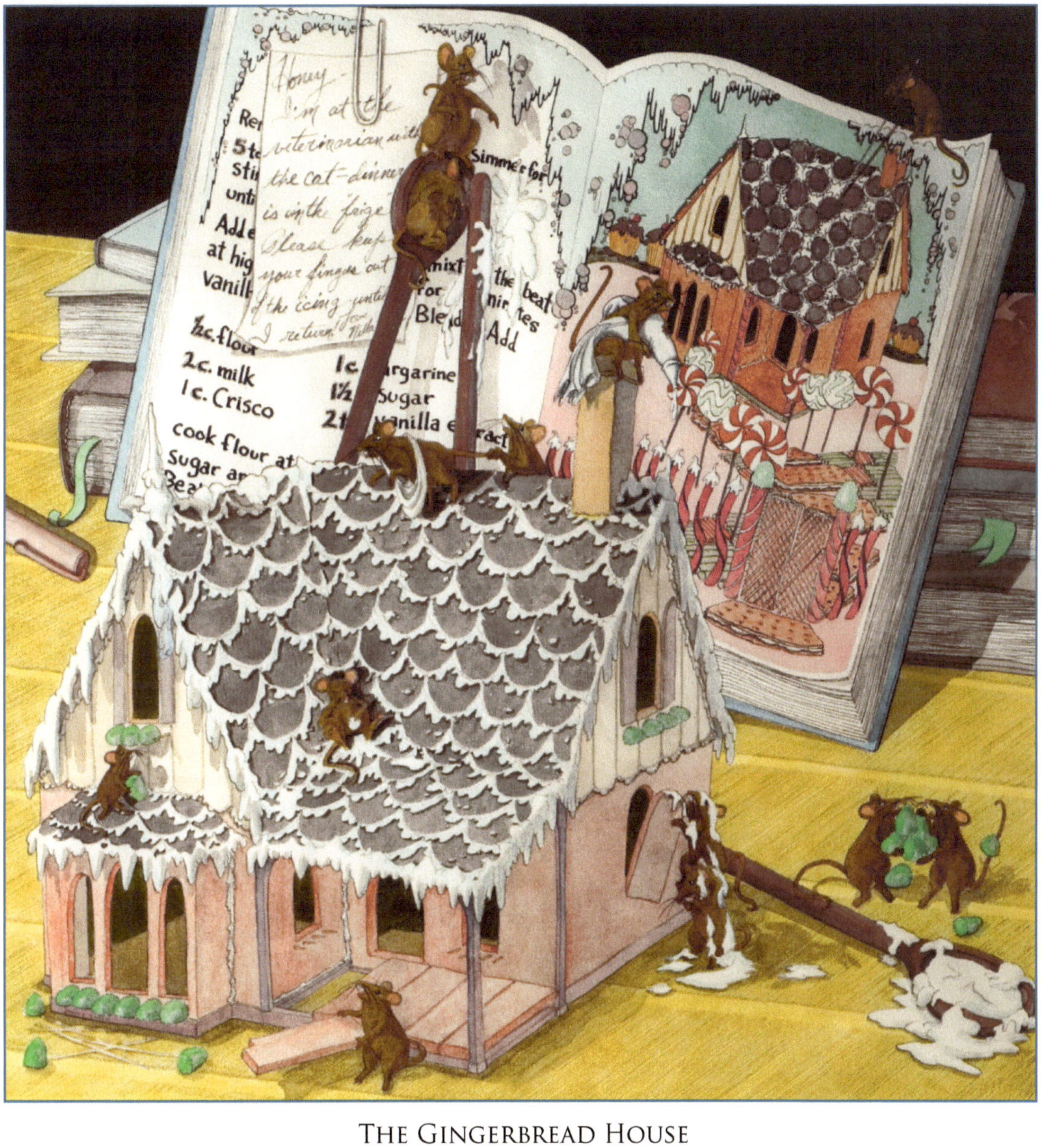

The Gingerbread House

It was intended as a gesture of good will - really it was: complete the decorating, and the humans would see what fine fellows they were. Out would go the mouse traps. Out would go the cat. All would be harmony but the mice's enthusiasm pitifully lacked organization.

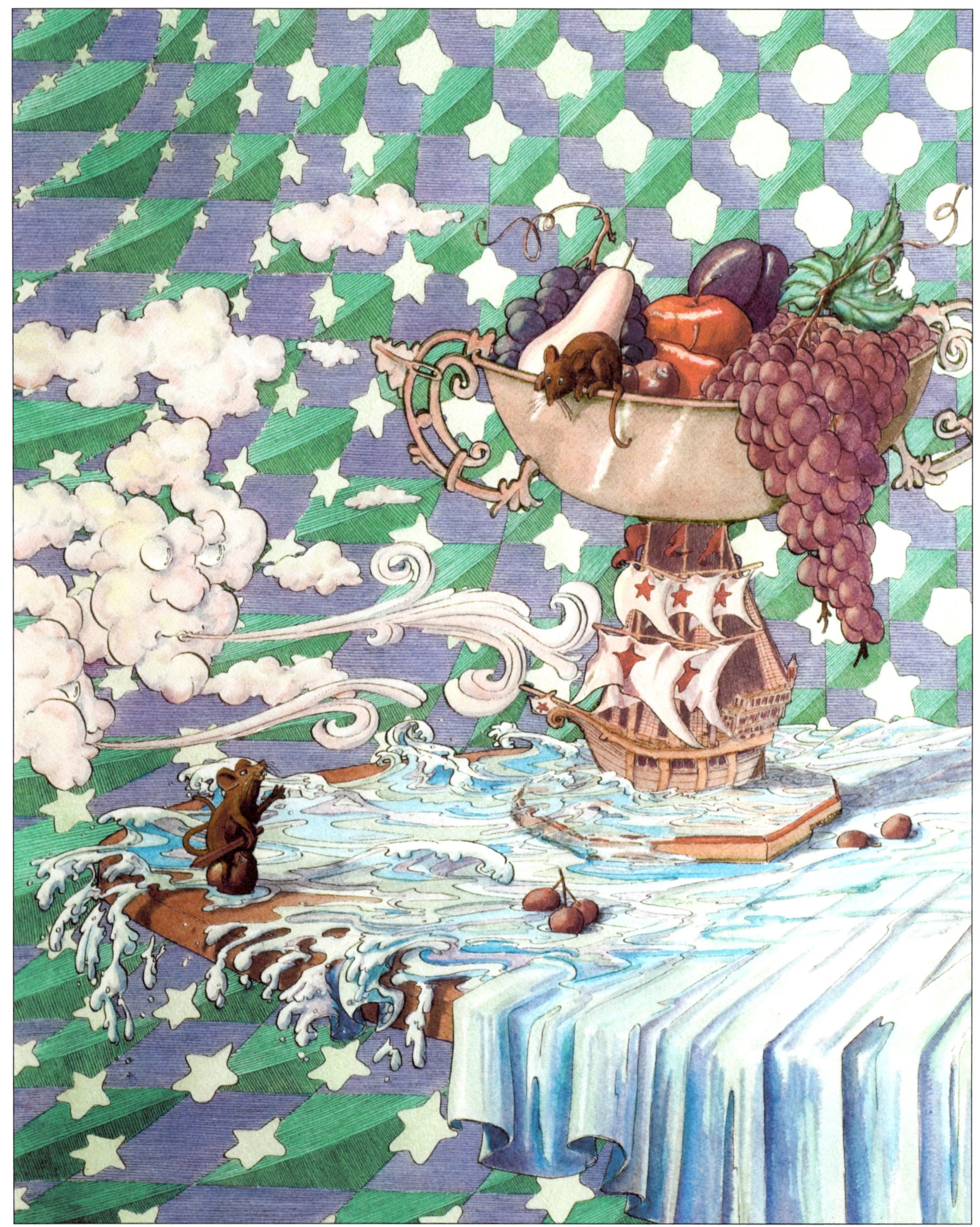

Roesen Still Life

This was no Roesen still life, Topher observed, and it isn't very still, Linz replied, as she bobbed along on the crabapple.

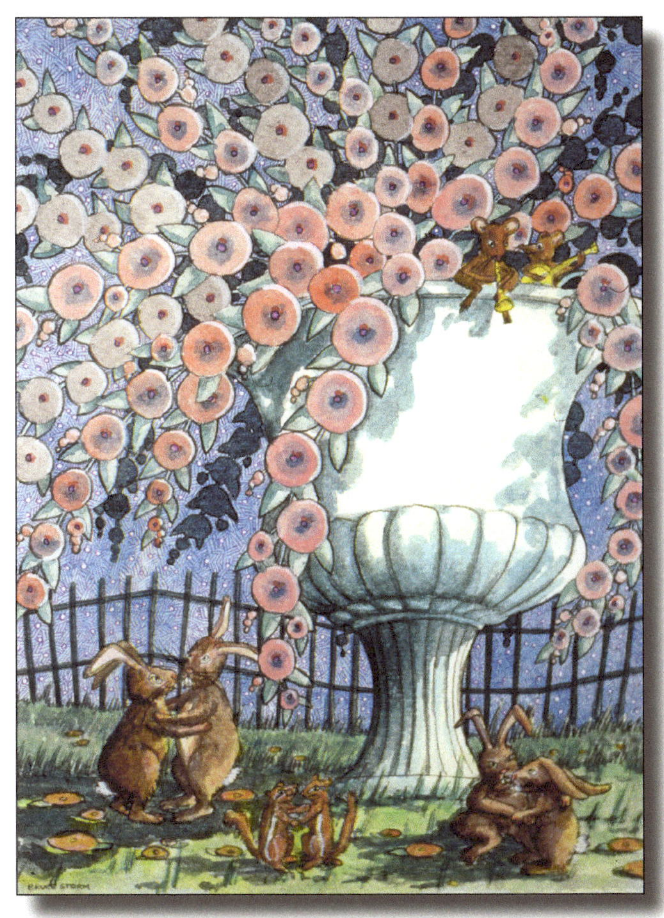

Romance

Bed Time Froggy

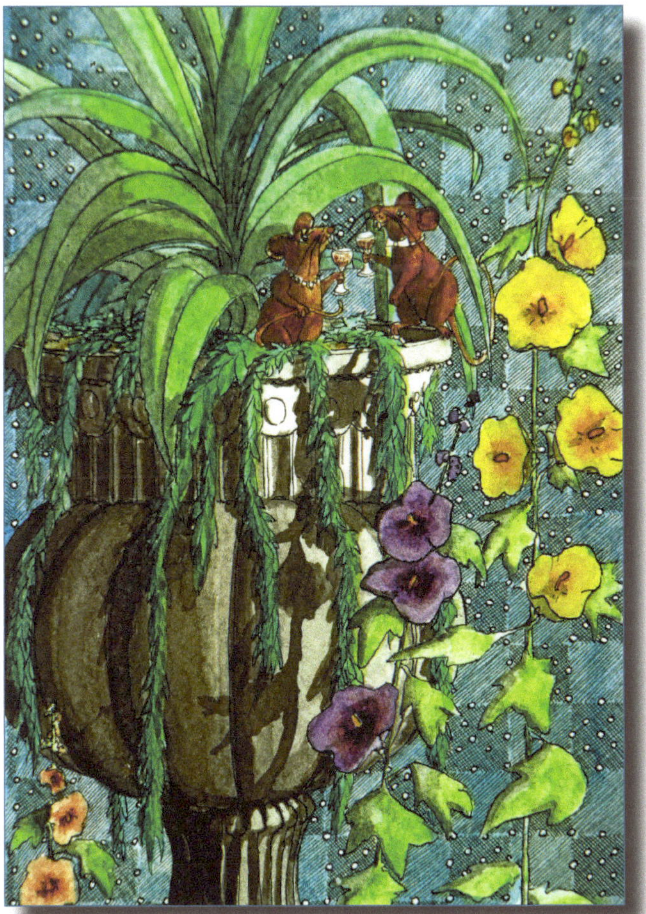

Anniversary Toast

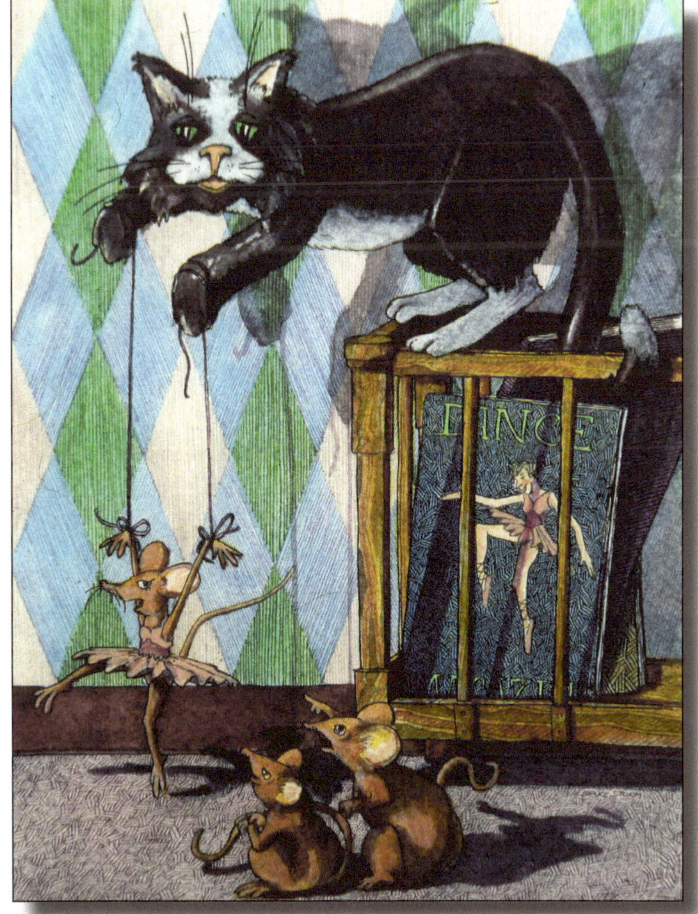

Dance

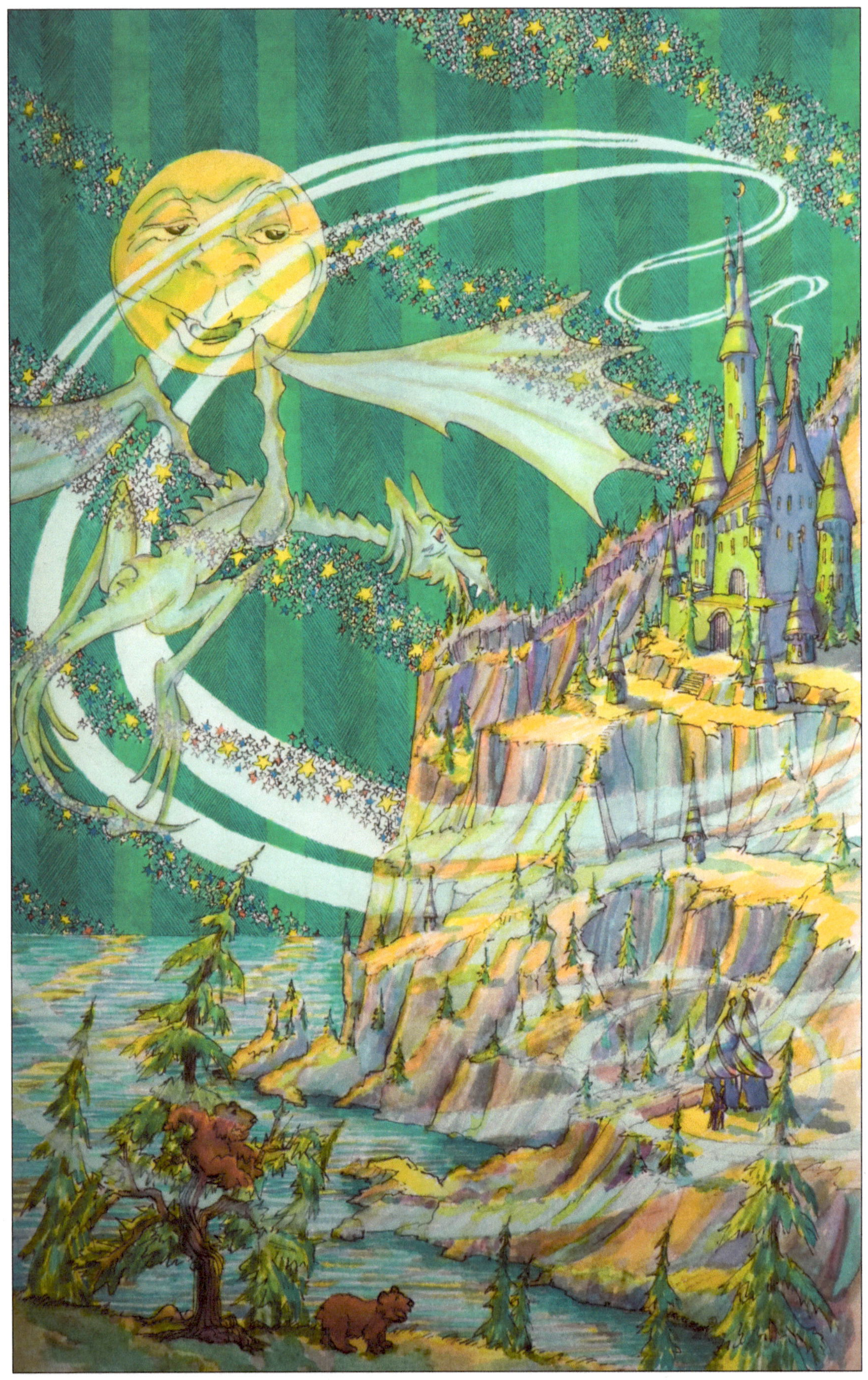

Dragons Don't Tell

Through the heavens the dragon soared unfettered. Mischievous bears, flickering castle lights, the little dancing stars; the dragon knew all their stories and wishes, but you know dragons never tell.

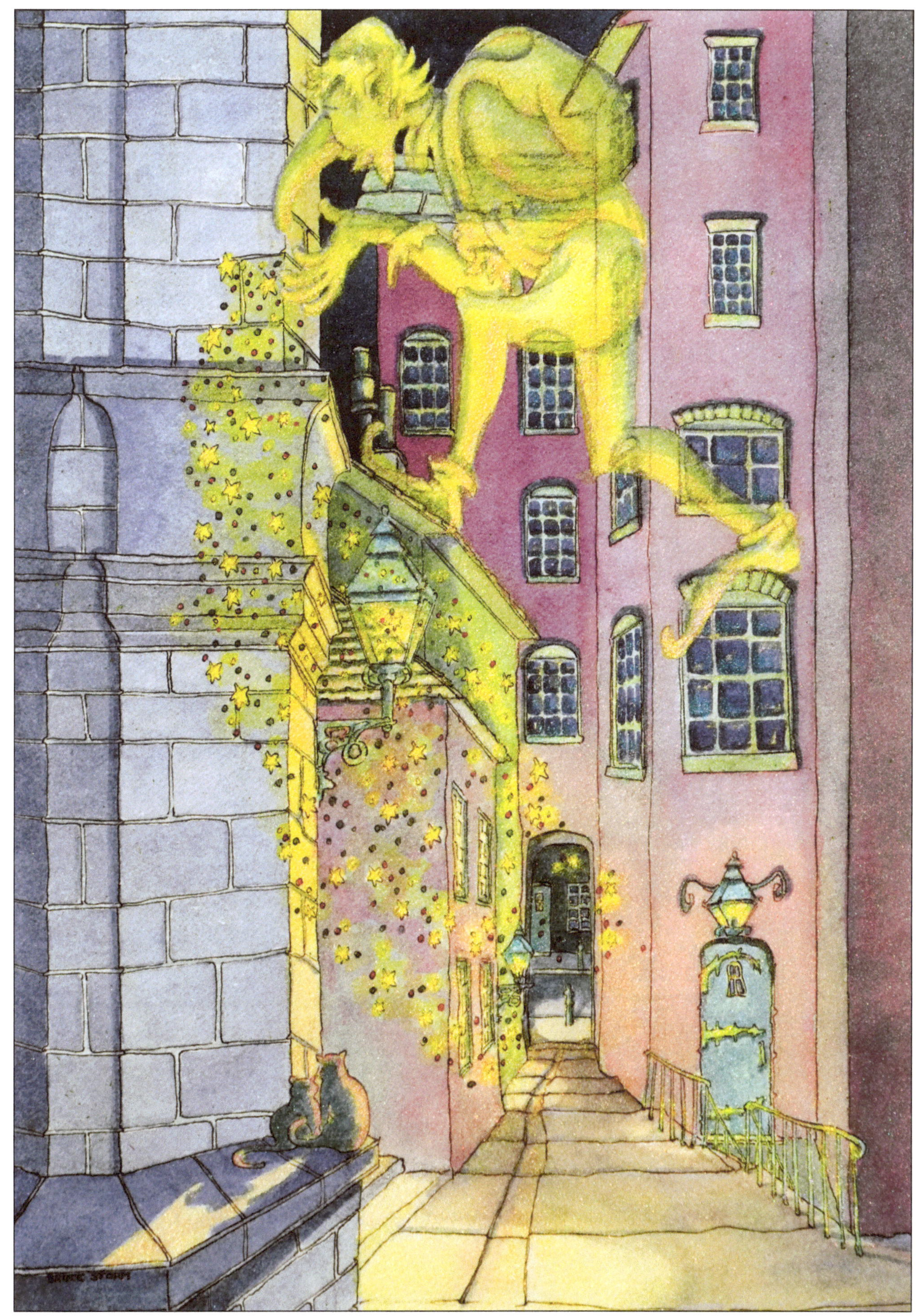

Sandman City Scene

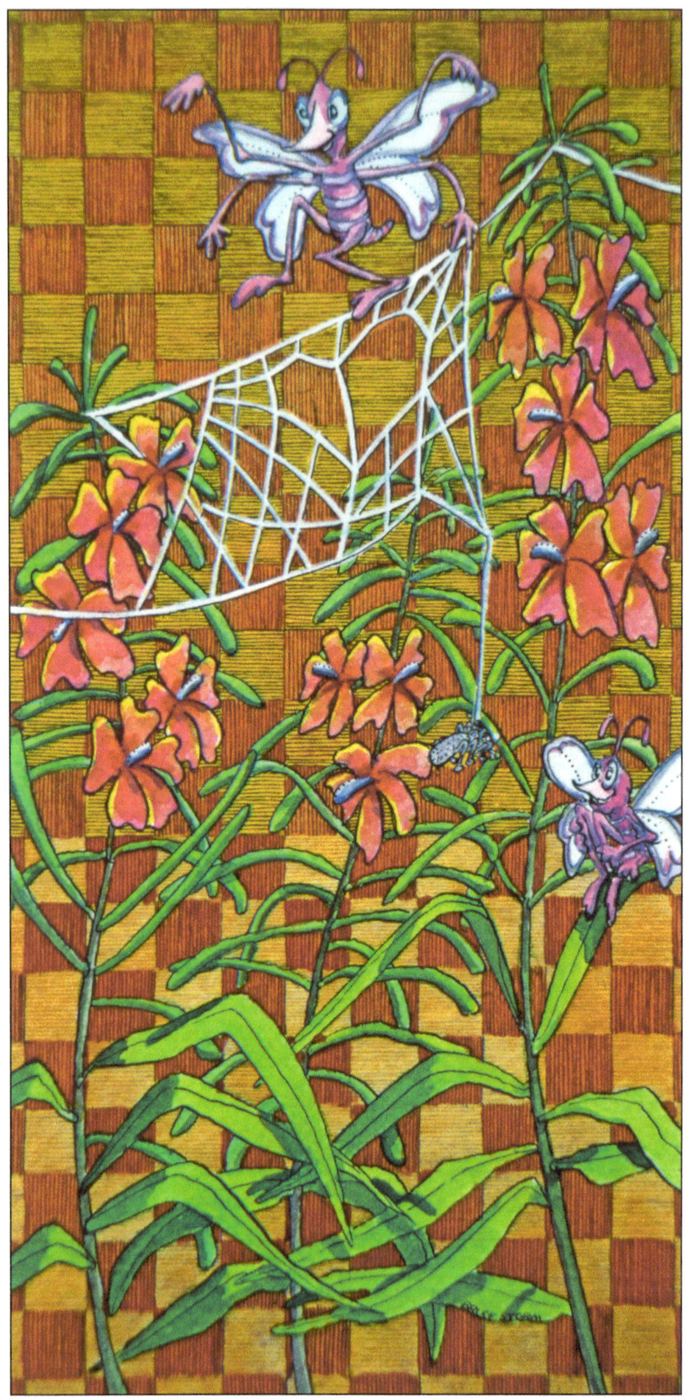

Love Bugs

She gazed breathlessly at the weed. Henry was such a romantic. How ever had he convinced the old spider to do it?

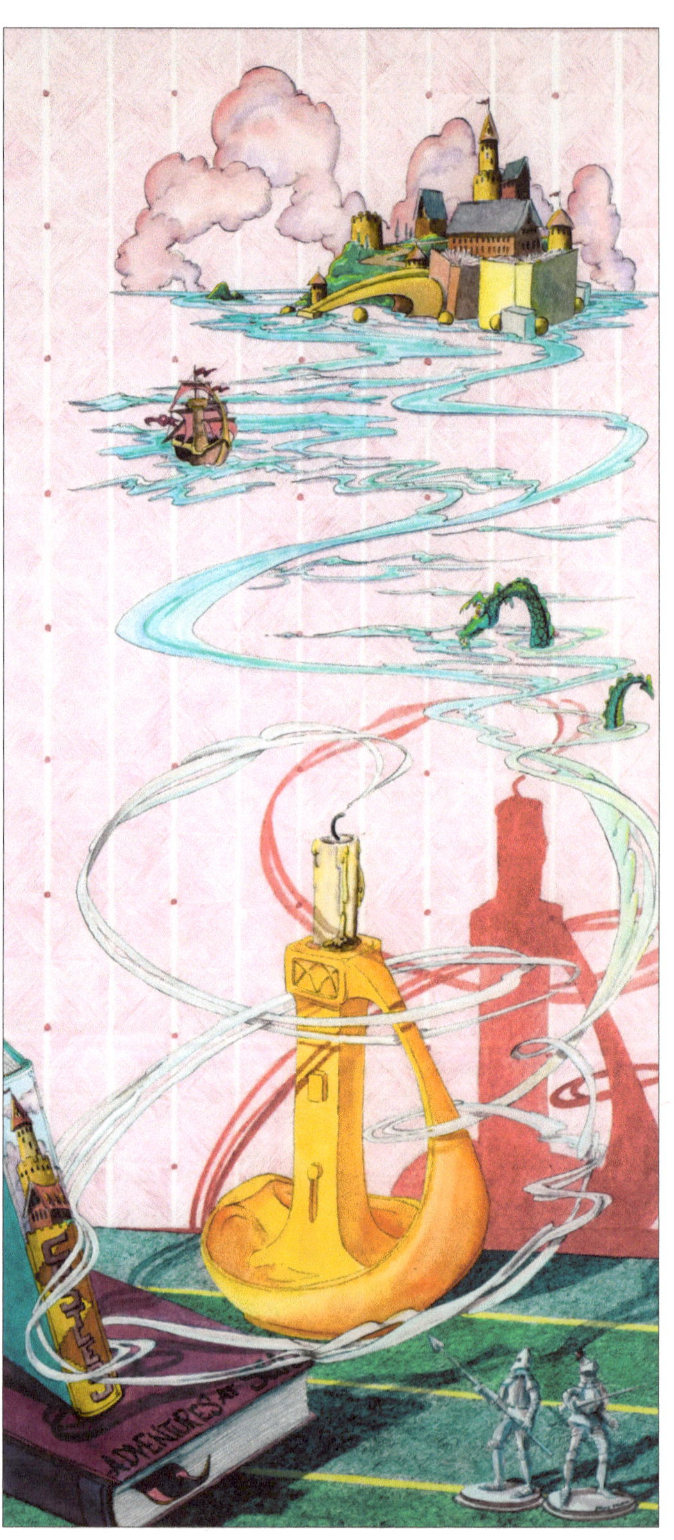

Novel Approach

Take the words, infuse with private realities, spark with remembrances, drift into the dream.

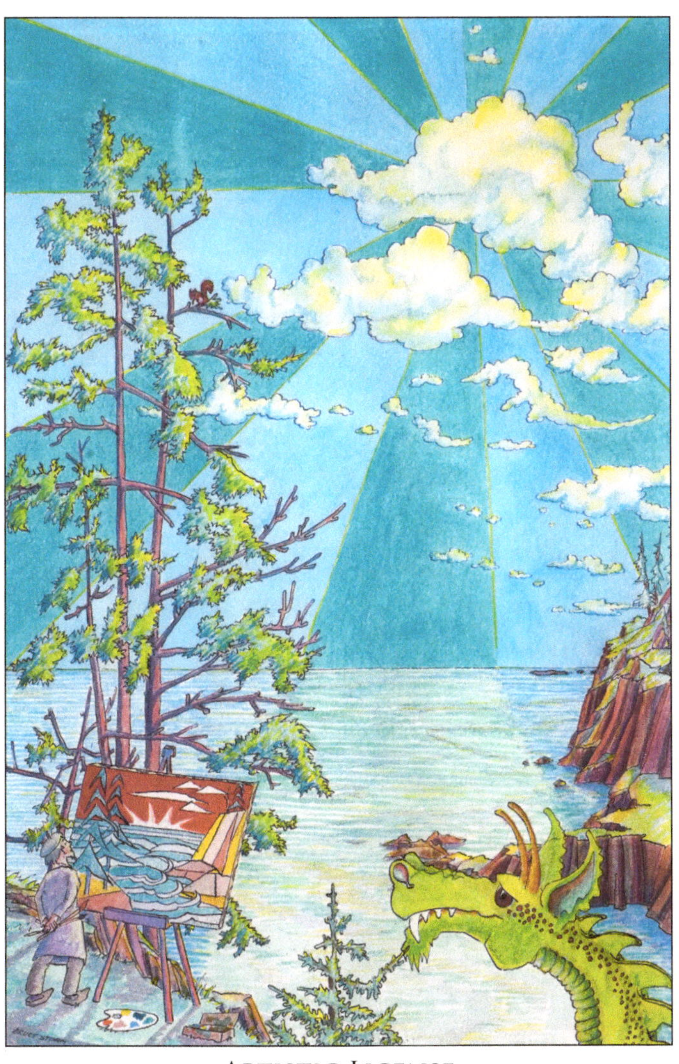

Artistic License

"Change what you will - it's your world. Your life - your art. Don't want to paint the dragon cloud - don't. Still a dragon adds a certain "je ne sais quoi" The painter's observer mused.

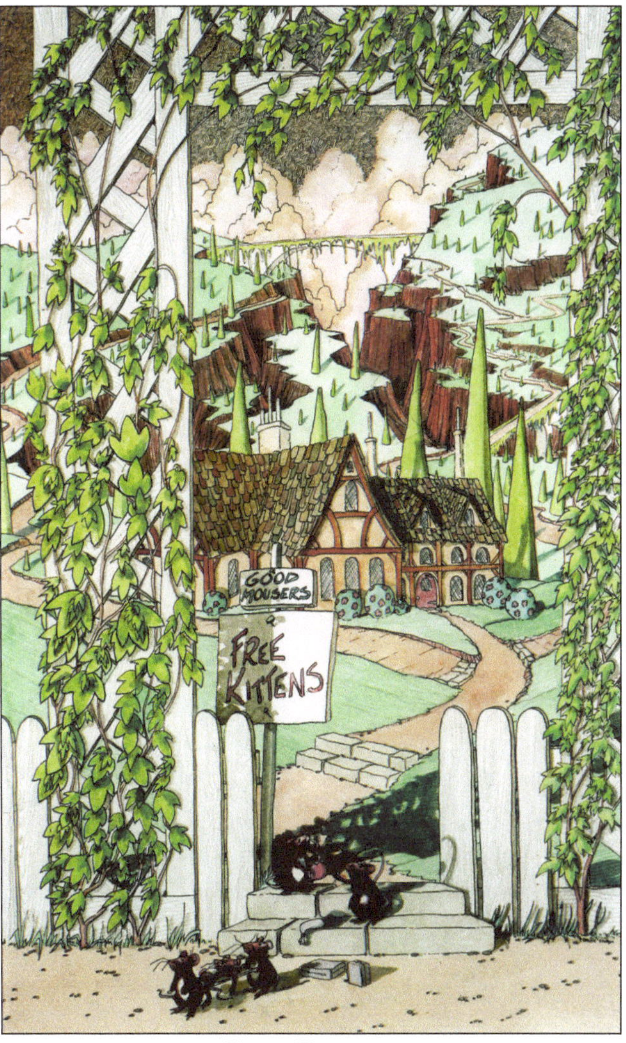

Free Kittens

Everything was idyllic, serene, a haven from the world's turmoil, absolutely their cup of tea, tip-top, yes--blissful, perfectly blissful. Then, the sign went up and all hell broke loose.

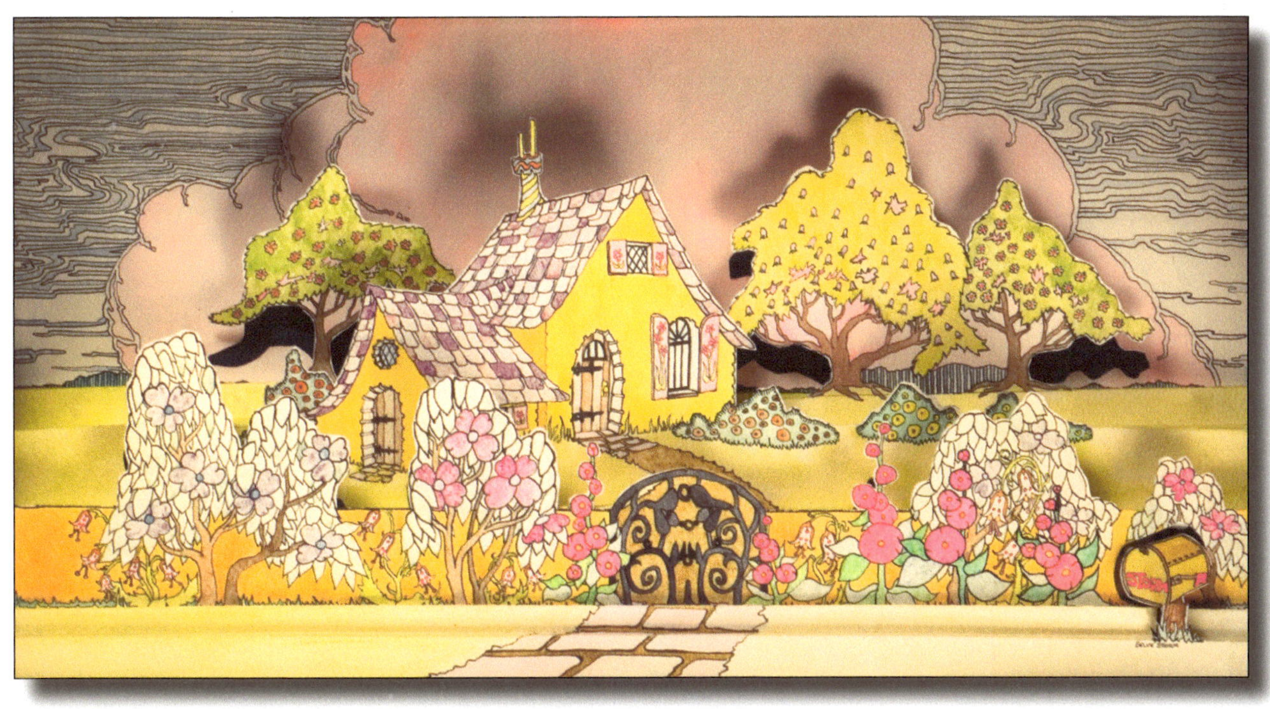

Hollyhocks and Whipperwills

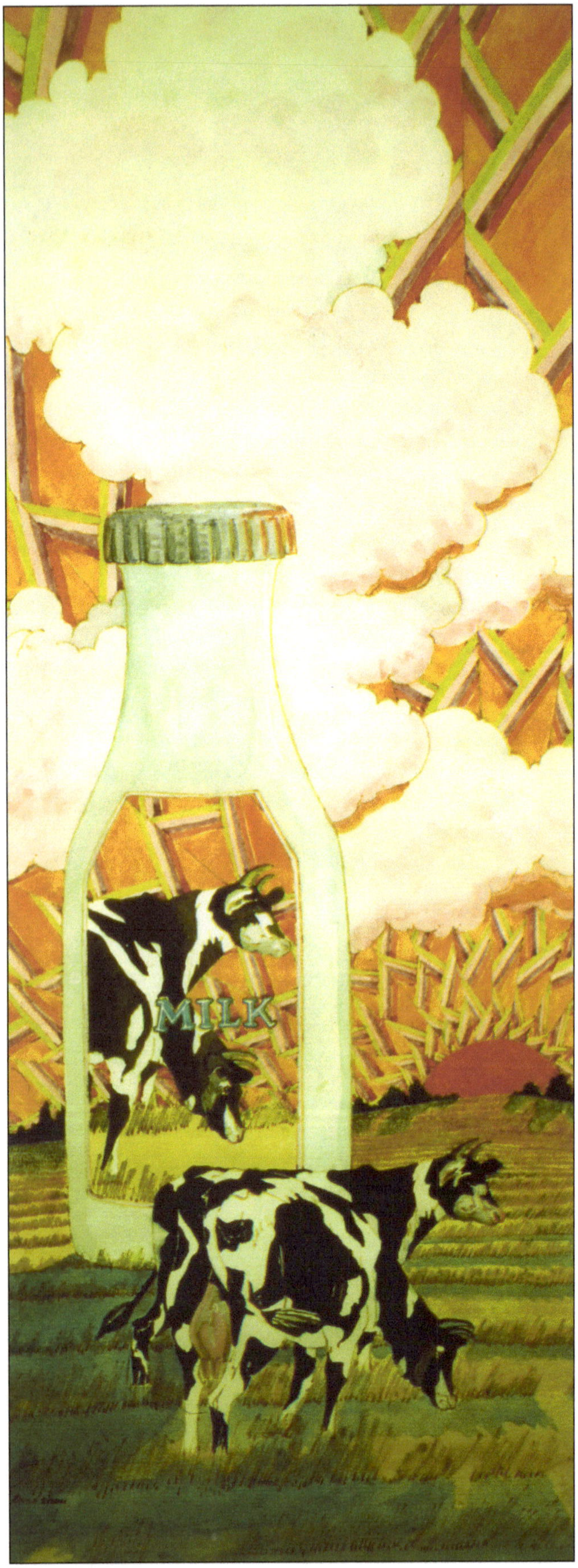

MILK

MILK

Morning Cows

Lift off the cover, pry up the cardboard cap. Pour out a morning of childhood rememberances...cows and the sun...glory of youth.

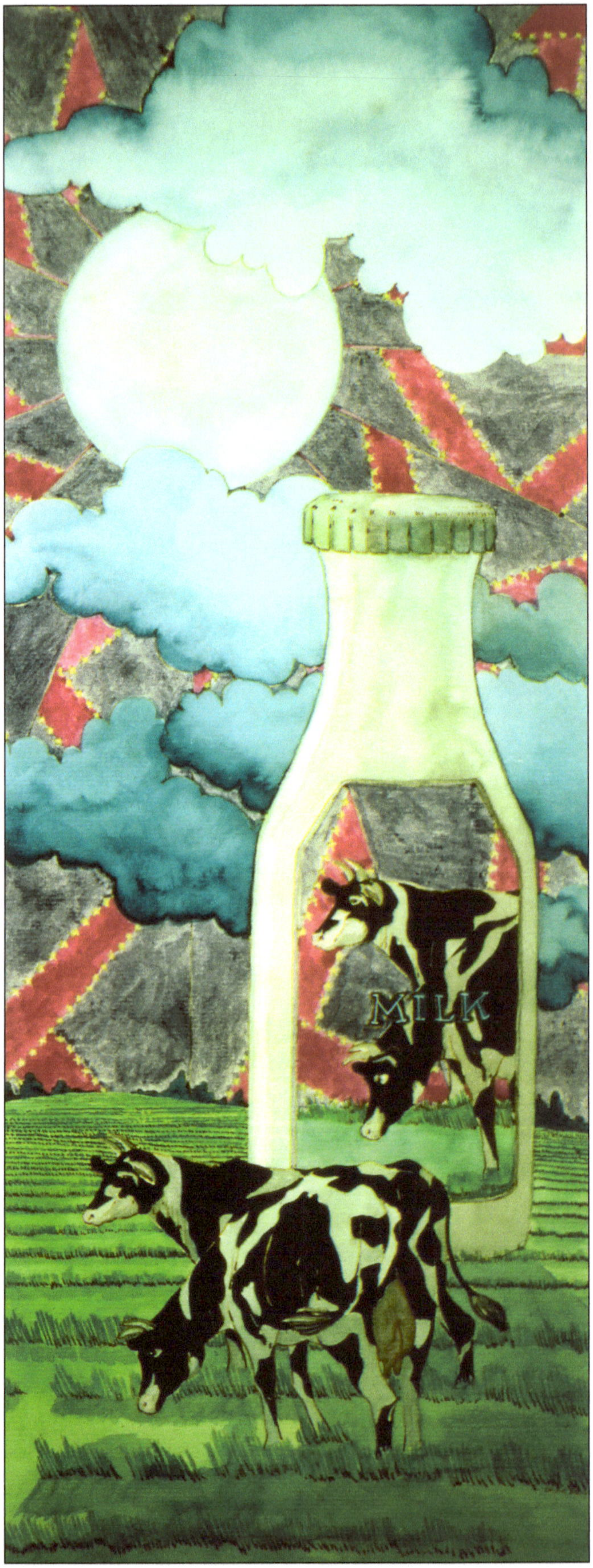

Night Cows

Lift off the cover, pry up the cardboard cap. Pour out a night of starry innocence...cows and moons and wonderment.

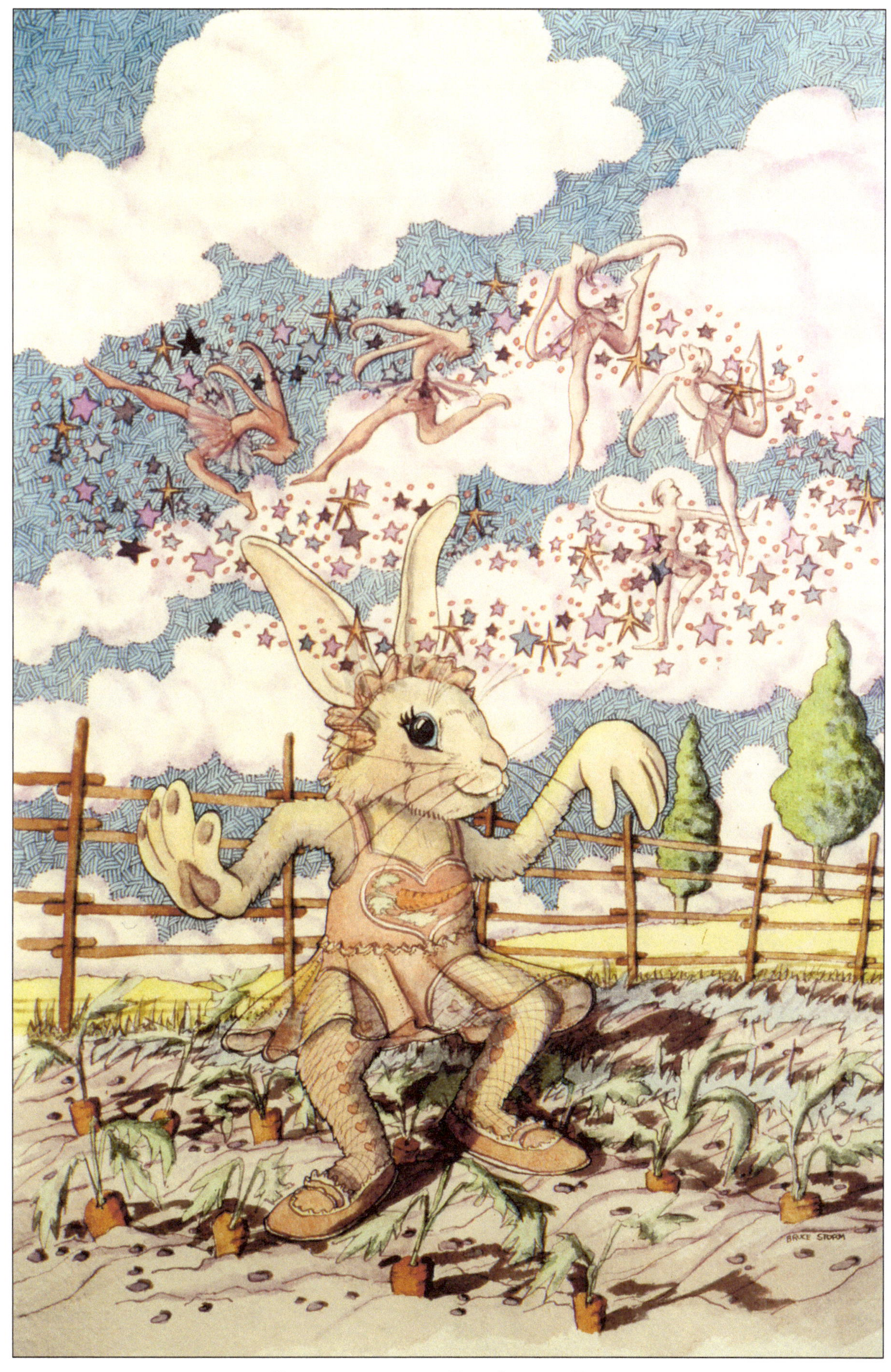

Dancing down The Bunny Trail

Posing and turning, leaping and swaying, the young rabbit performed with her troop of airy ballerinas. Oh, how graceful she was in her imagination.

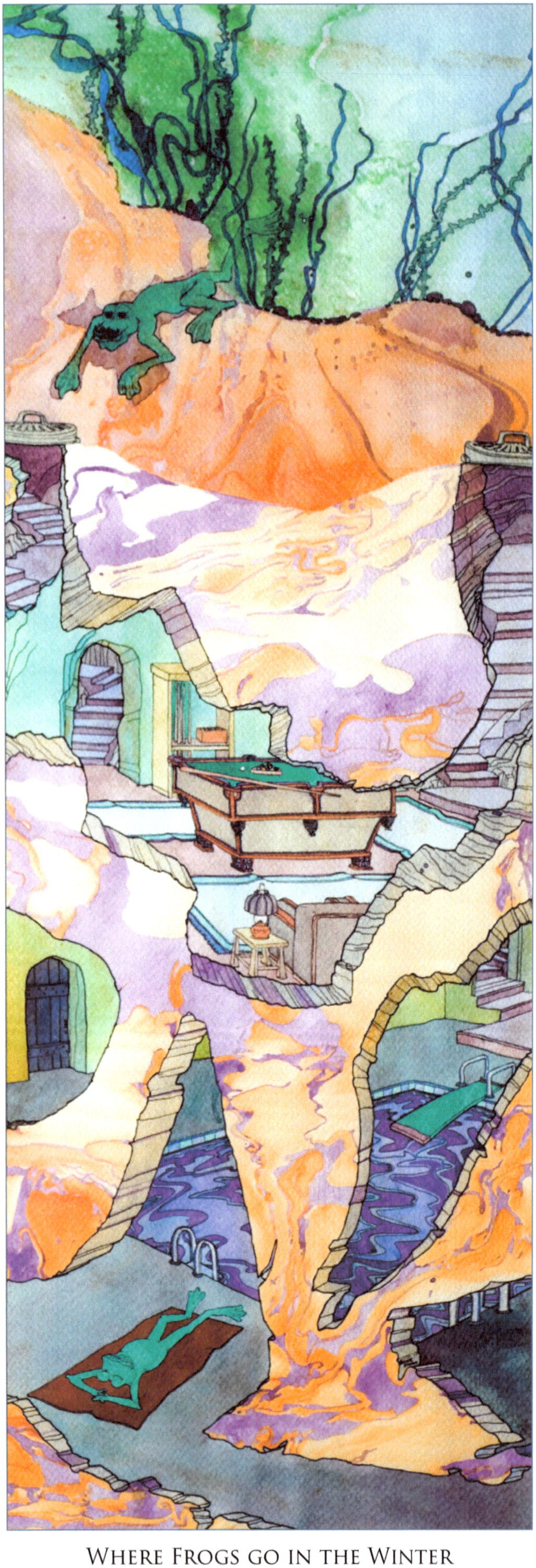

Where Frogs go in the Winter

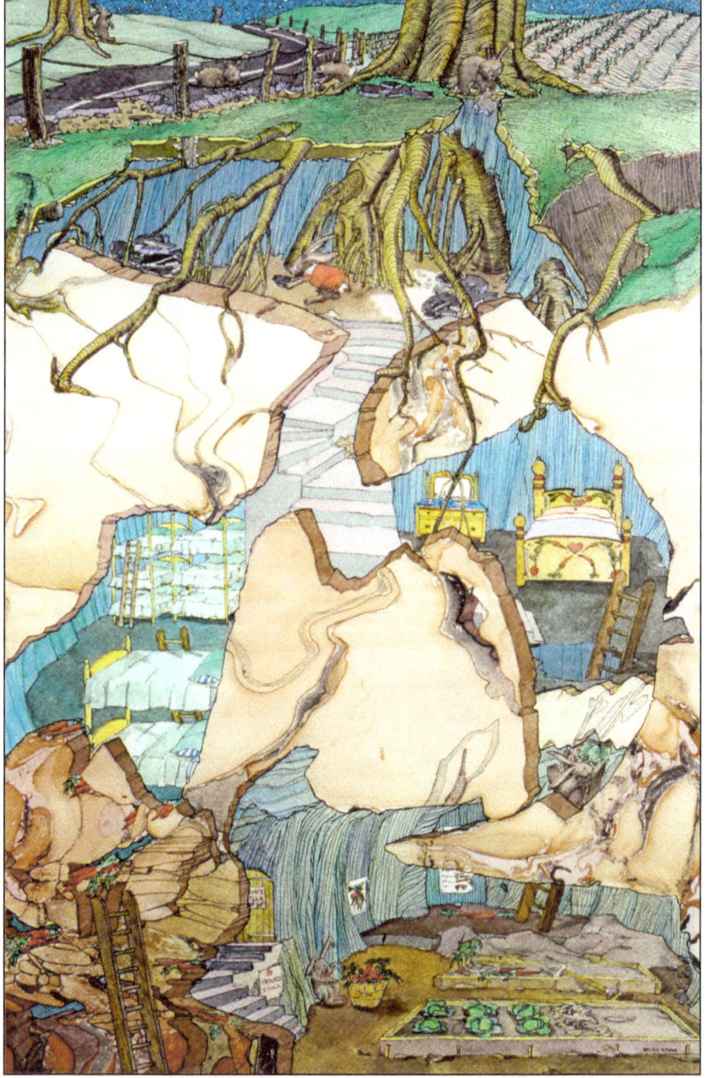

Pot Holes

In an attempt to impede traffic, the woodland creatures skillfully removed chunks of the macadam and stored them deep inside their burrows. A vast network of sentries was deployed to sound the warnings of oncoming headlights through the brisk night sky.

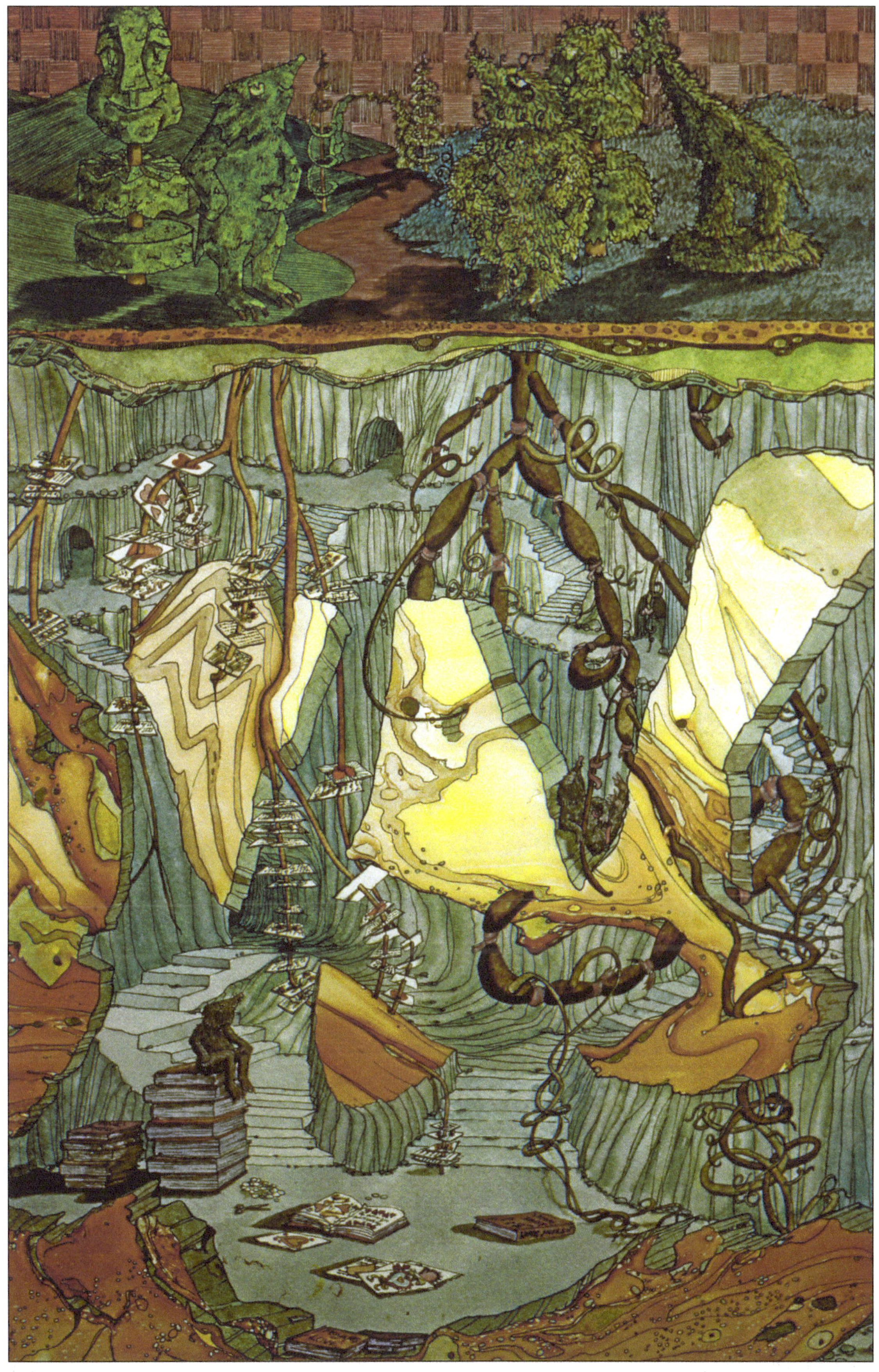

Topiary Competition

The rivalry had gone on for sometime when the moles decided on the topiary competition as the best way of settling the dispute. Utilizing old handkerchiefs and stray rubber bands, one tortured the roots into submission while the other gently removed old Rachmaninoff and Strauss sheet music, placing them in the proper juxtaposition with discarded valentines and sonnets, thus creating peerless topiary.

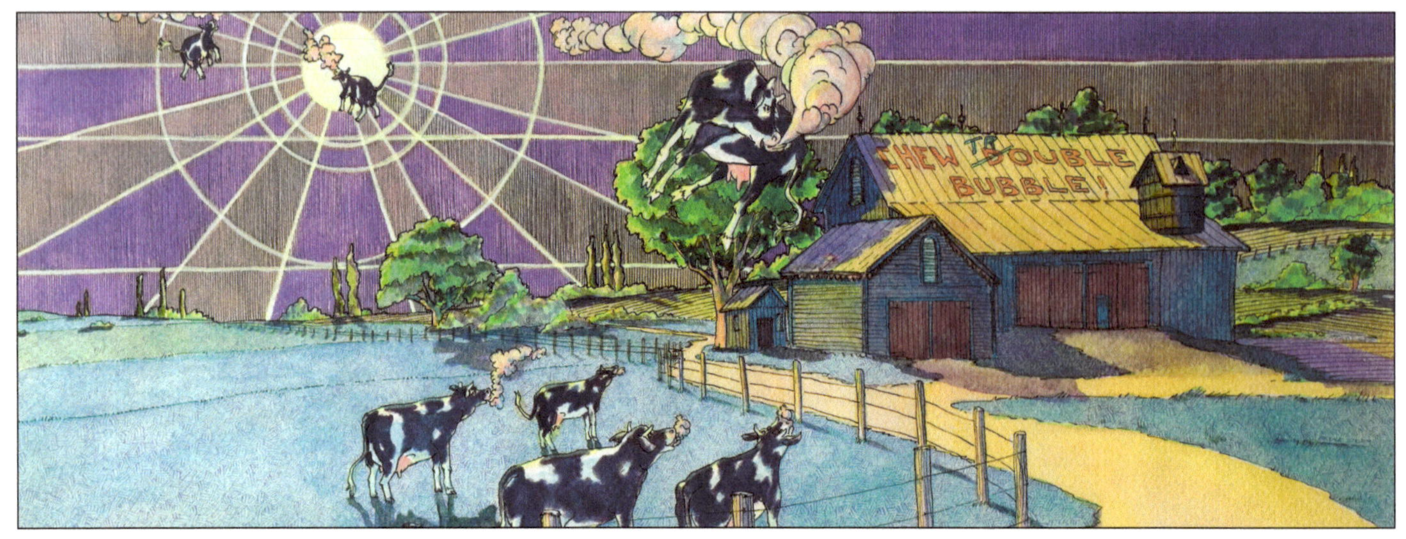

South Pasture - Trouble Bubble

Out on the south pasture Blossom Betty and Buttercup had discovered the old carton of trouble bubble. under the full moon's glow the trio led the group in arabesques and introduced the much touted mooooon walk.

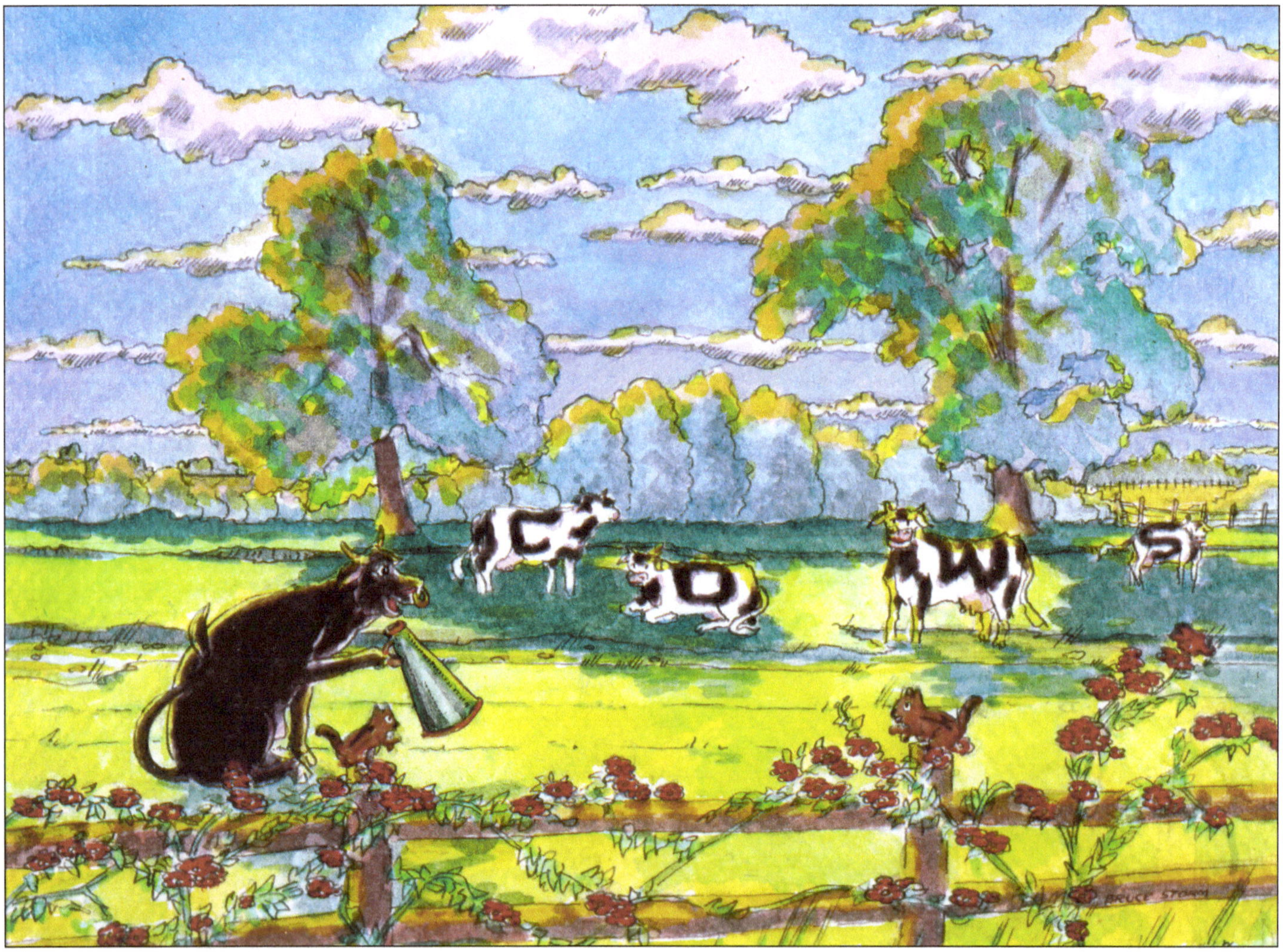

Places girls

Radio City or Vegas, then maybe a European tour. Wally had to wonder what cosmic force had brought those four cows into his pasture. Fate or coincidence. Did it matter? They were all high kickers.

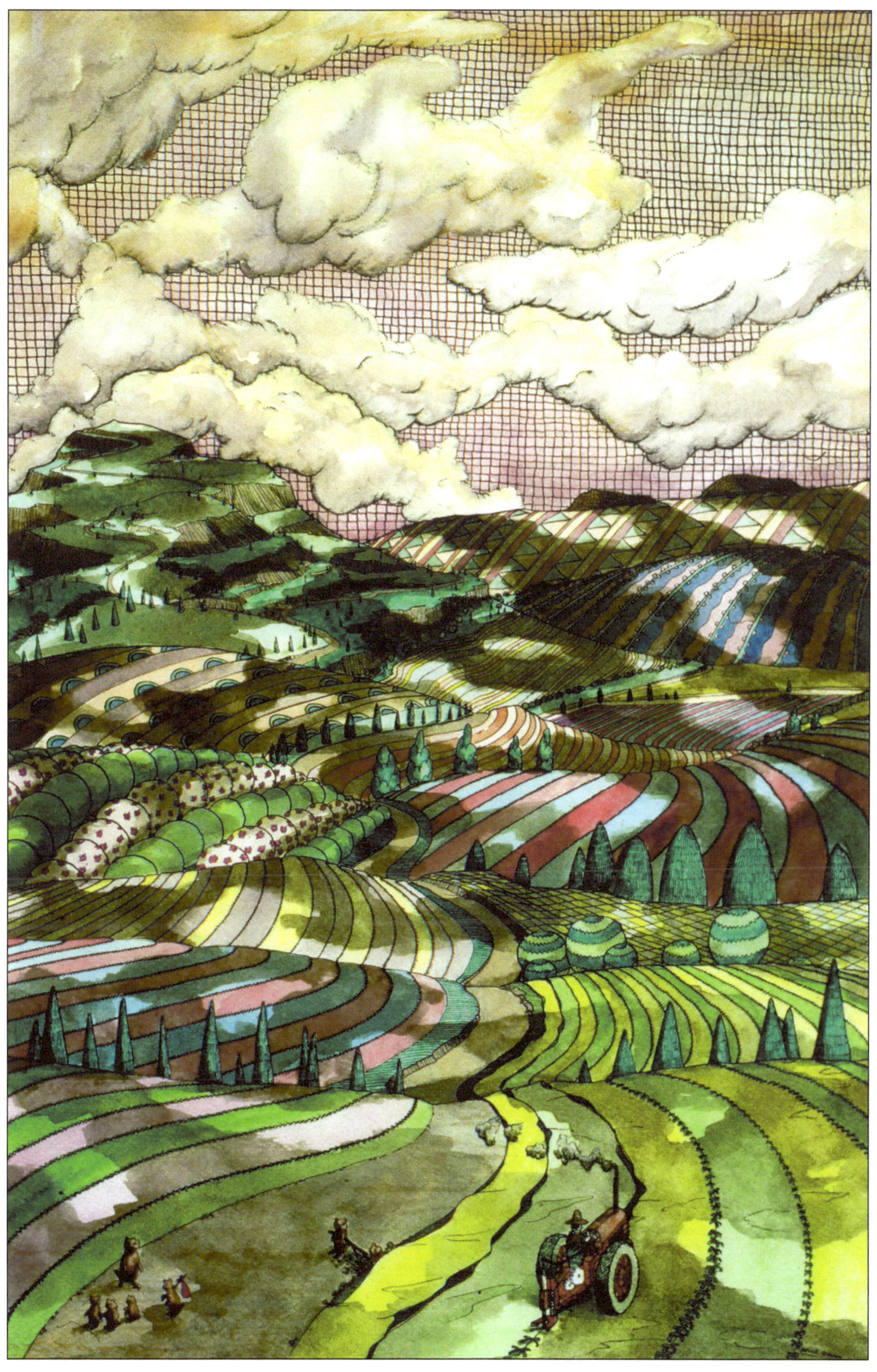

Cross Stitch

Their burrow was about to be sewn up. Now "Thorton" and the family found themselves facing the endless quilt of fields without a plan.

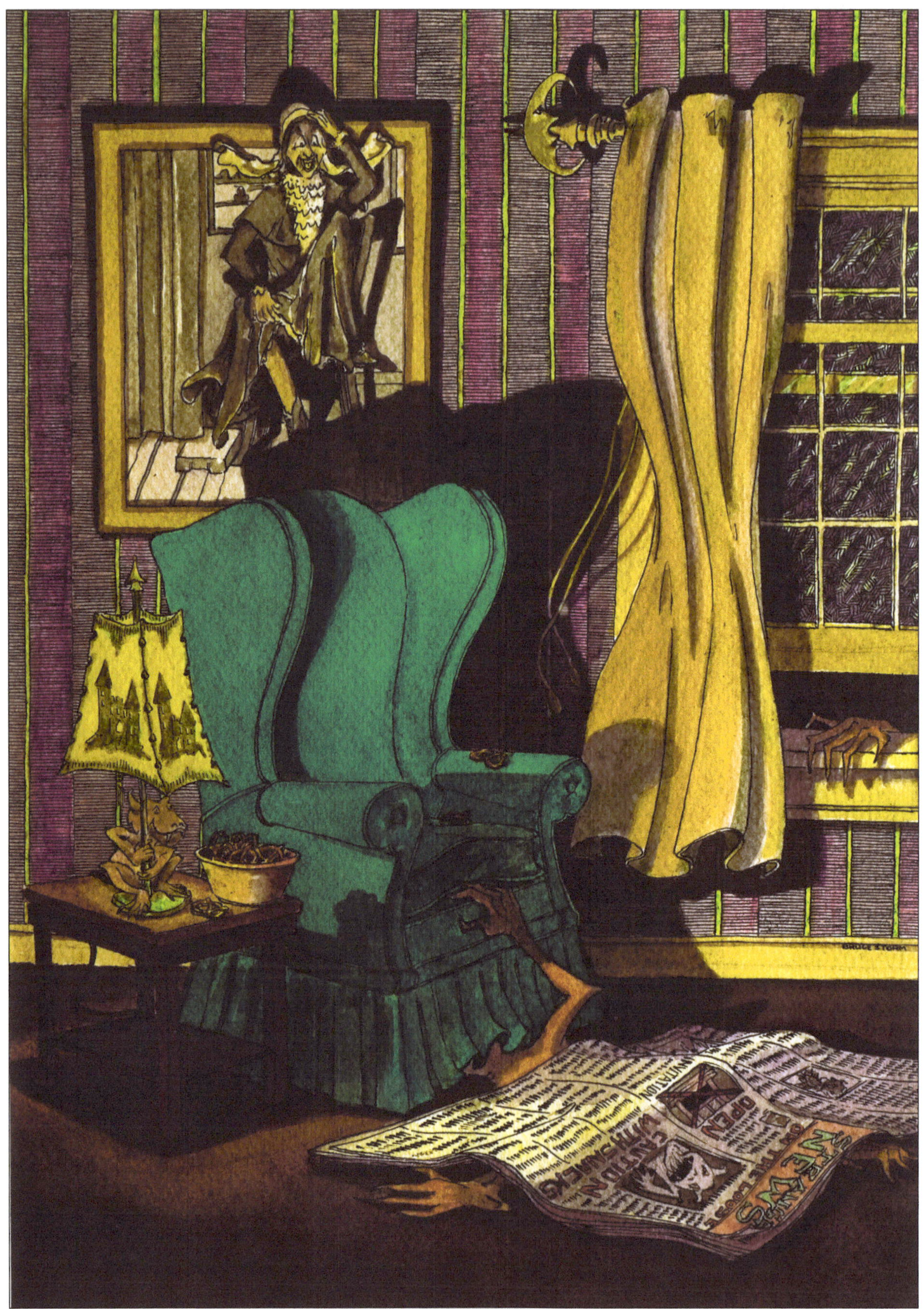

Caution

Look under the chair...
Lift the cushions...
Close the windows...
Check the closet door...
Turn on the light...
Then eat all the pretzels!

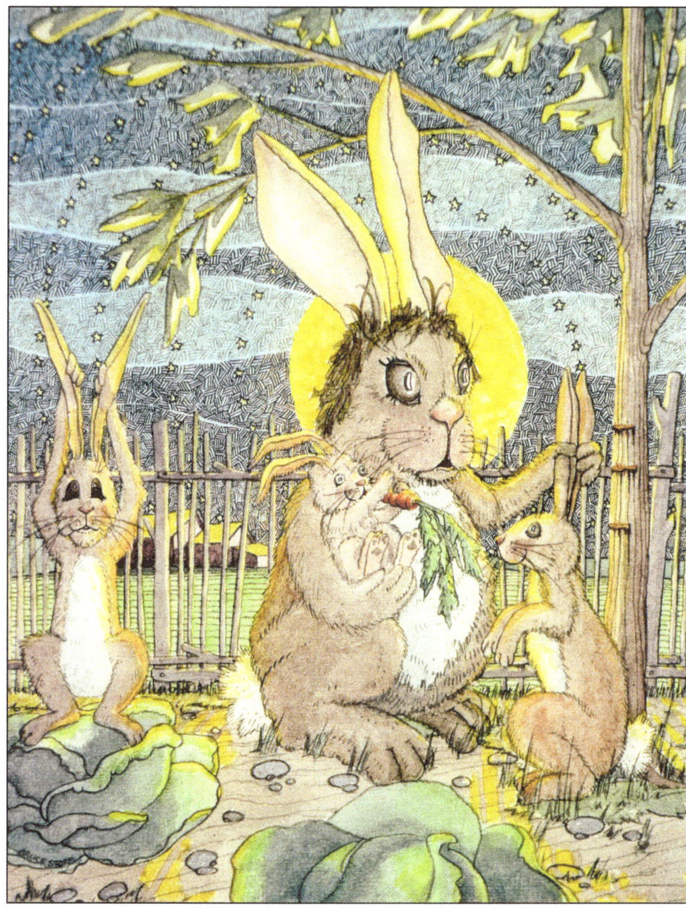

Measure Up

Old Mama Rabbit knew his ears would never measure up, but Little Brown Eyes stretched and stretched hoping to surpass his brother.

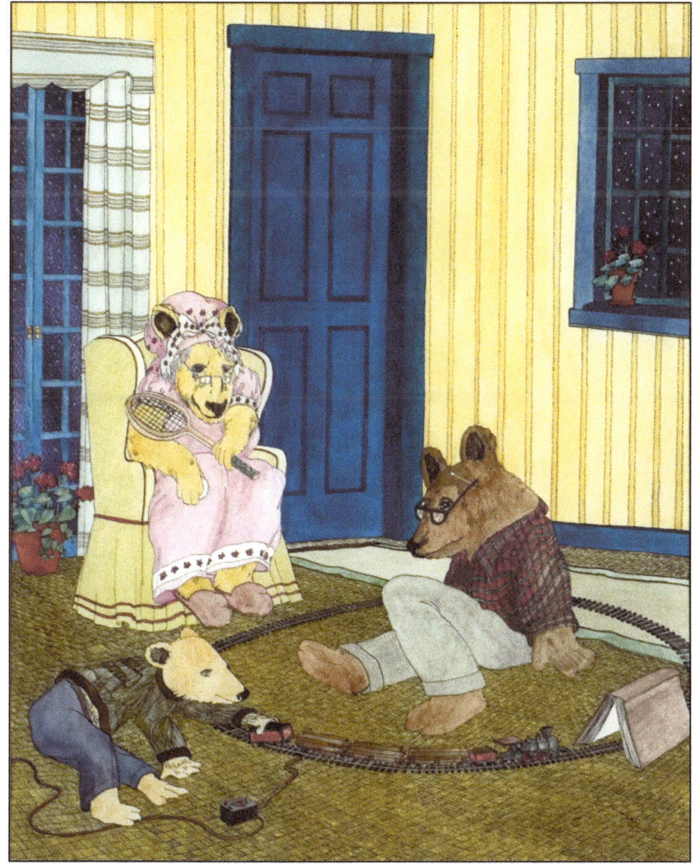

The 'Tabears'

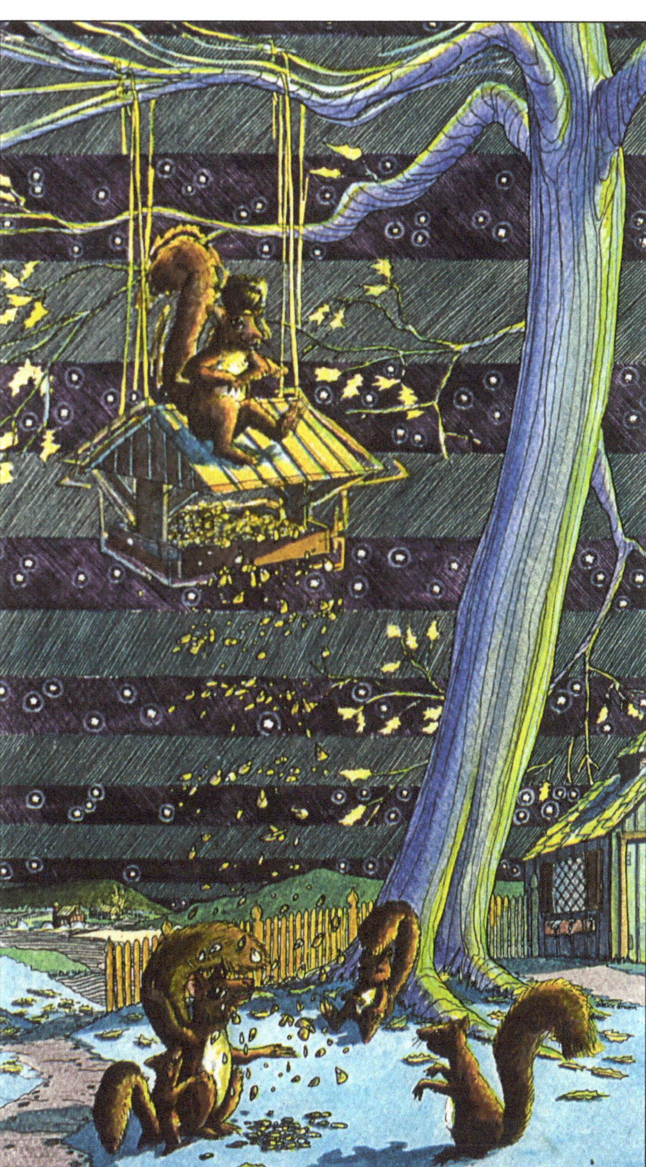

Feeding Frenzy

Buster would spring and leap, his furry feet flying, showering the bounty to those below. But, how he longed to go on a grand tour with the Bolshoi. But if nothing came of it, there was always the bird seed.

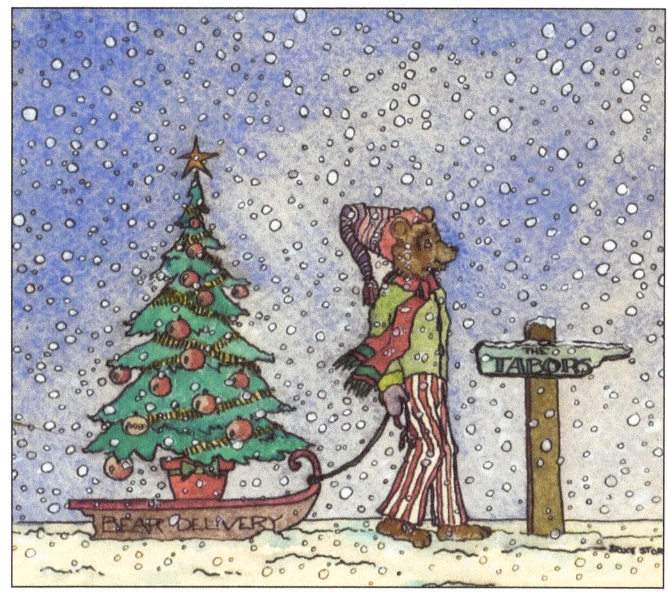

The Tabers' Christmas Card

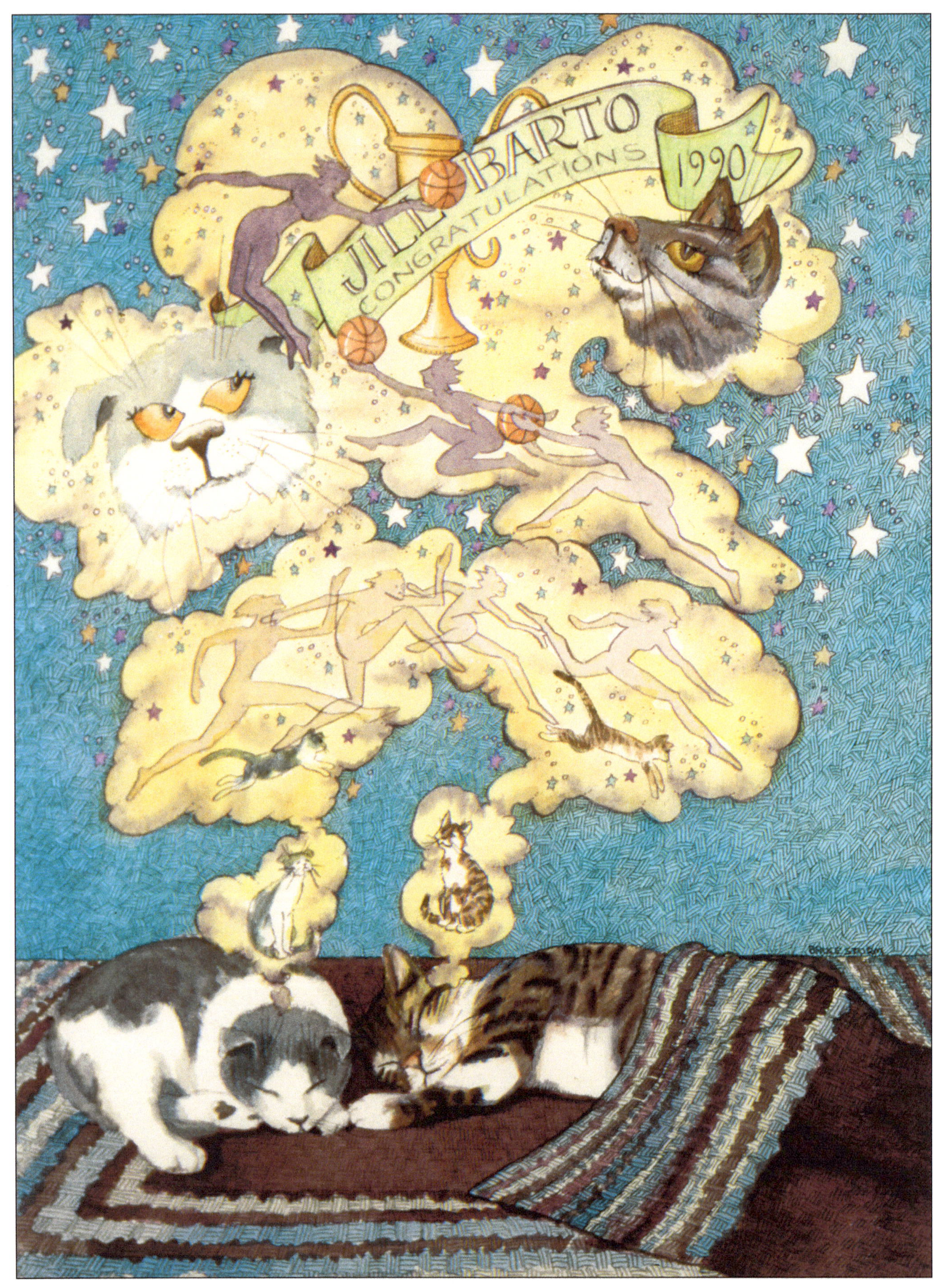

Congratulations Jill Barto

From her furry feline friends - Cookie and Kelly

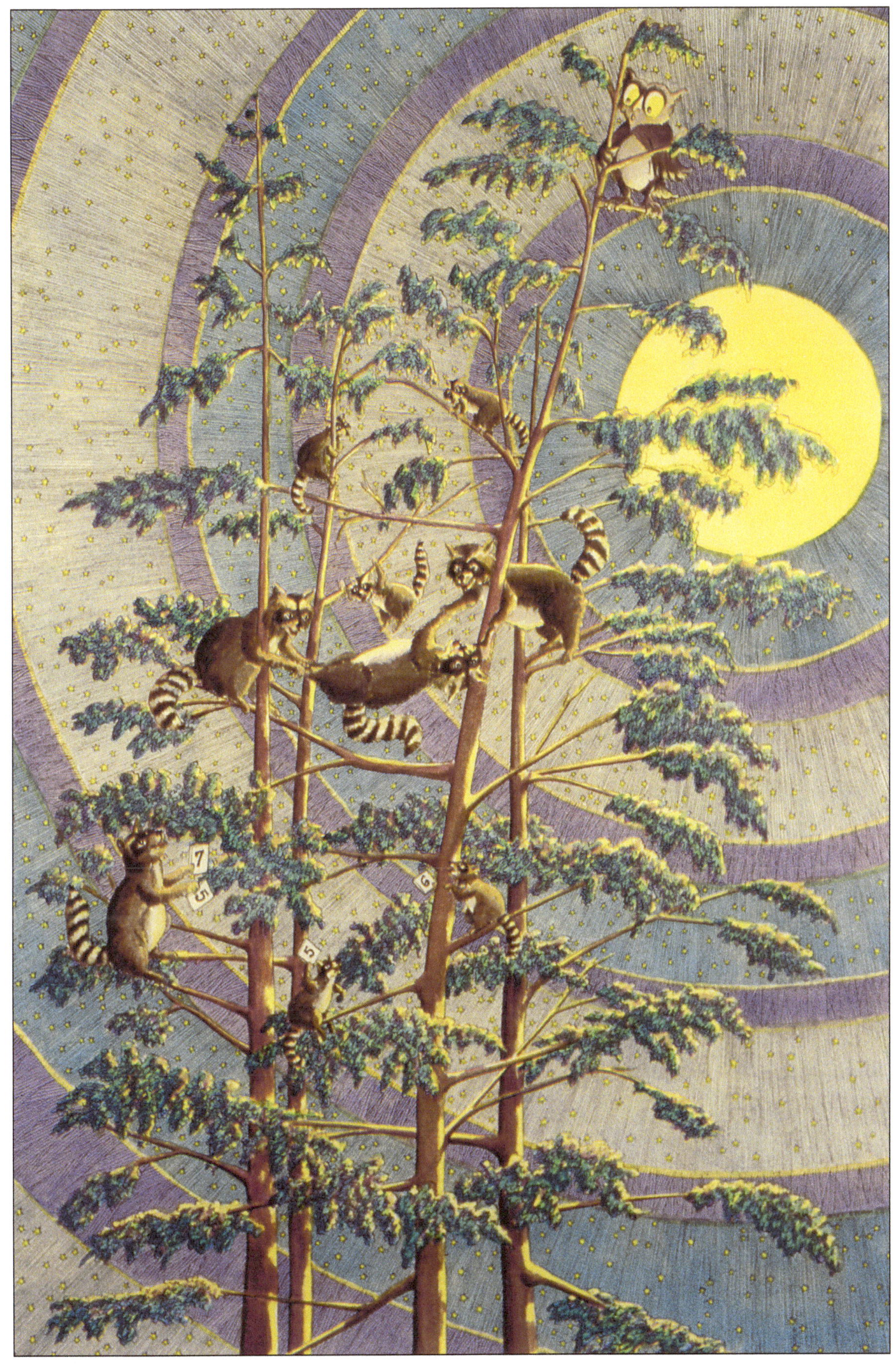

Lunar Olympics

Shocking, unbelievable, thought the owl as the raccoon children vaulted off of grandpa's belly while their cousins judged the height, style and degree of difficulty. A clear case of Olympic mania he hypothesized

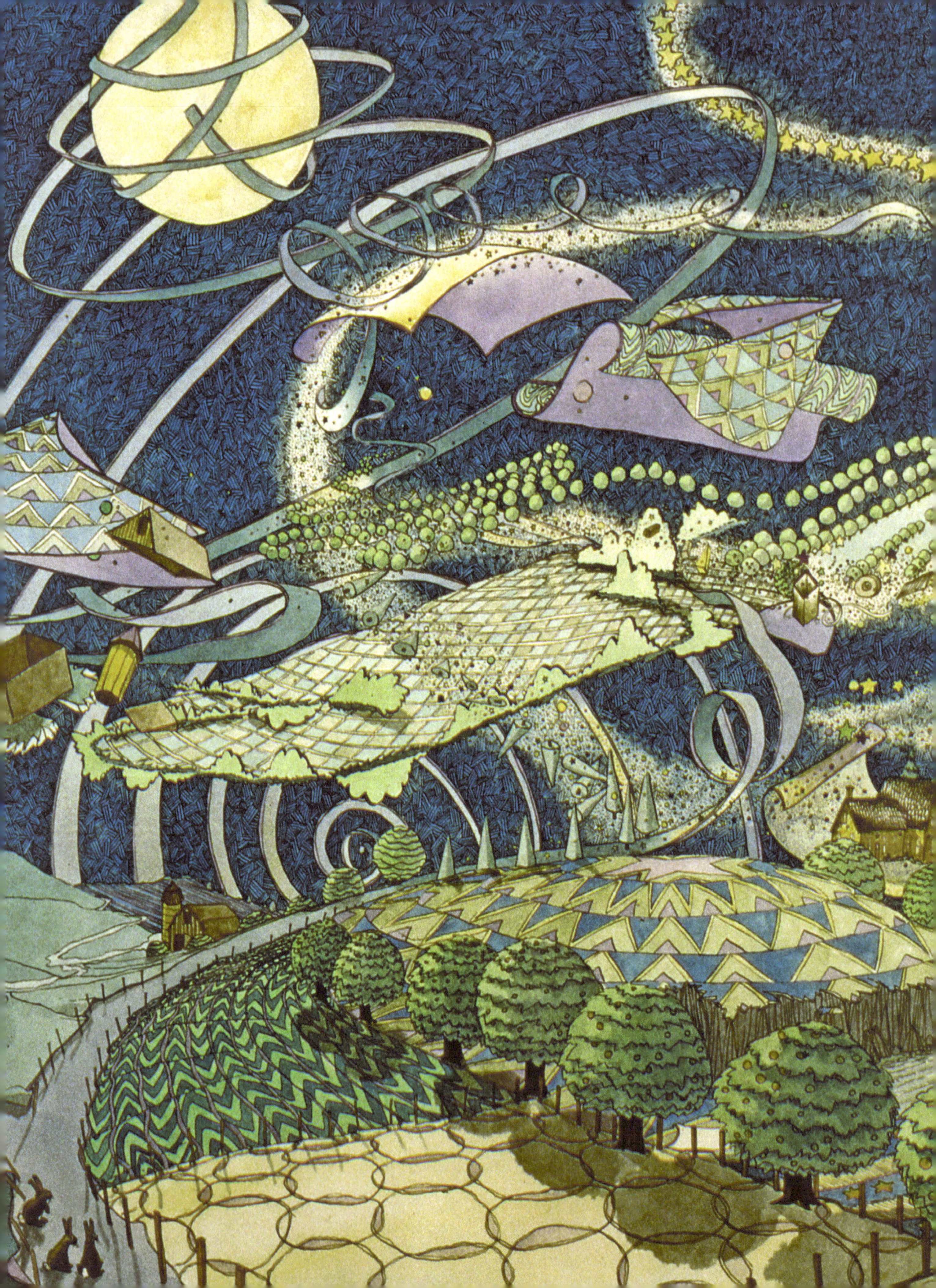

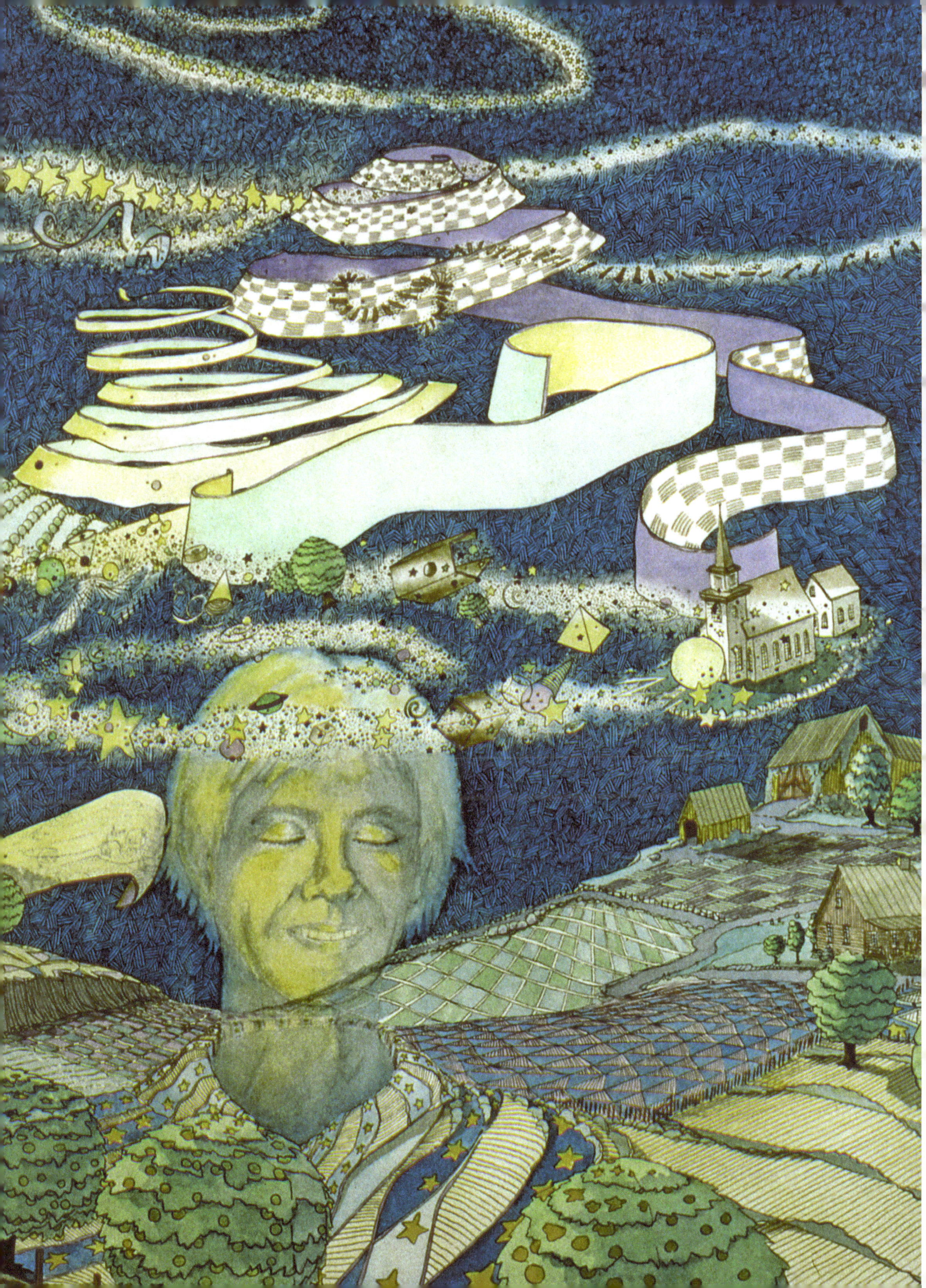

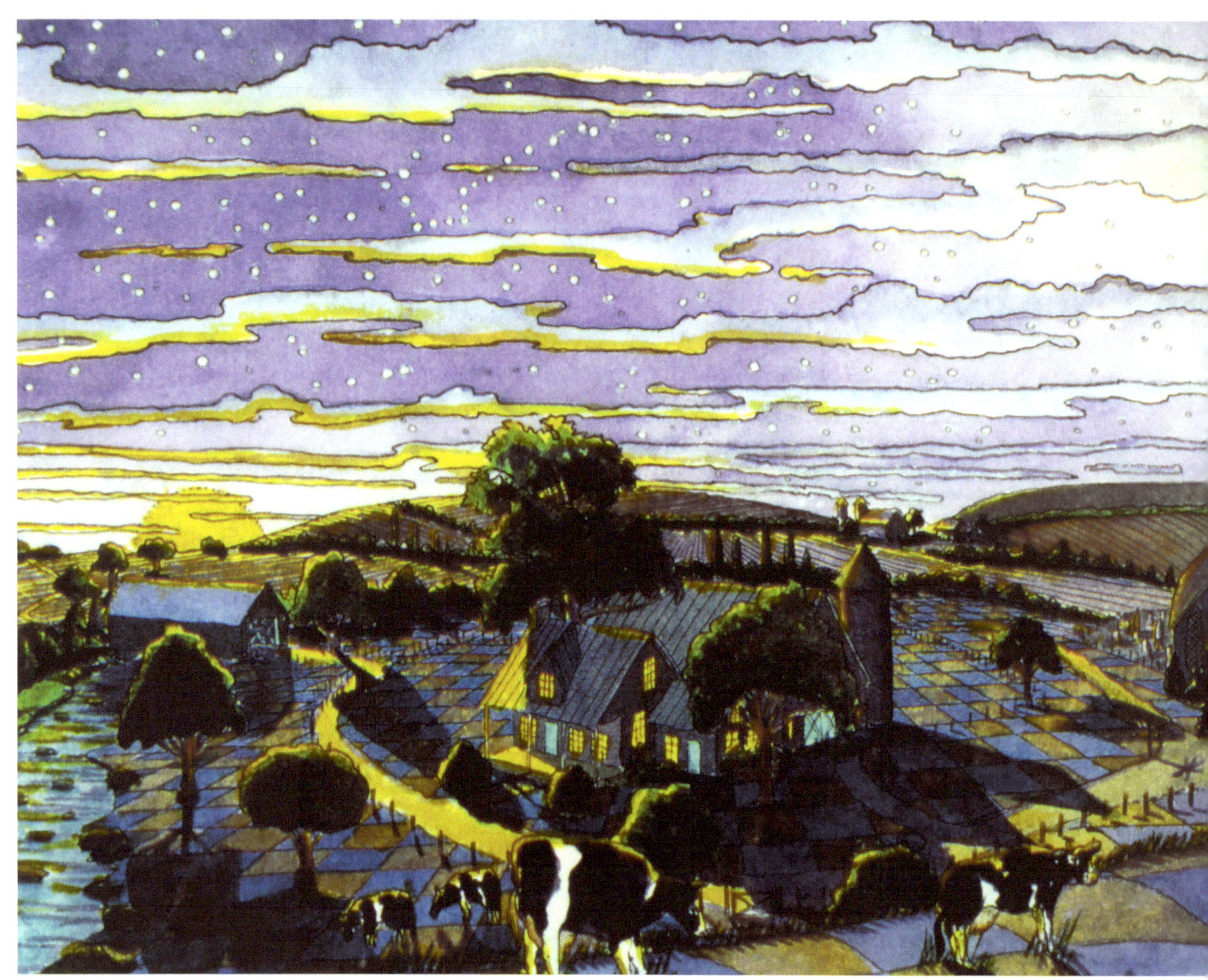

Not Much Happens in Checkerville

The cows meander down the hill and sashay back again, while the sun and moon exchange dominance above the checkerboard fields. Not much happens in Checkerville.

Previous page:

Composing

Images unravel and float as he composes the night painting. Sometimes they seem real, and he is the dream. Shapes and colors fold as the artist adjusts them into place. Quietly the patterns begin to set, while from the corner the little rabbits wonder if it is time for them to hop into the cosmic landscape.

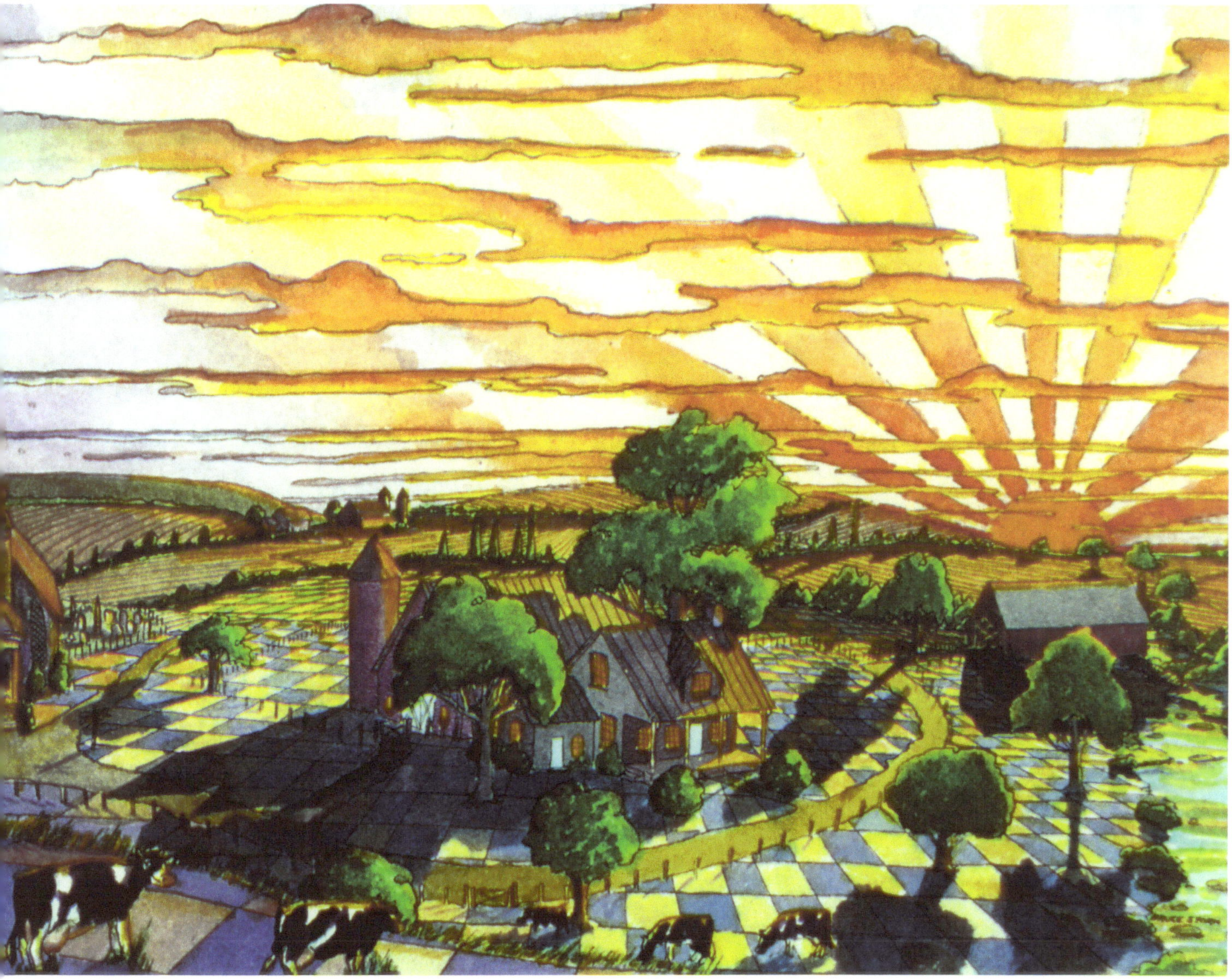

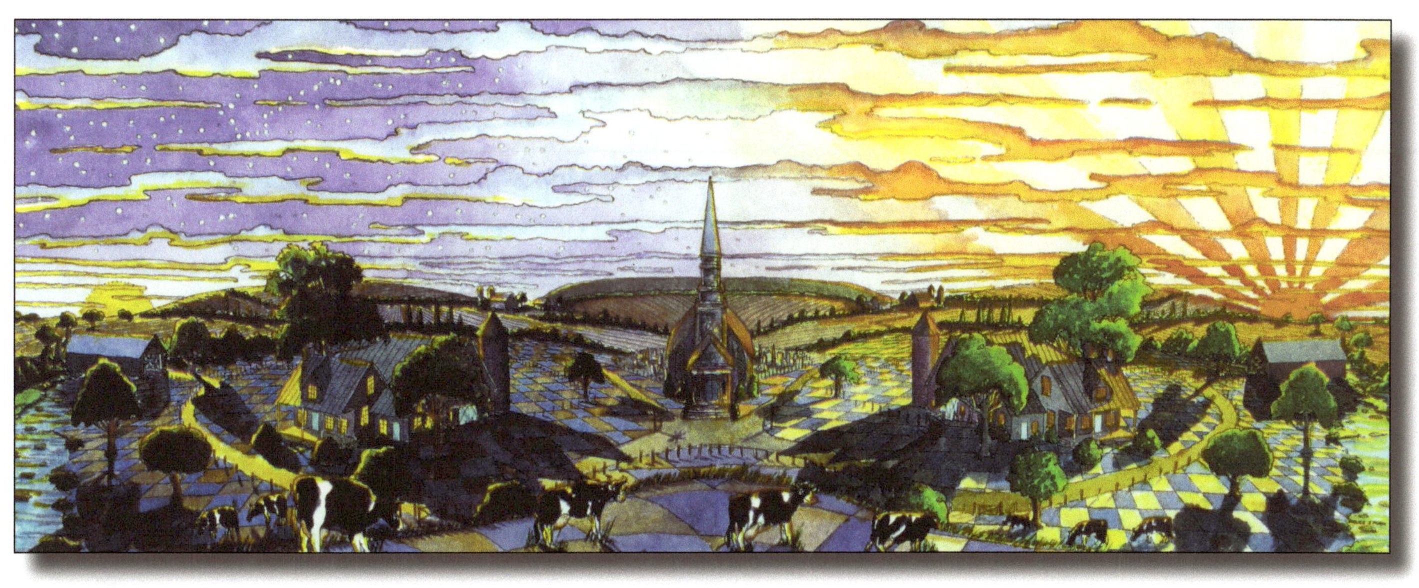

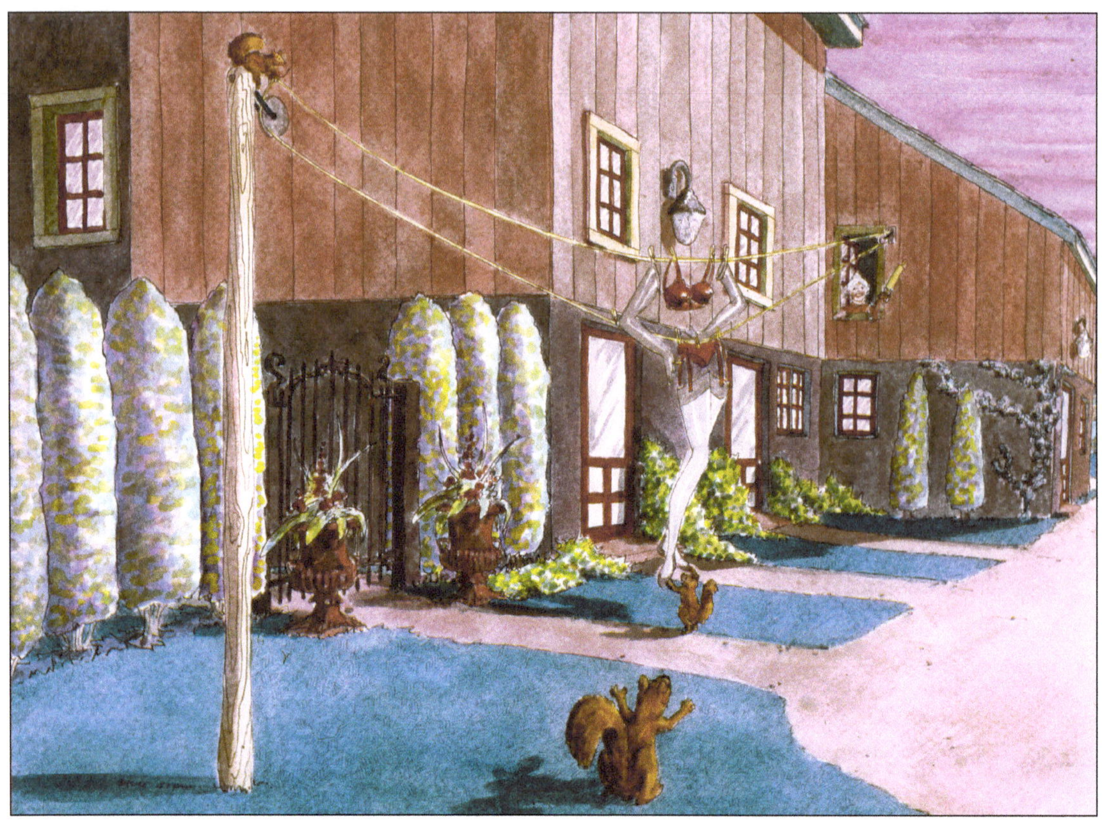

That was no lady-That's my wash!

Duchamp would have been proud - A happening, performance art. Line, form, zesty color, and when Harry yanked that pulley - movement.

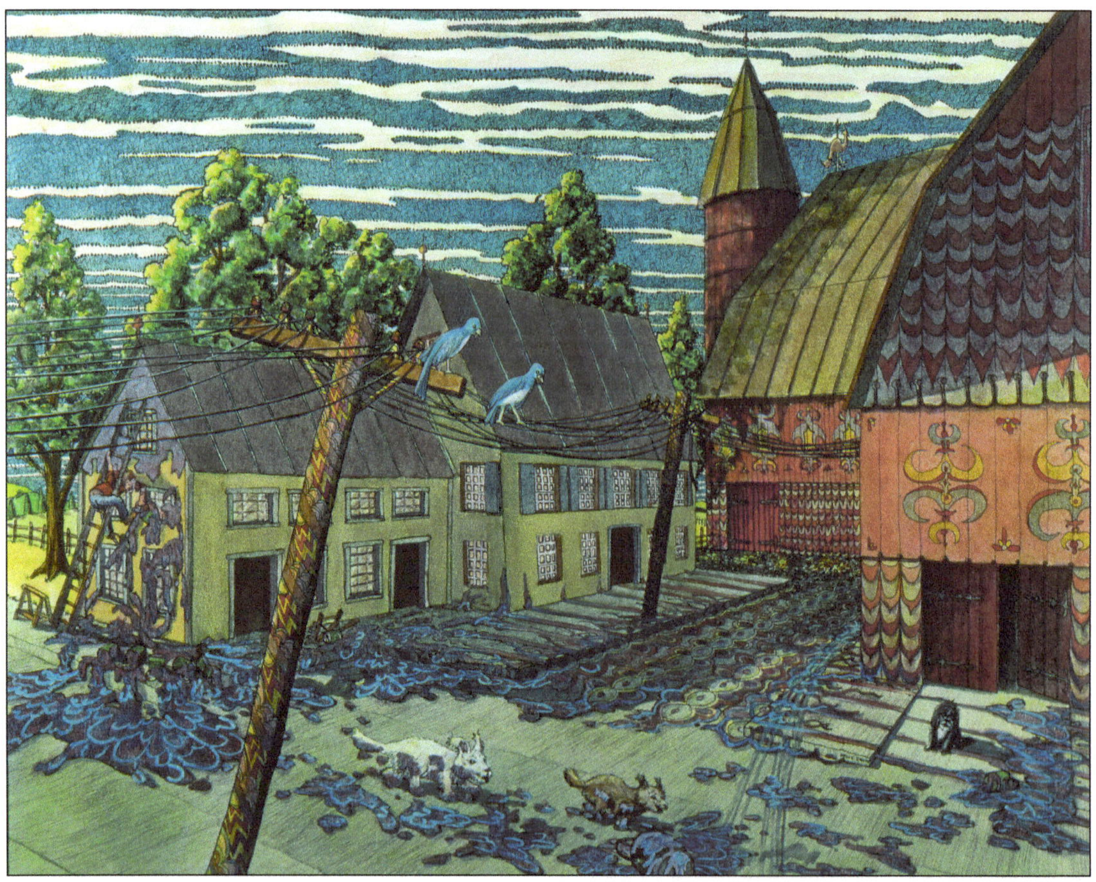

Dutch Barn - A Semi Self Portrait

Luna and Wifee scampered through the paint buckets leaving a disastrous mess in their wake. As the painter ranted at the merriment, Mr. McSnutter observed that something extraordinarily Pennsylvania Dutch was happening to the paint.

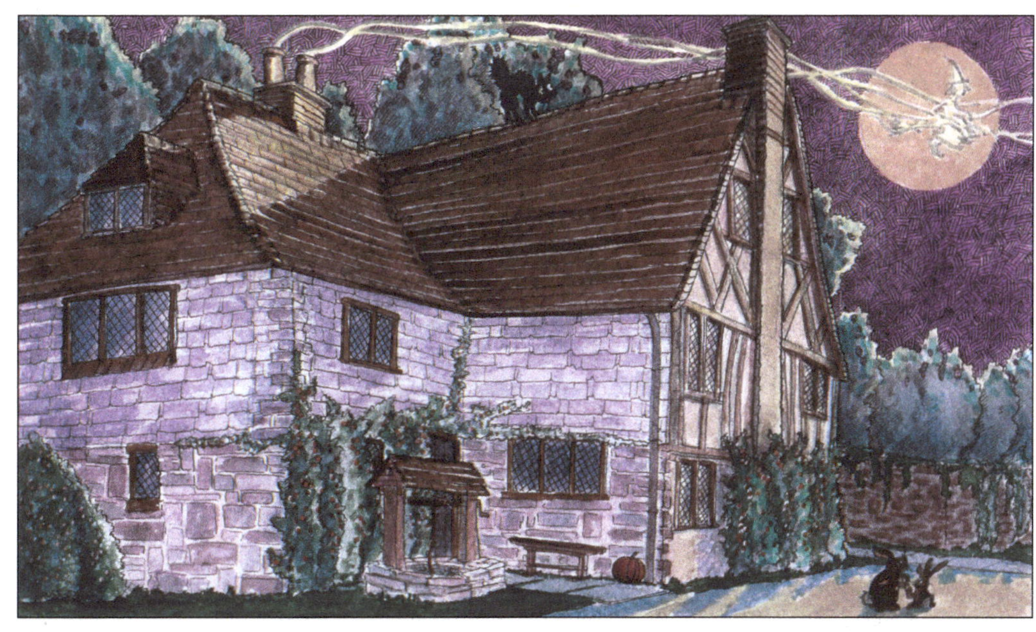

Unsolved Mysteries

Against the lunar glow there seemed to be a form. Why was midnight so alarmed, pondered Bissy and Kate?

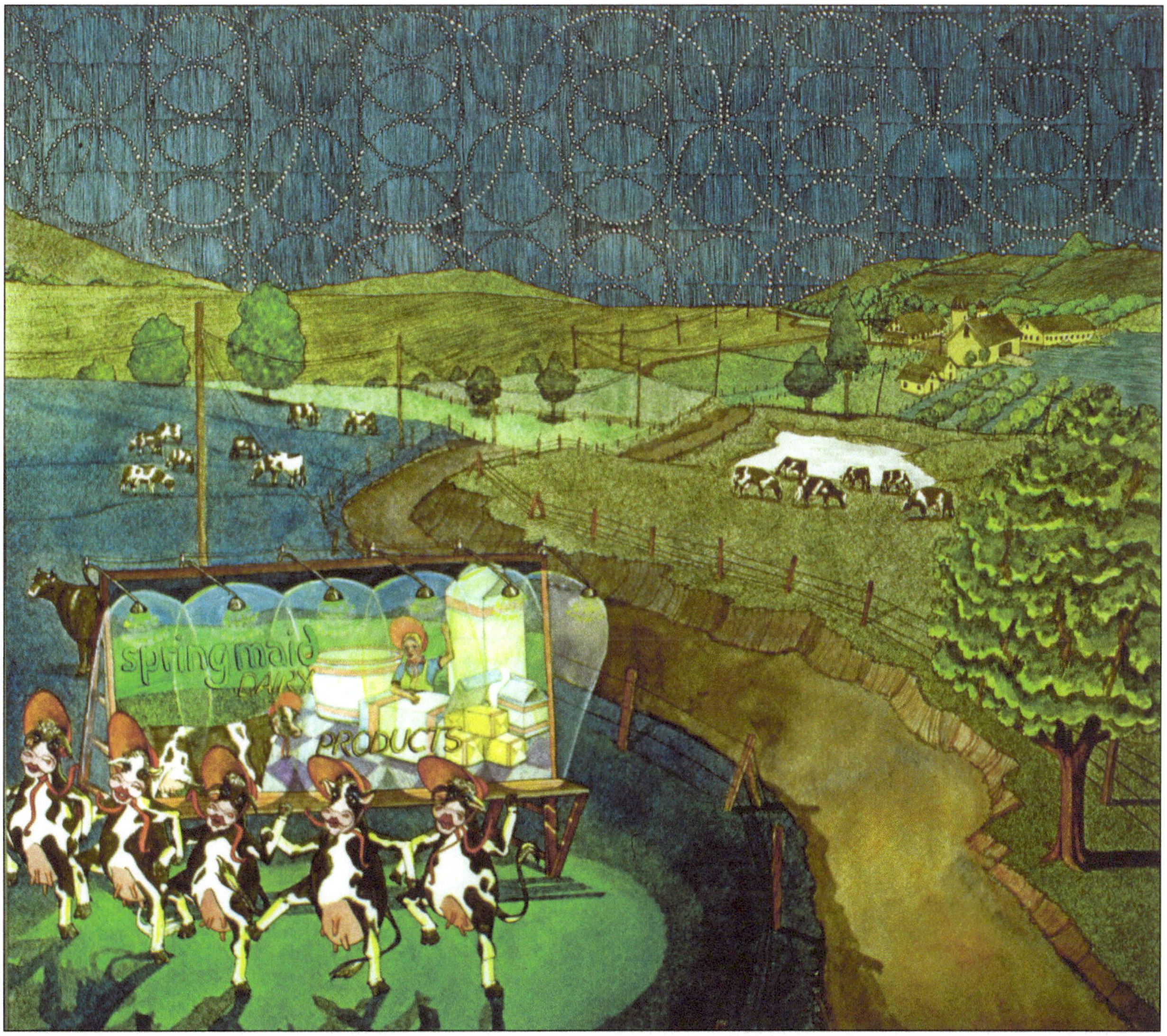

Spring Maid Dairy "Okay Perhaps..Moo Kick"

Shaka shaka moo kick, shaka shaka moo, Any flavor that you want, That's the flavor that we got, shaka shaka moo kick, Long into the night.

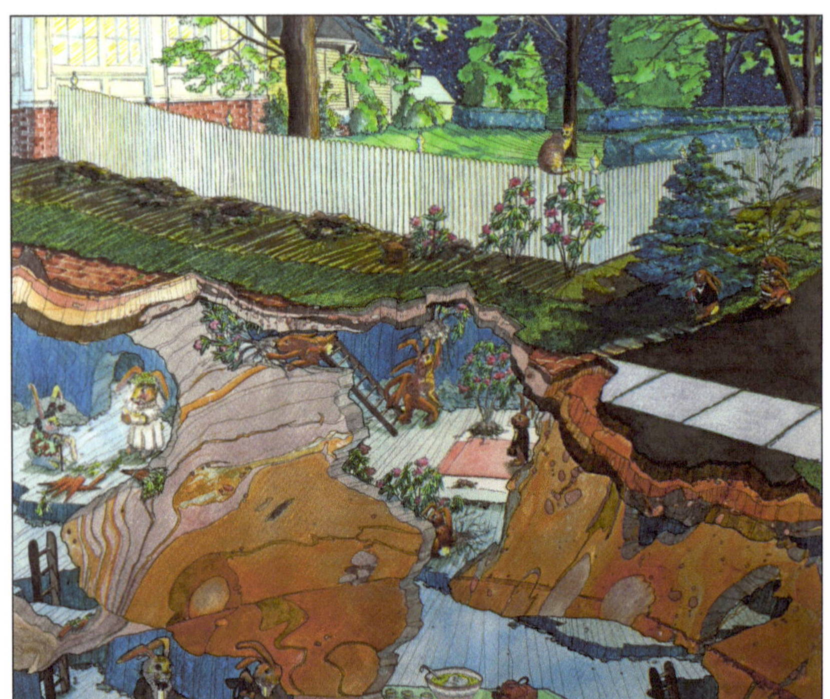

Uninvited Guest

They had used the path by the Tabor's drive so familiar to all the rabbits but now were delayed by the presence of a large orange uninvited guest who watched with amazement as the rhododendron rapidly disappeared from the Williams yard. The befuddled cat was quite unaware of Carol and Scott's wedding preparations. She knew only that the evening was cool.

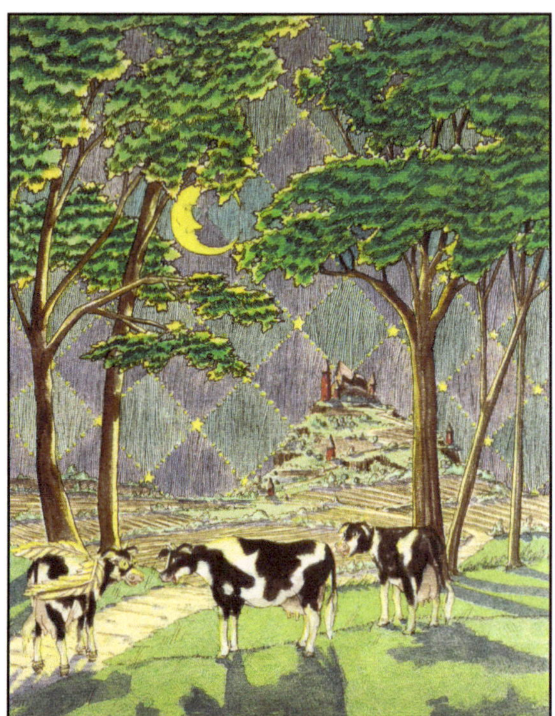

Moon Jump Spring Shoes

Holsteins have joie'de vivre; Lauretta's spring shoes seemed the perfect touch to turn her dream into reality. Bea and Gladys were full of encouragement and awe.

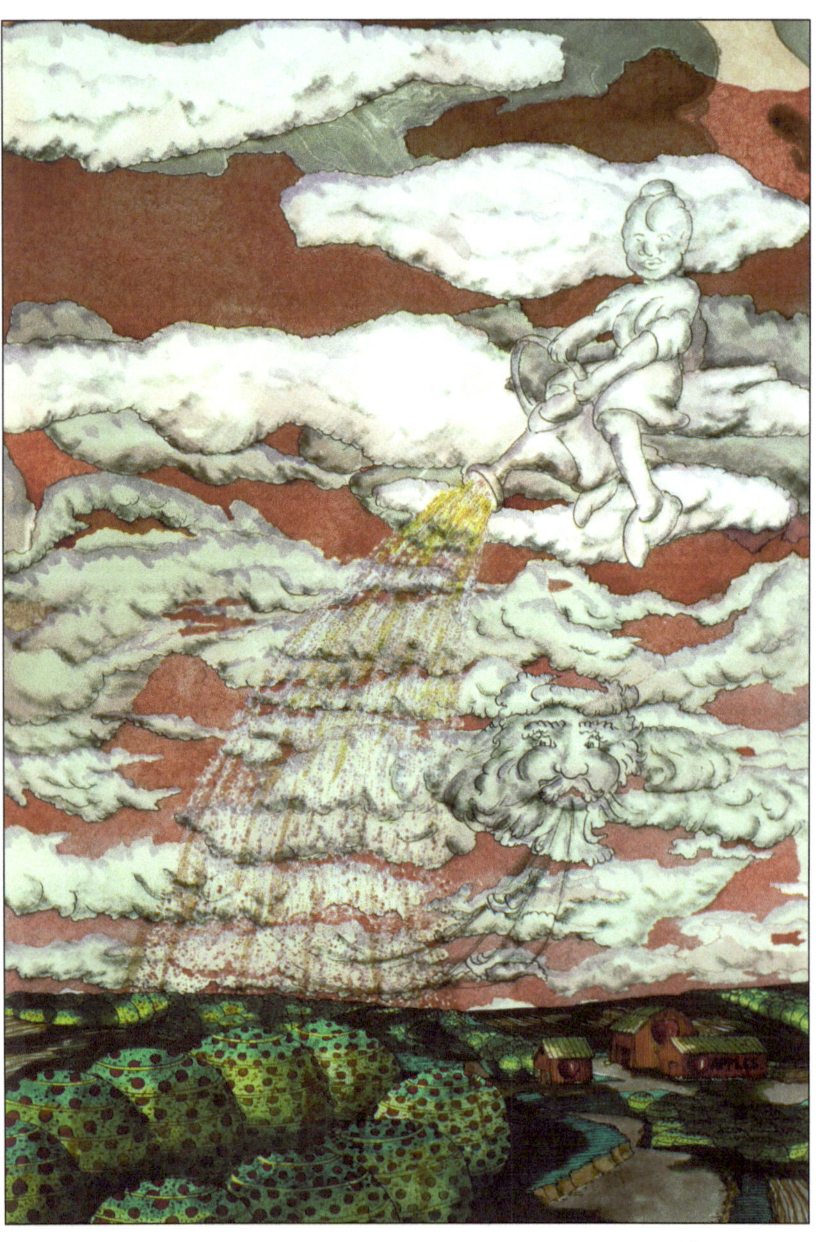

Coloring the McIntosh

He moved her there on a current of air just in time to water the McIntosh trees. What a joy to watch them color up. There were days when a cloud wanted to be an alligator floating in the blue or a great elephant charging across the evening sky, but nothing really compared to sprinkling the Macs.

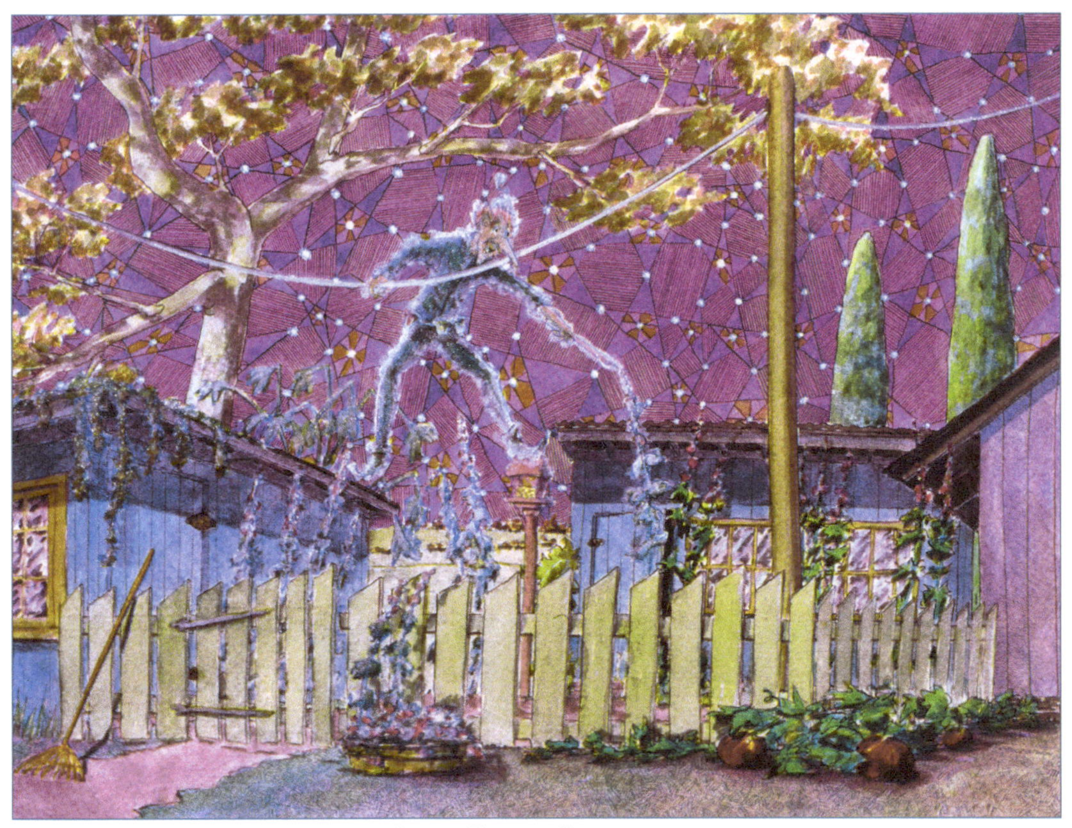

Jack Frost Returns

With every stroke he crystallized the garden green stems to silver pink blossoms to silver, silver, silver, silver so chic, so now every wire, roof and fence would be silvery by morning. How they would glitter in the morning light!

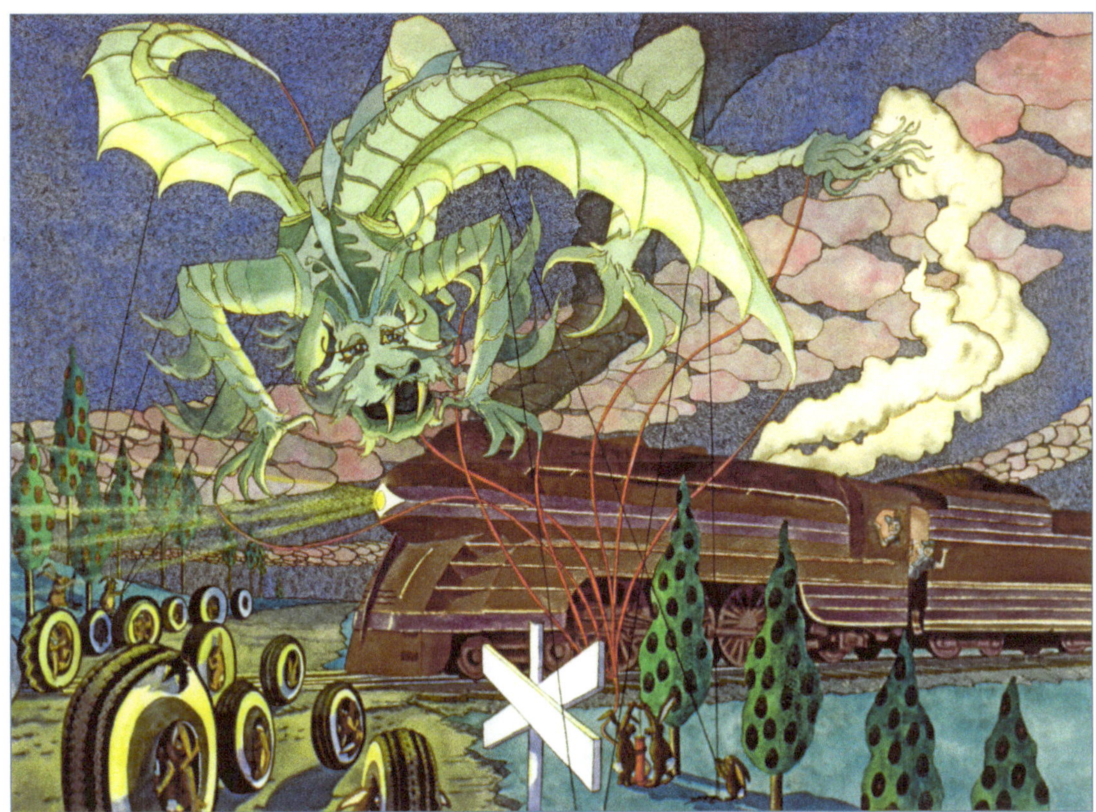

The Great Tire Race

Annually the rabbits held their great tire race. Bouncing along the country roads with wild abandonment and exuberance, they only feared the railroad crossing. In an attempt to halt the train, the rabbit officials created a diversion by utilizing one of their famous balloons, which usually did the trick.

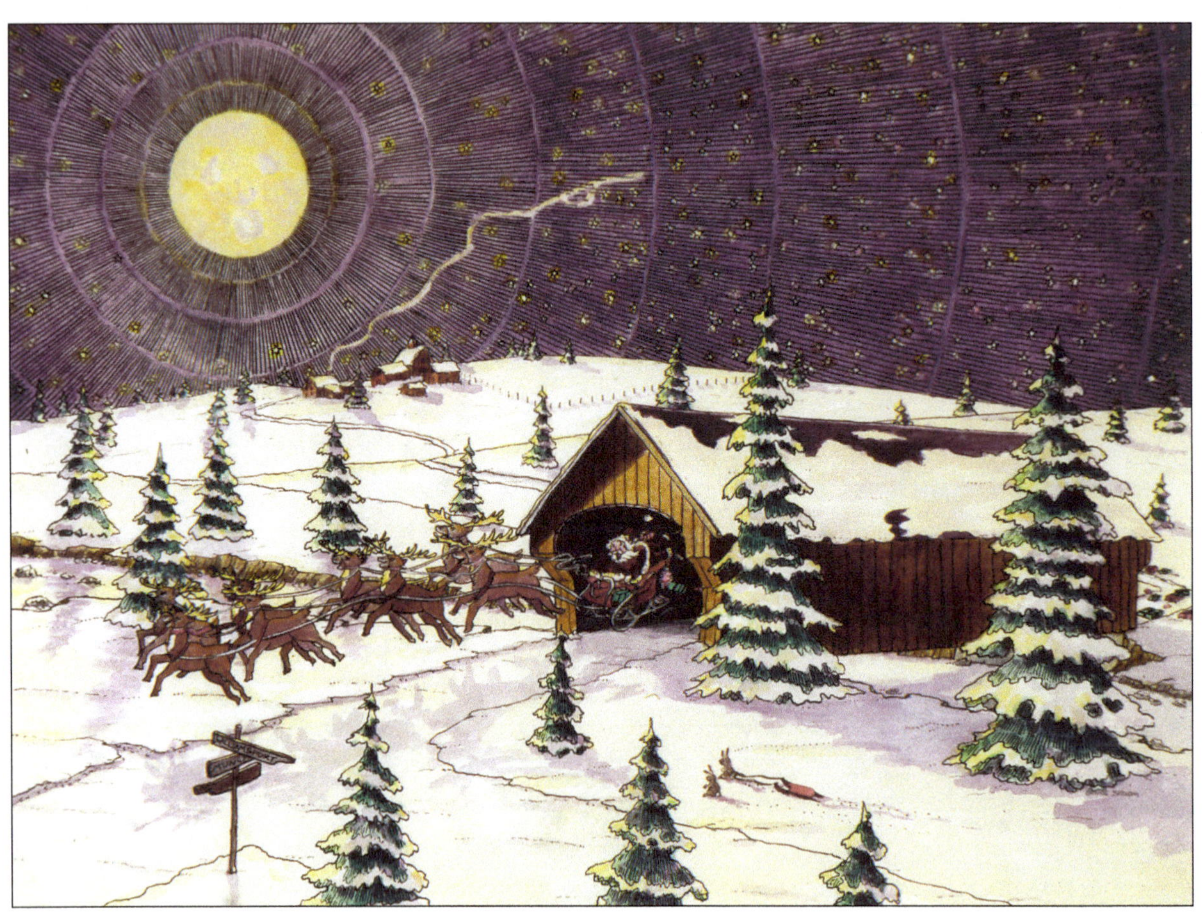

WITH RECKLESS ABANDON

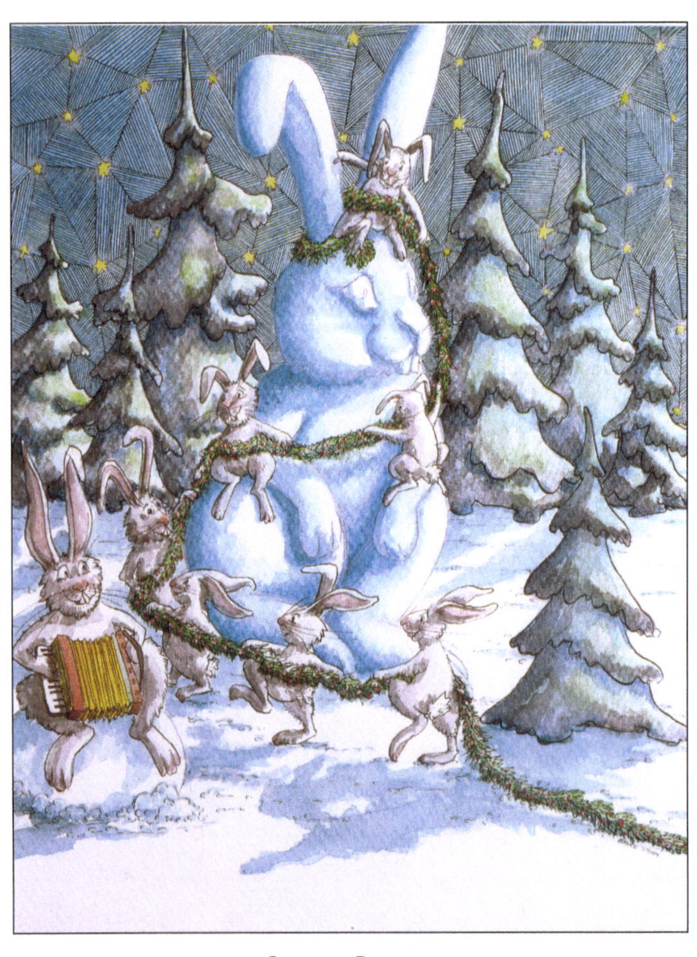

SNOW BUNNY

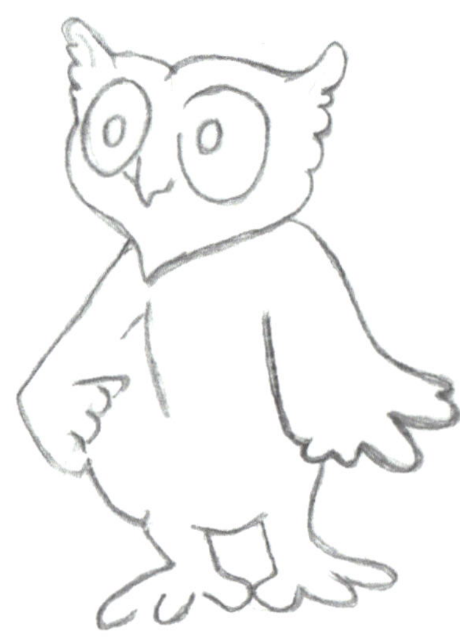

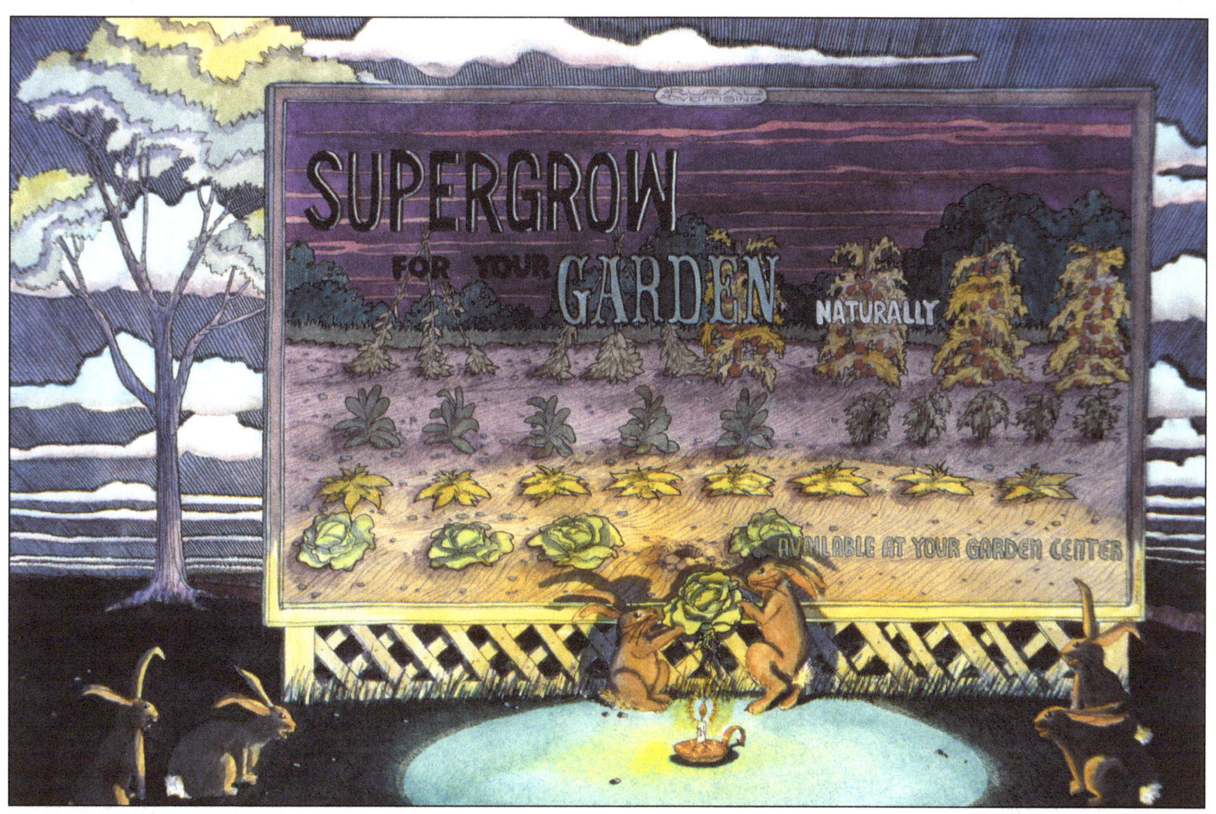

Super Grow For Your Garden

Thaddeus said it had worked but they were all skeptics. Yet there it was - quite undeniably: a cabbage.

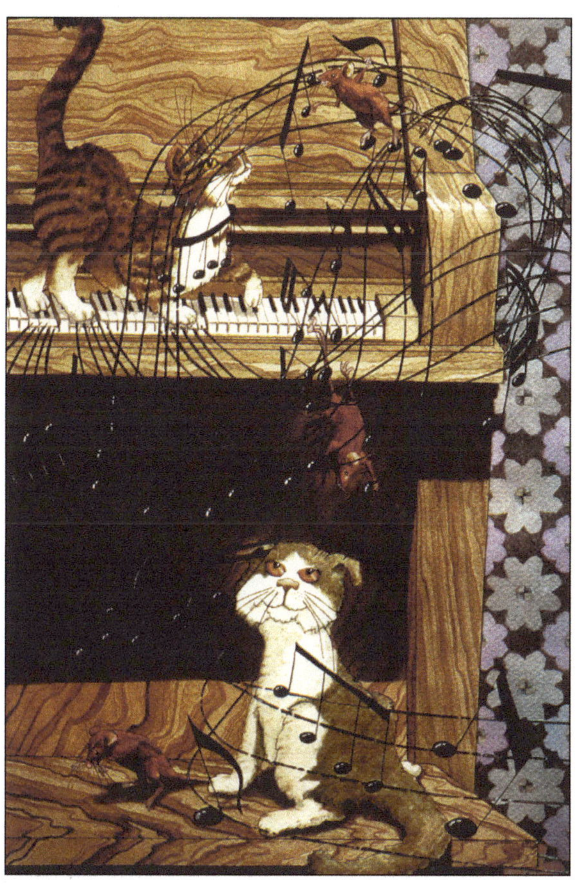

Cookie's Discovery

When you step on the keys, the music comes out—and so do the mice. Cookie and Kelley (a Scottish fold purebred) plotted to nab the mice as the notes faded away.

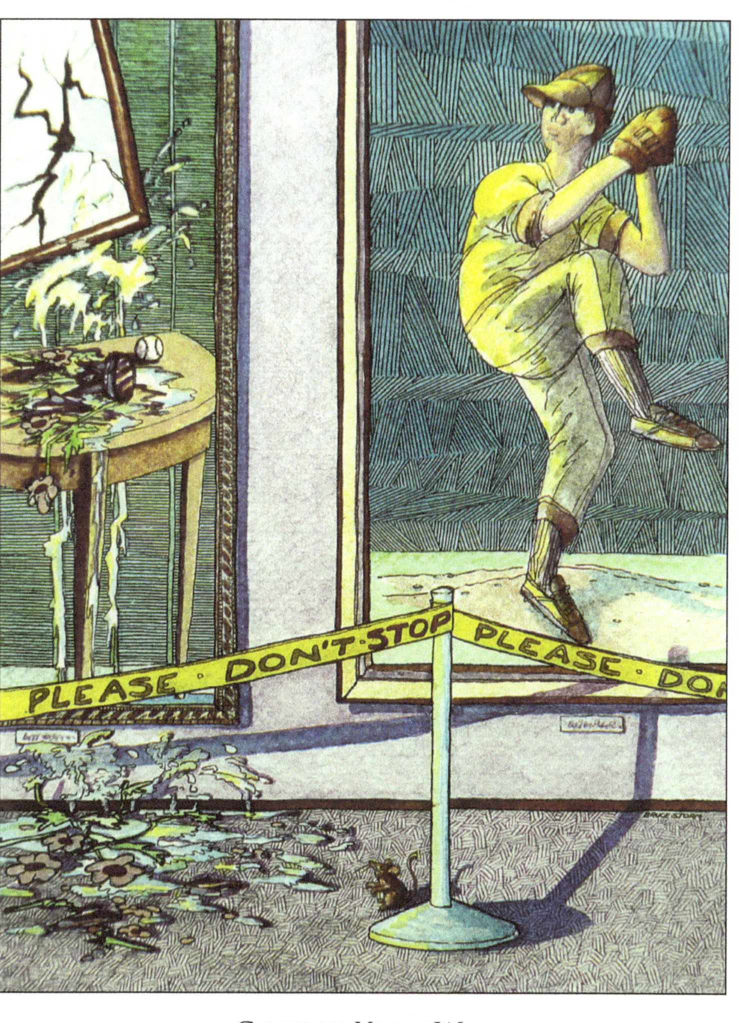

Coming Your Way

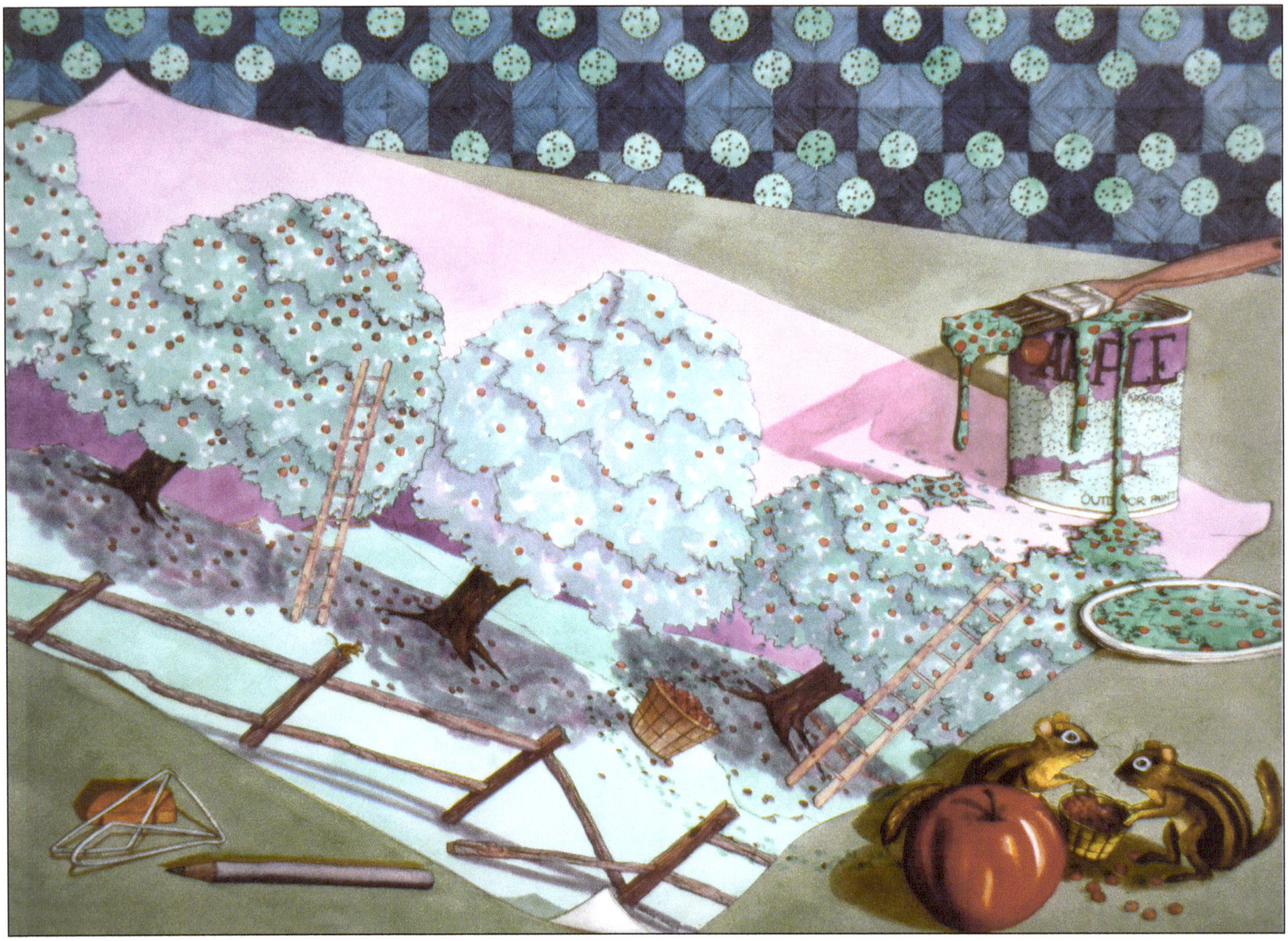

Apple Brand Outdoor Paint

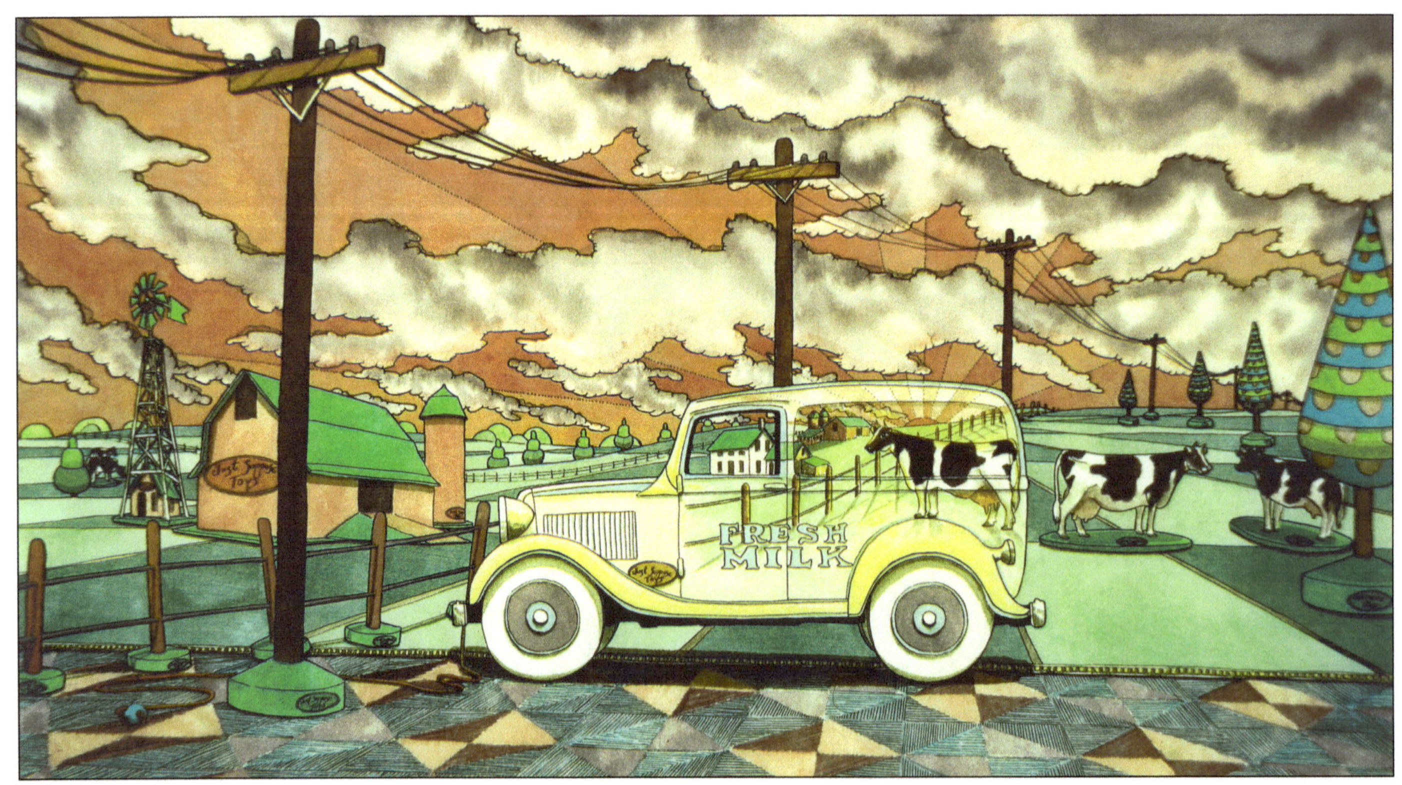

Fresh Milk

The rubber cows and wooden trees seem so real upon the old quilt. You could almost feel the sun rising.

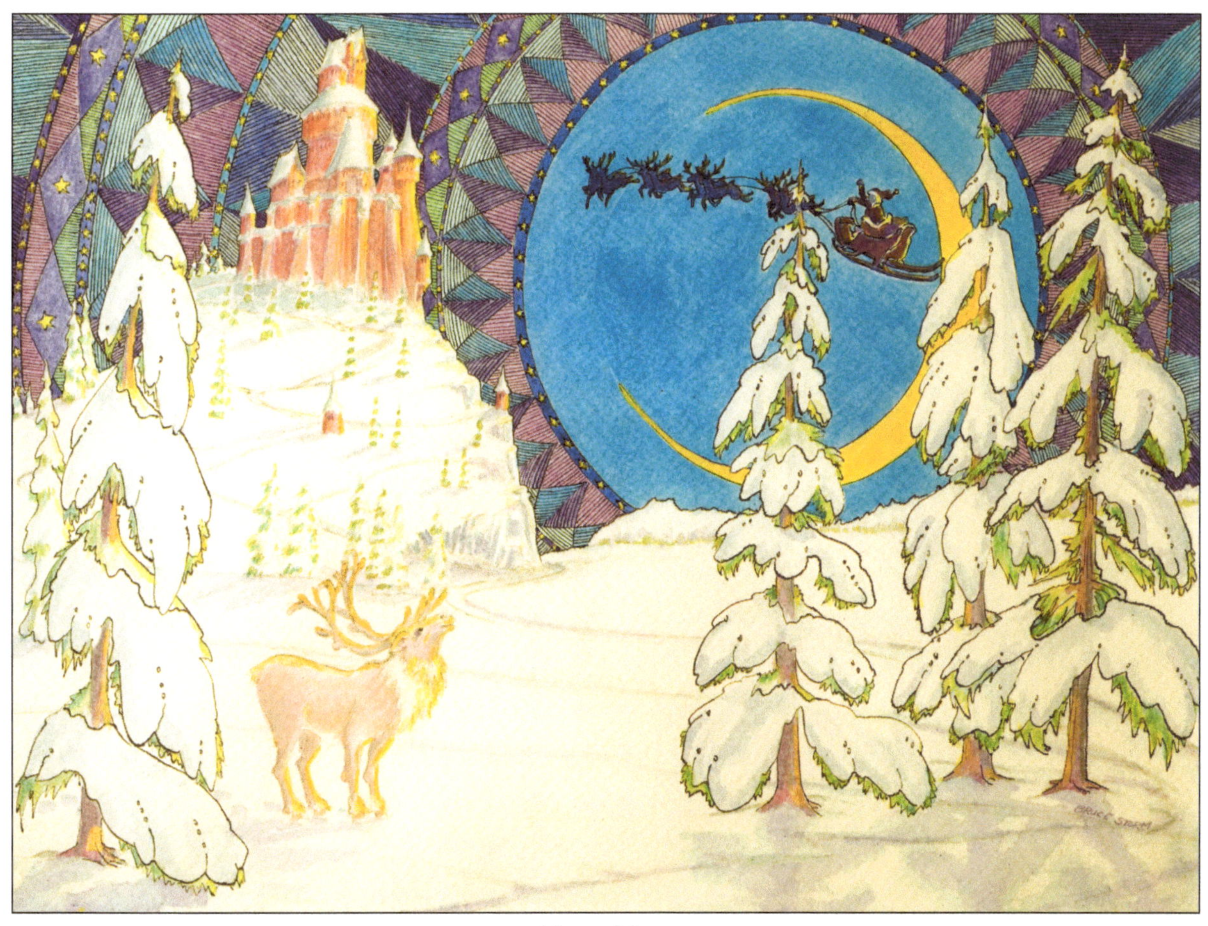

NEXT YEAR

FONTAINE AND NUREYEV HAD NOTHING ON THOSE DEER MAGICALLY DANCING ACROSS THE COLD NIGHT SKY. EVERY YOUNG DEER LOOKED WITH PRIDE ON THEIR PERFECTION AND DREAMED NEXT YEAR IT COULD BE ME.

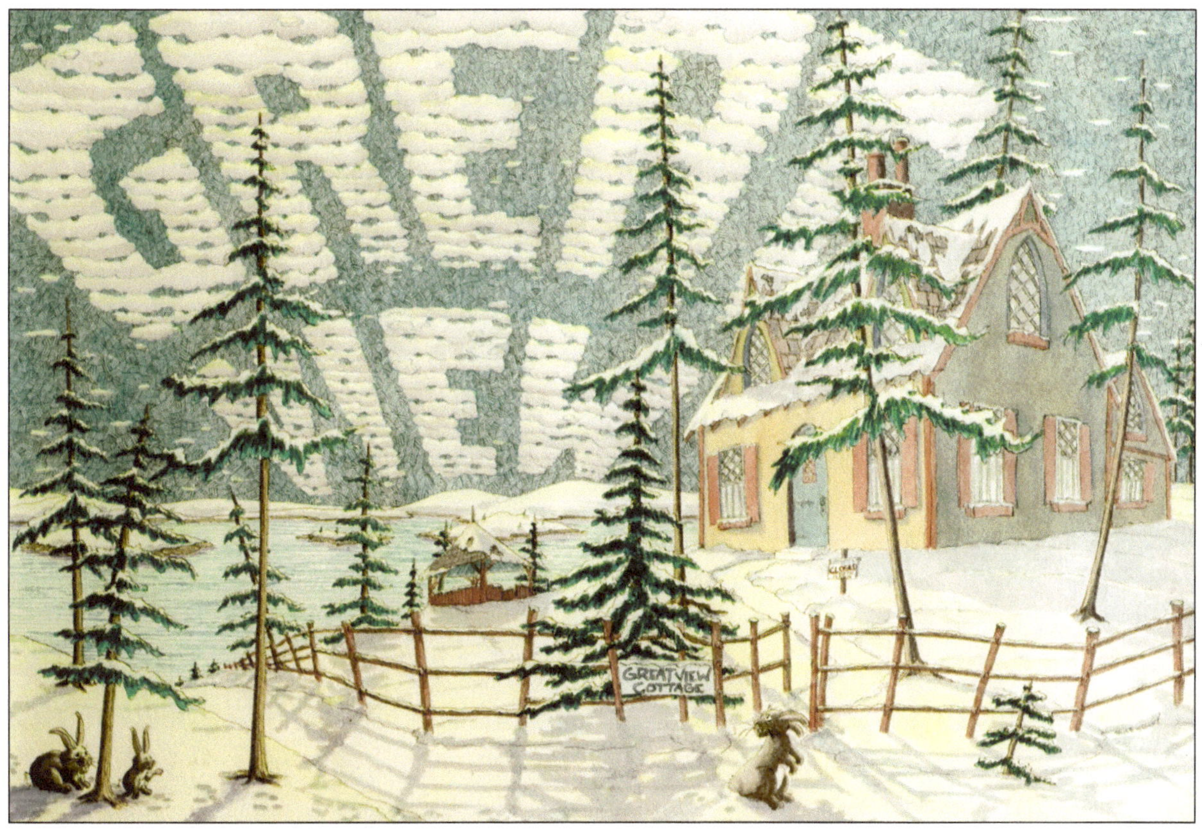

GREAT VIEW COTTAGE

"DID THE OTHERS SEE IT, TOO?" OTTO TURNED TO ASK AS THE GREAT VIEW BECAME A TOUCH MORE LAVENDAR.

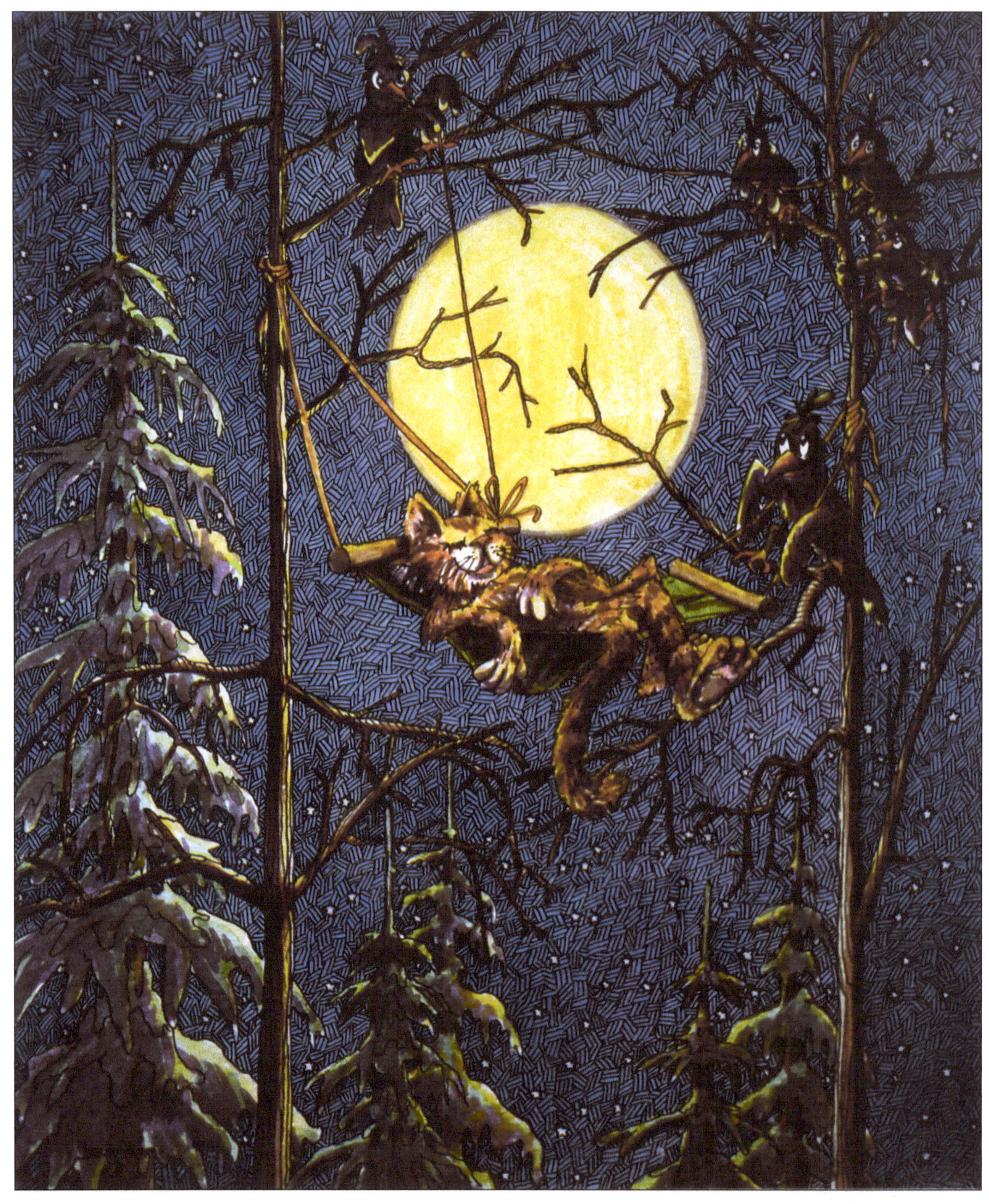

Catastrophy

The silence was about to be broken.

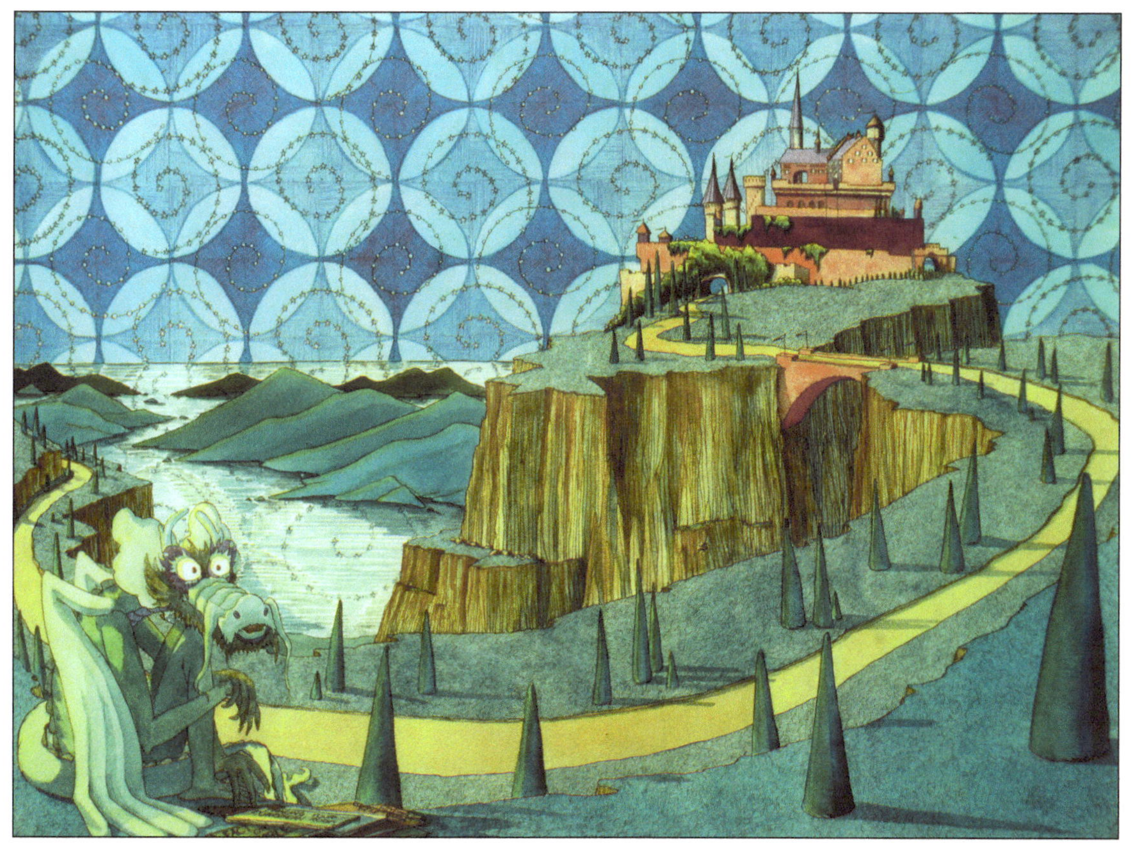

Tracing Your Roots

The dragon stared into the starry night awestruck that this was the very spot where his foredragons had lived so long ago - how enchanting!

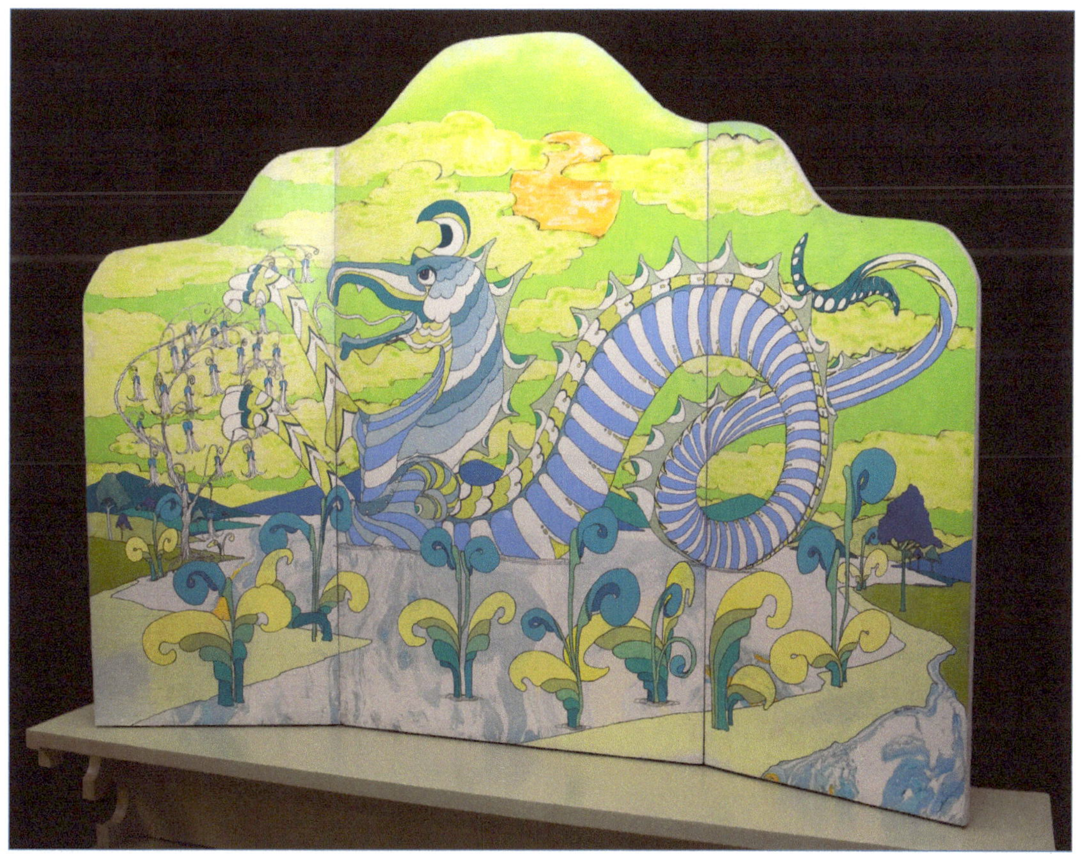

Tryptic

Friendly, warm and playful the Chinese dragon paws about in the lake. The landscape is quiet as another day in another millennium begins.

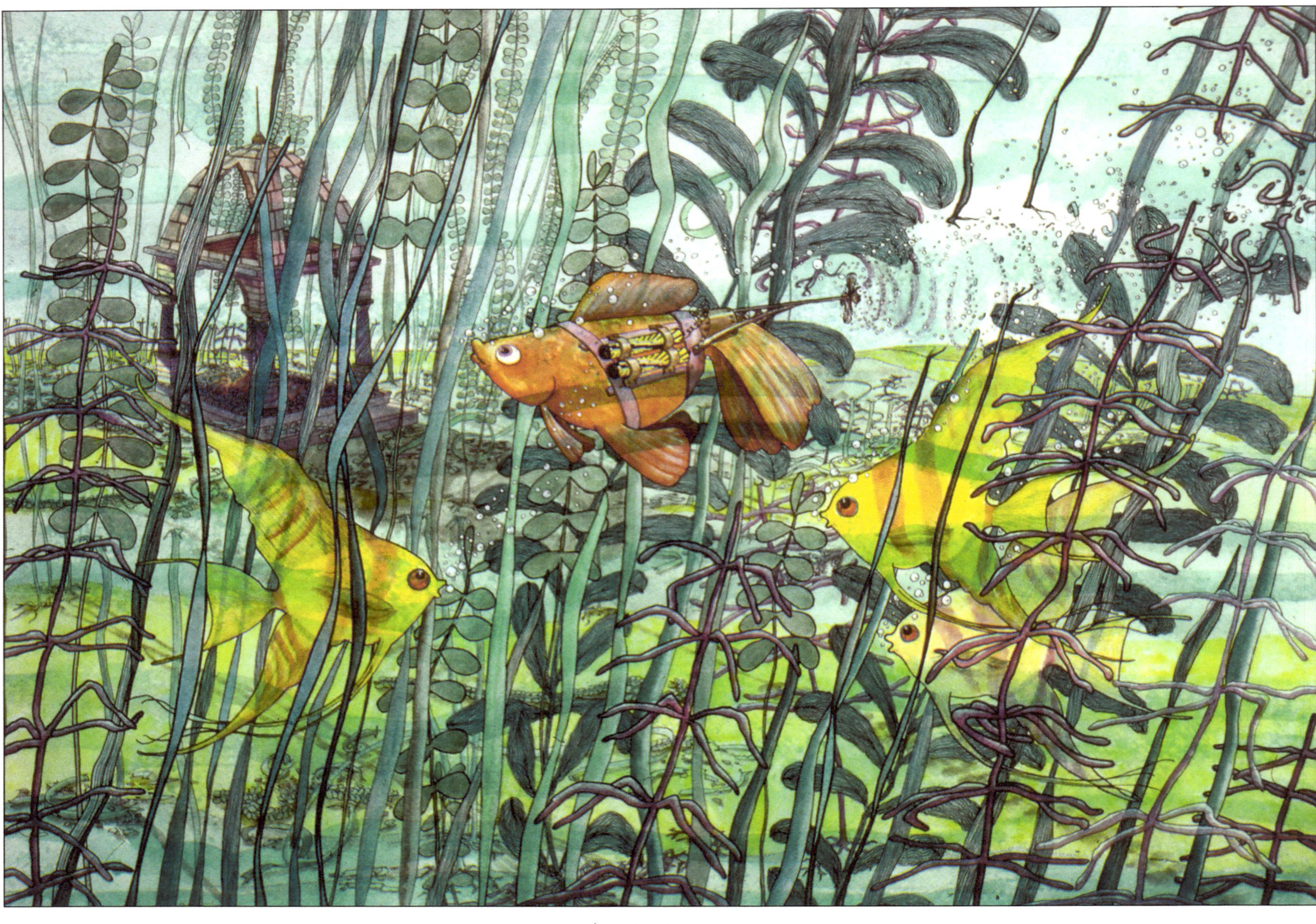

I'm No Angel

Dissatisfied with natural movement and with total disregard for the rest of the school, "Lionel" creates elaborate devices which introduce raucous noise and speed to his previous silent world in an attempt to impress his peers.

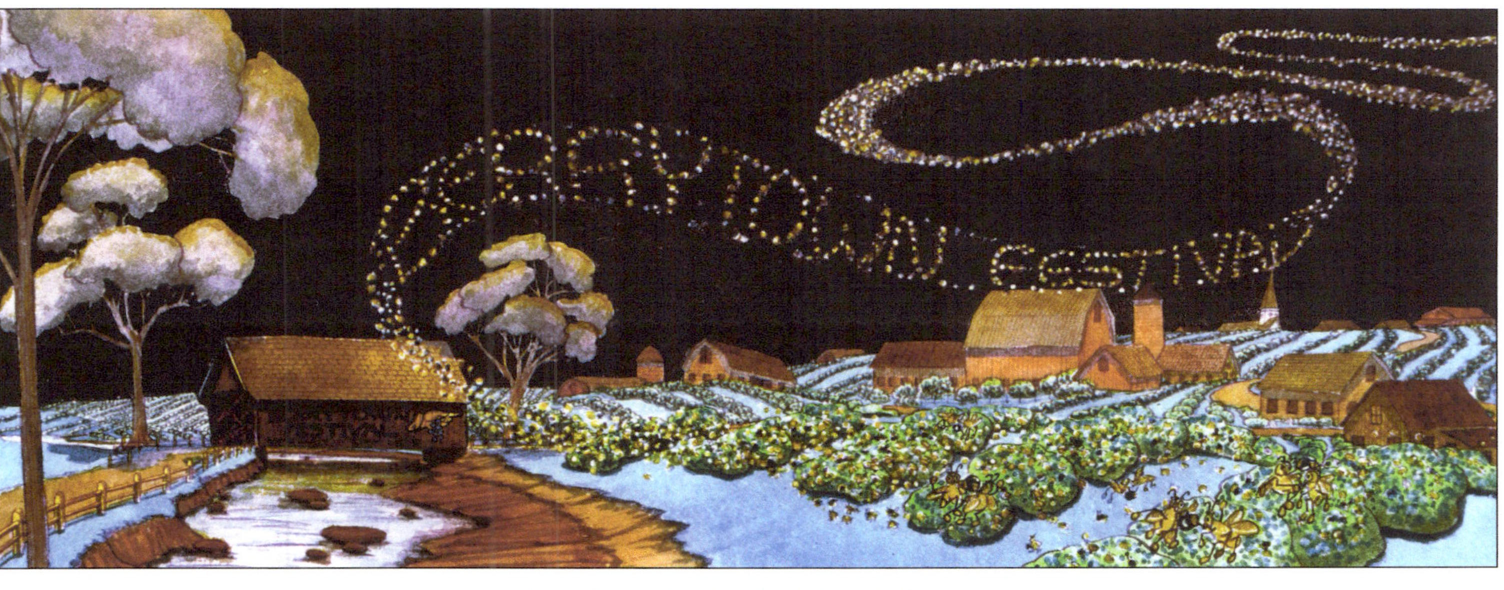

THE BUGS WERE BAD THAT YEAR

STEAMY DAYS, BALMY NIGHTS, BERRIES AS BIG AS YOUR THUMB AT THE MOONLIGHT FESTIVAL DOWN AT THE OLD BERRYTOWN - BUT, OH, THE BUGS WERE BAD THAT YEAR.

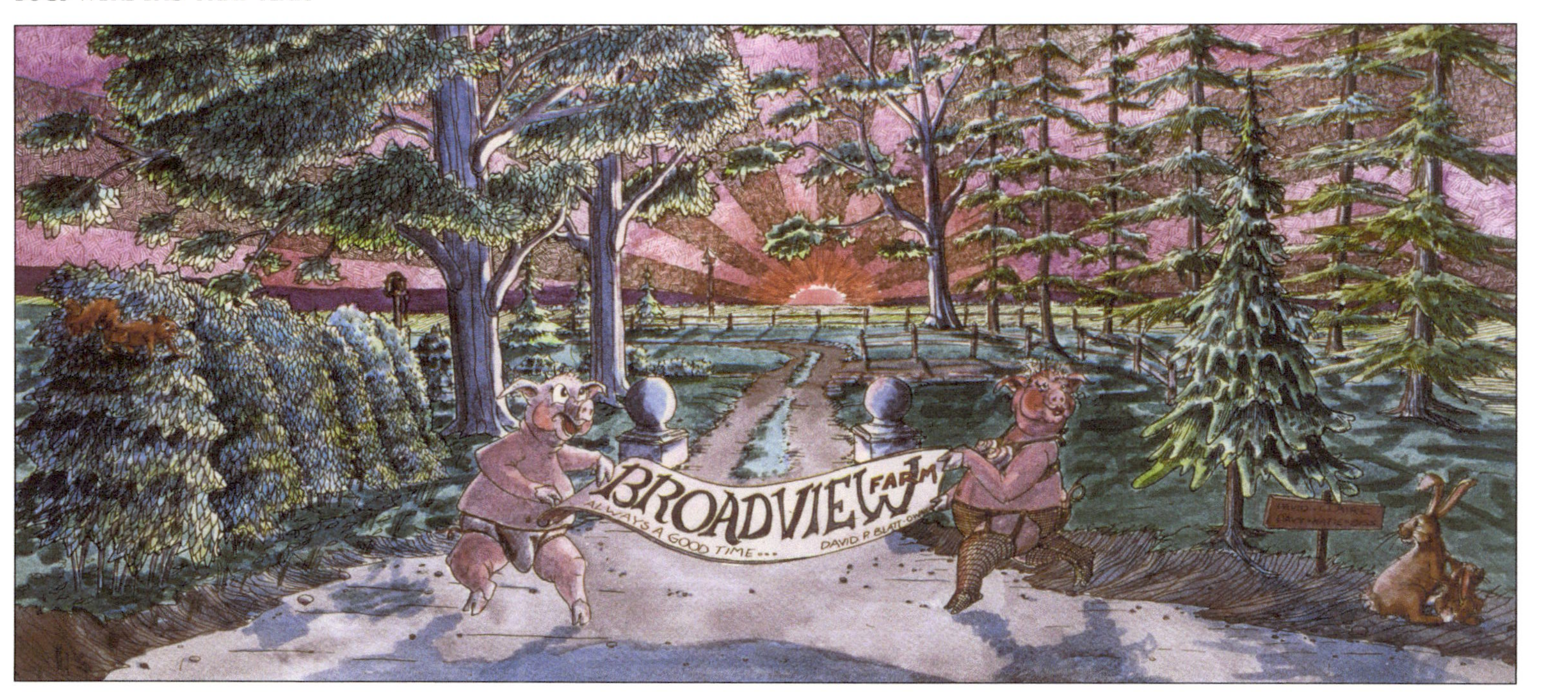

BROAD VIEW FARM

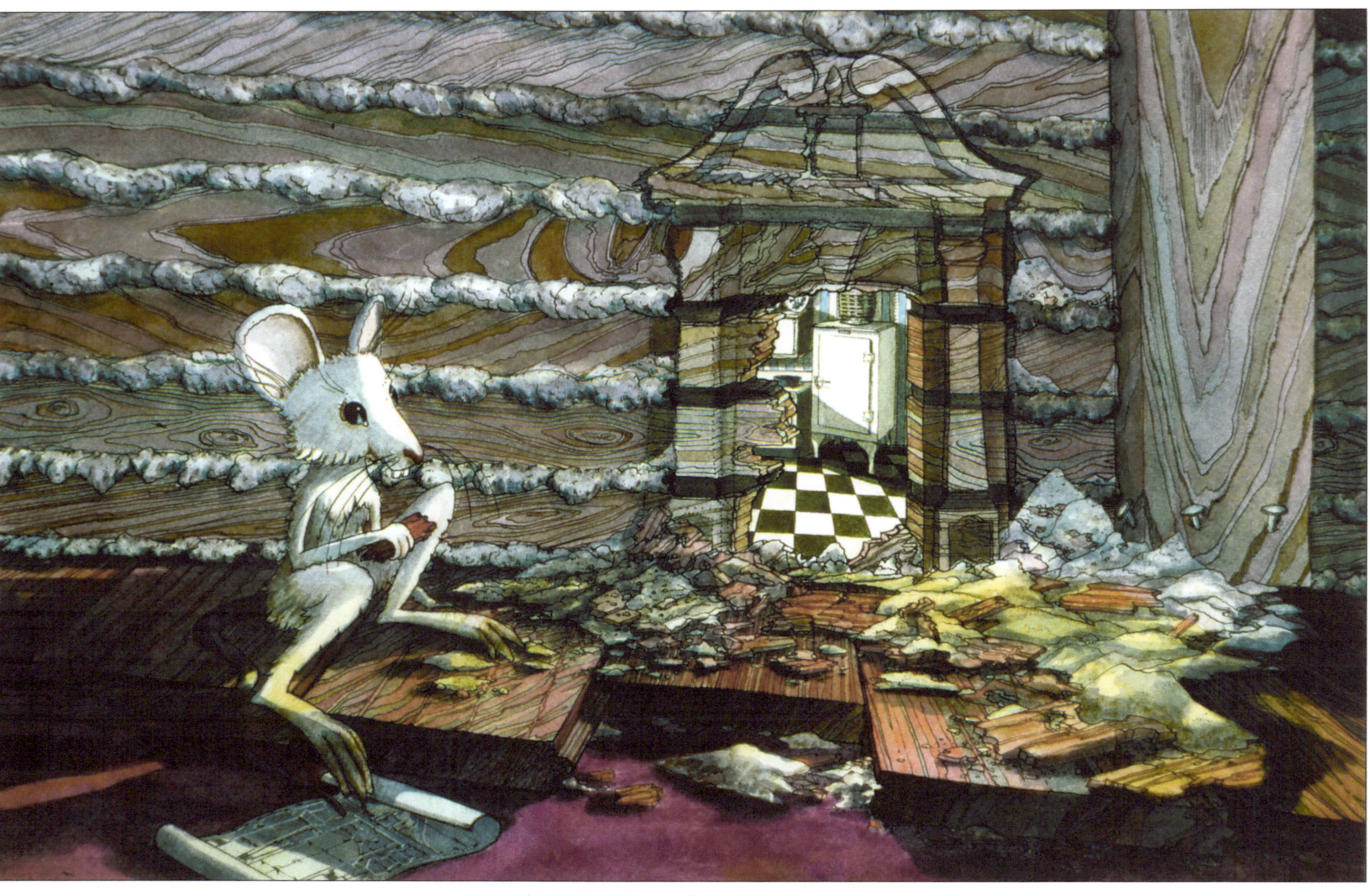

Architectural Improvements

Clever and always good with his paws, "Rollo" fashions a broken-arch pediment for his home. A devotee of Palladio, he wonders why the bungalow kitchen outside his door lacks the elegance he envisions for his own domicile.

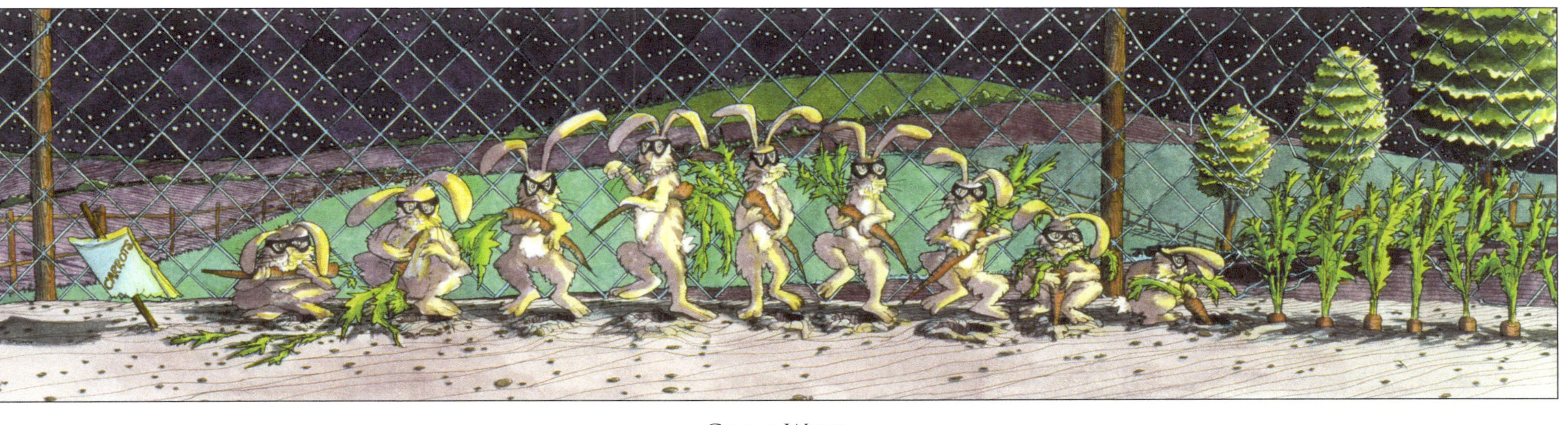

Crime Wave

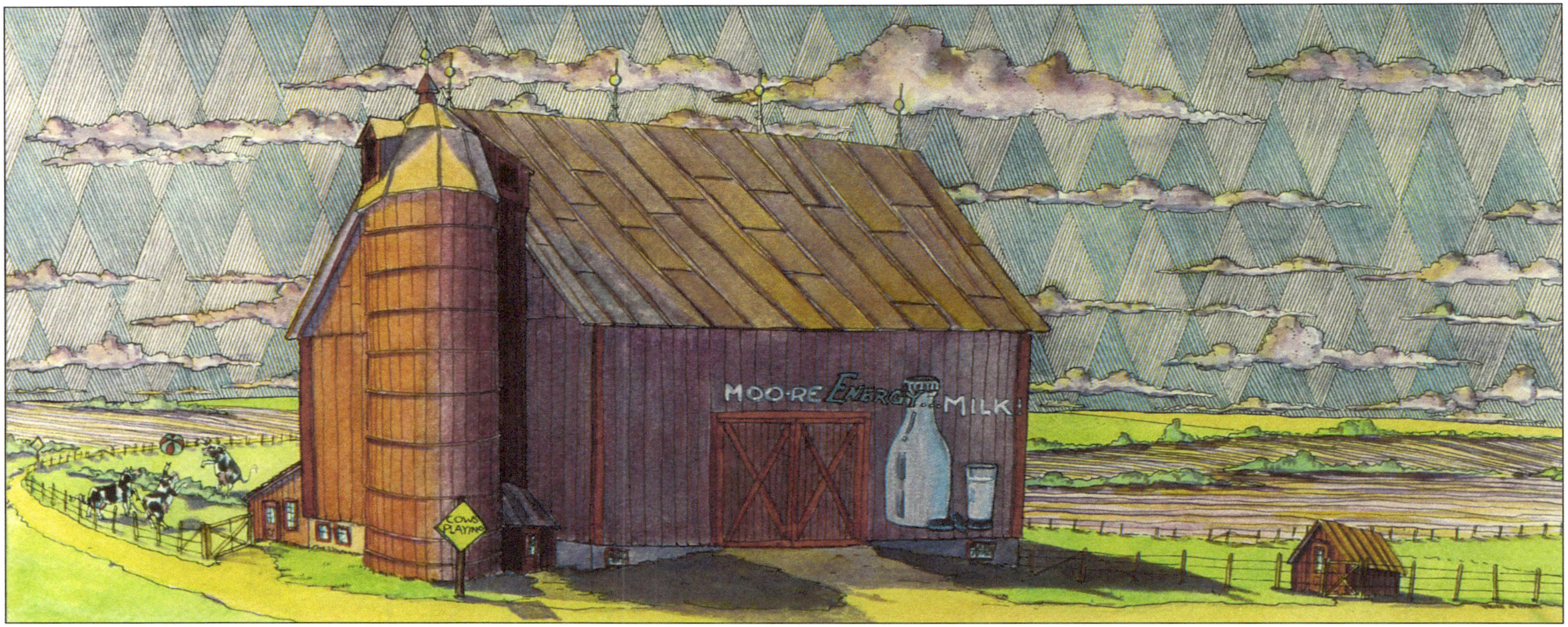

Cows At Play

All those golden days of sunshine when life is as light as a beach ball and as sweet as milk and cookies. Life can be Moovelous.

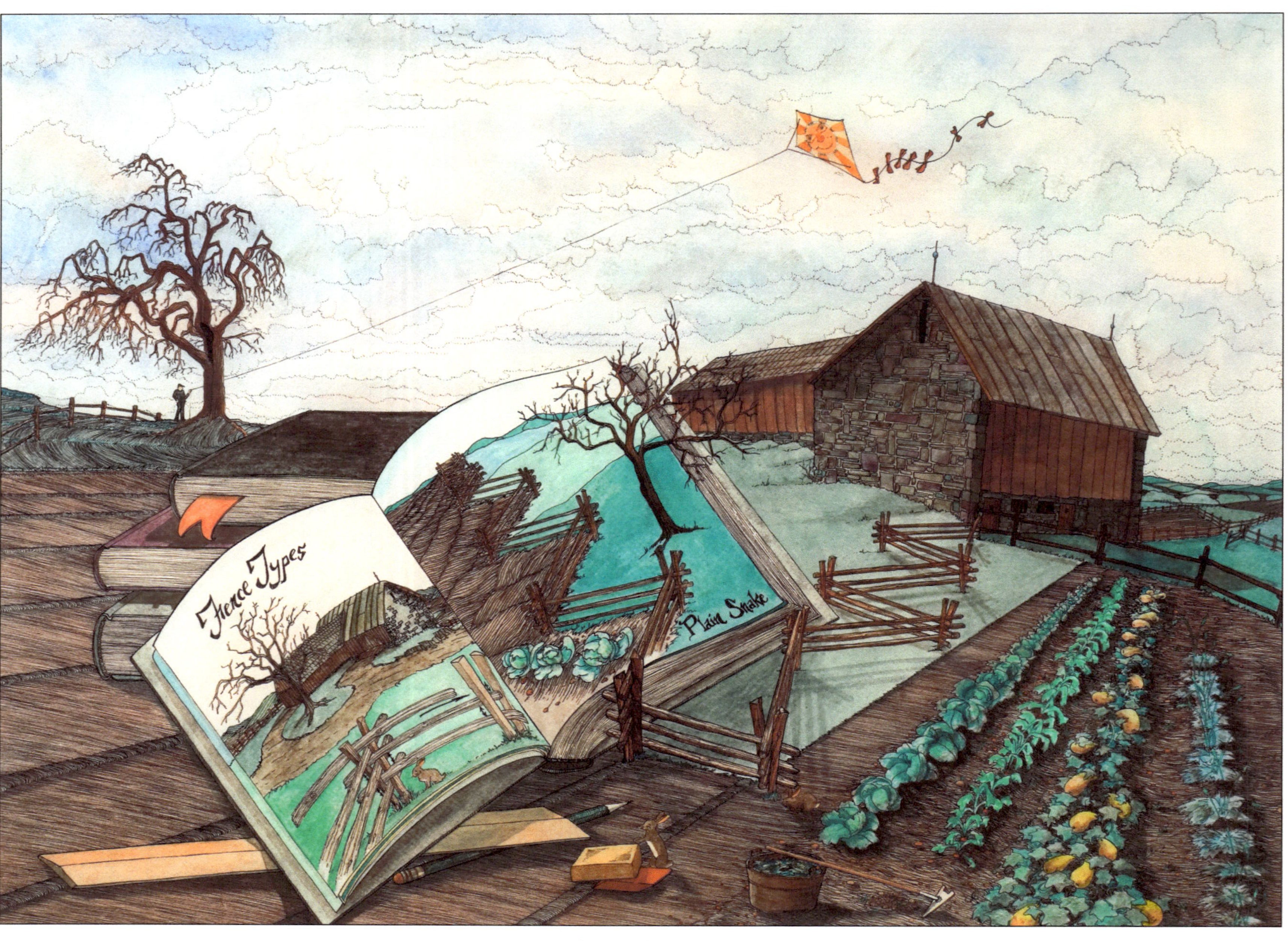

Plain Snake

THE INSTRUCTIONS ARE THERE - YOU NEED ONLY LOOK. AS YOU READ, THE IMAGES TAKE FORM - A PLAIN SNAKE FENCE. EVEN THOSE WORDS SEEM TO EVOKE A SIMPLE MAGIC OF QUIETER TIMES WHERE YOU CAN FLY A KITE IN RESTFUL HARMONY WITH THE BREEZE.

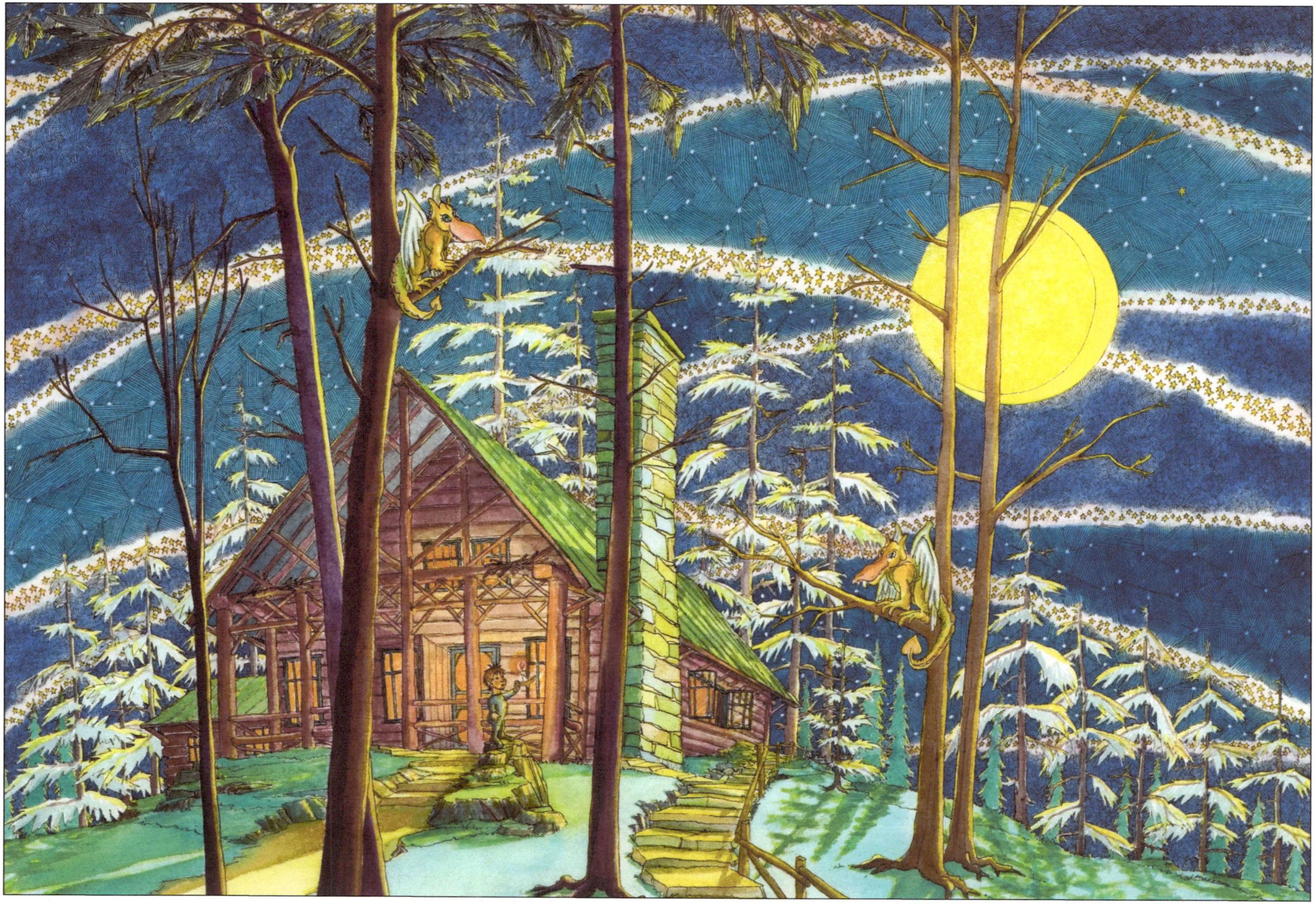

Time for Bed

Little dragons wanted to play under the full moon, tummies full of dragon chow. It is hard to go to sleep when stars are dancing and there are still moonbeams to be licked.

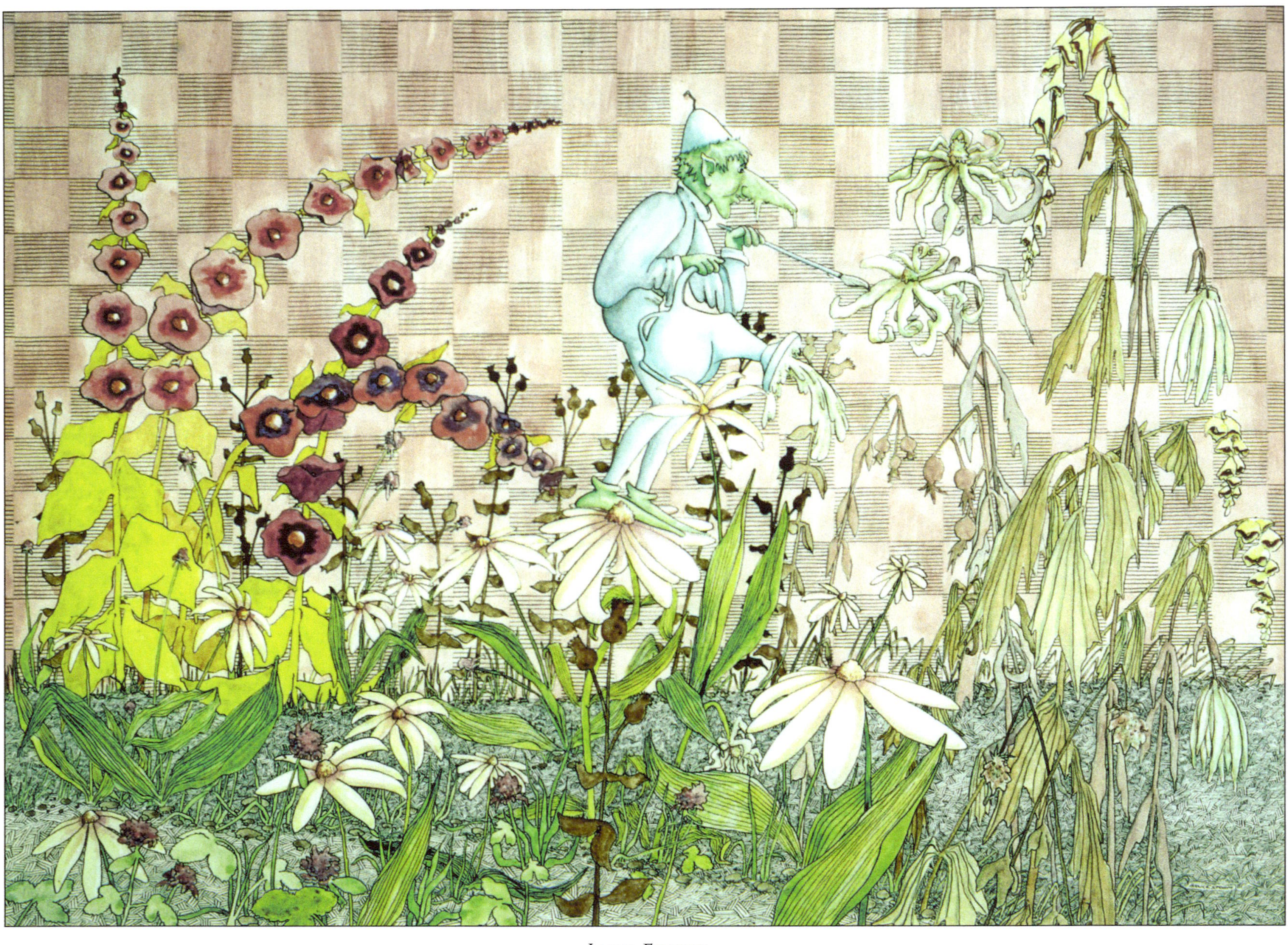

Jack Frost

Favoring Monet, he hopes to paint in the delicate shades of the impressionist. With his frosty brush he gently coats each flower. But the results are never quite what he anticipates. Still he persists. Winning rave reviews for his leaves, it is his flowers which he longs to improve. How did Monet manage?

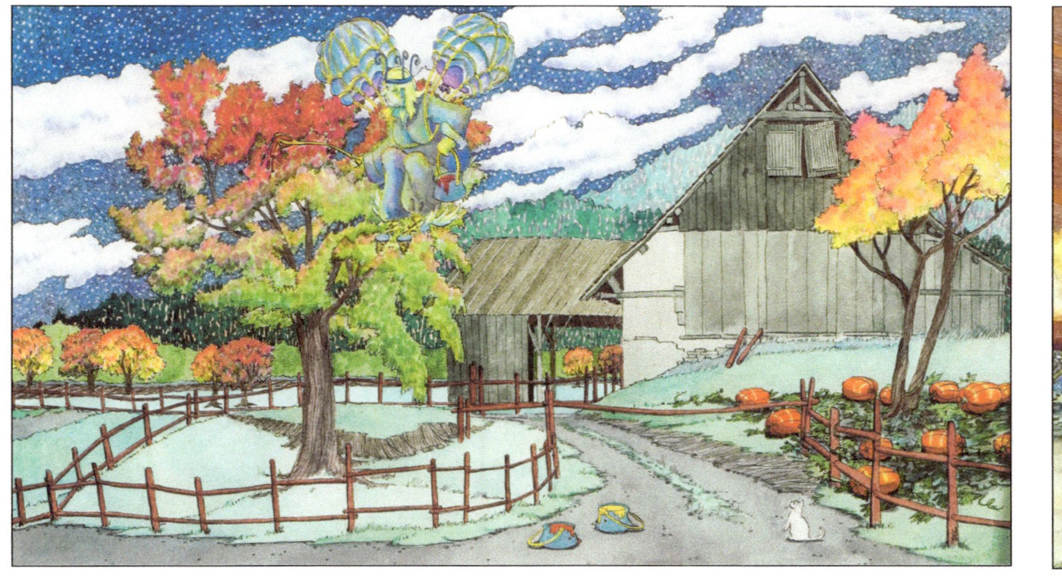

Heavy Frost

Spring shoes for lift, balloons for stability and the dear old girl was at it - enrobing each leaf with the colors only achieved by the experienced touch of a master.

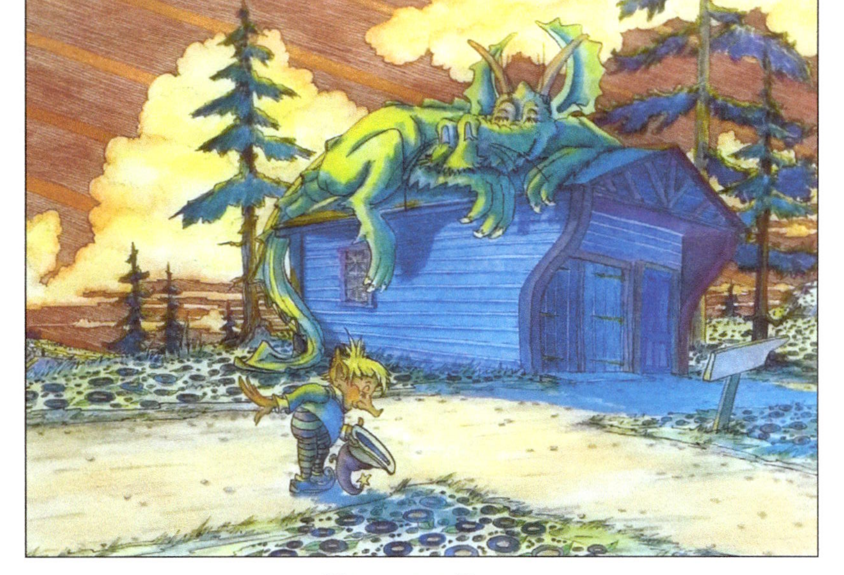

Dragon Dog

Good manners are essential when greeting a dragon dog. Bow, remove your cap and if he starts purring, then scratch his belly - you'll be friends for life.

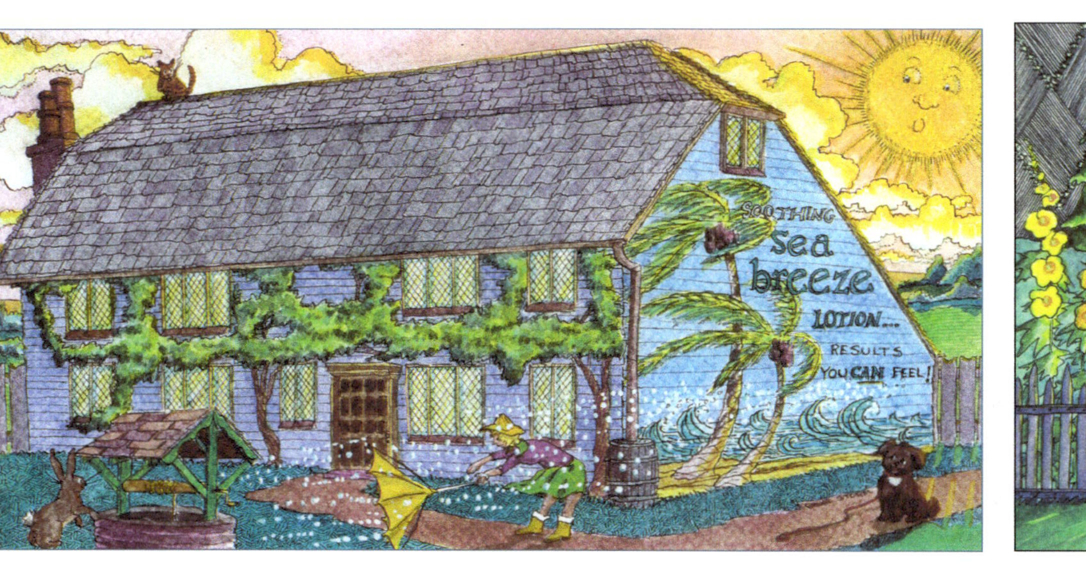

Truth In Advertising

Why had the artist painted that sign under the full moon? Since the sun had come up that corner had been nothing but trouble - cautiously thought Edward from his vantage point high on the roof top.

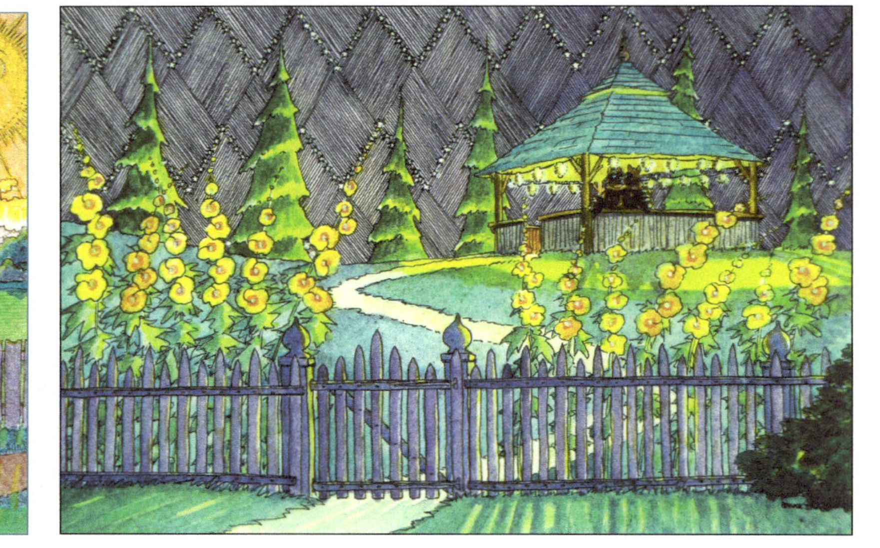

Dance Rendezvous

The Hollyhocks swayed to "Deep Purple" as it reverberated from the old Victrola. The night smelled of balsam and it was love at last.

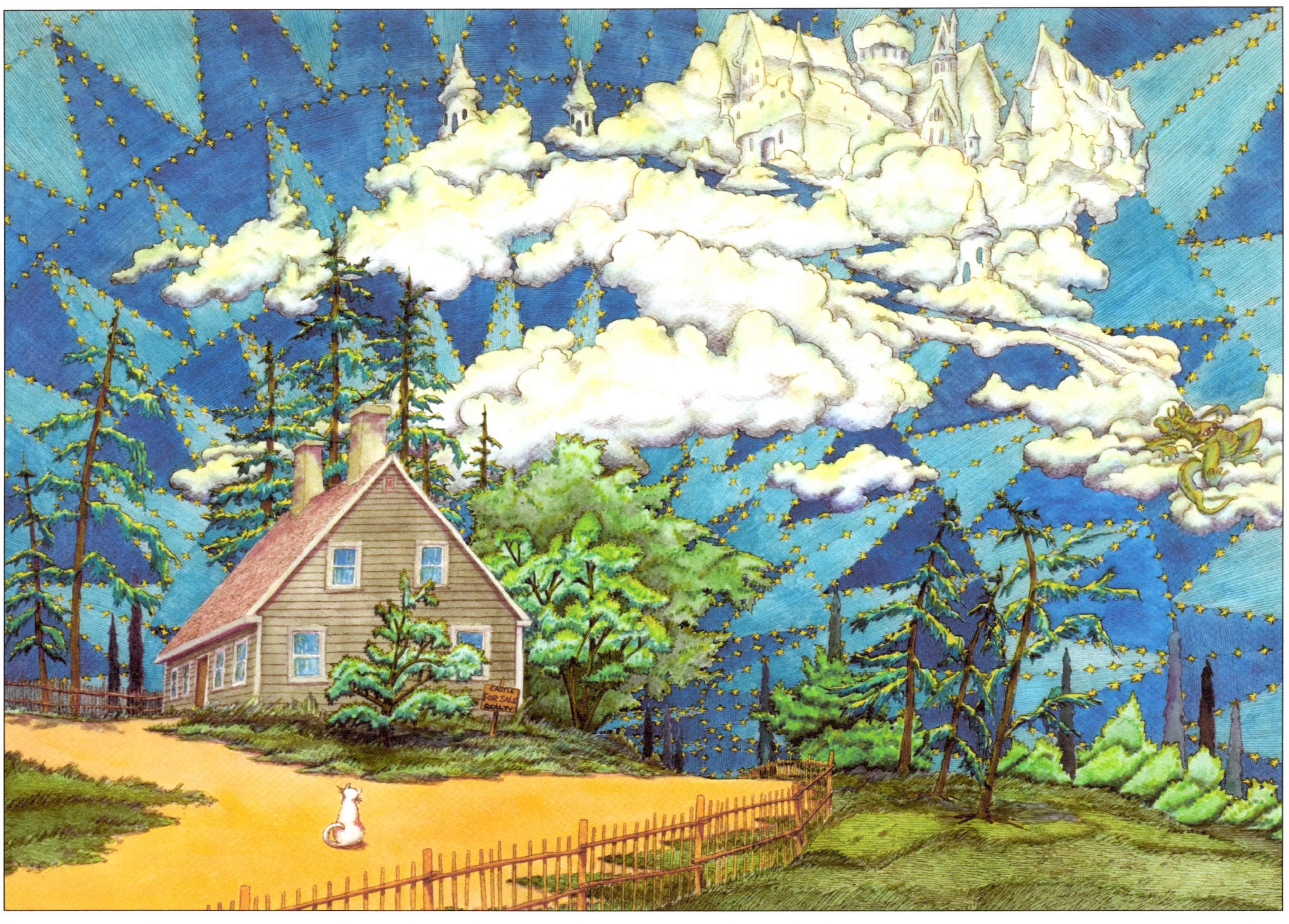

One Man's Home is....

"When the stars aline and magic is in the air, then the humblest of homes is a castle in spirit," whispered the dragon thoughtfully.

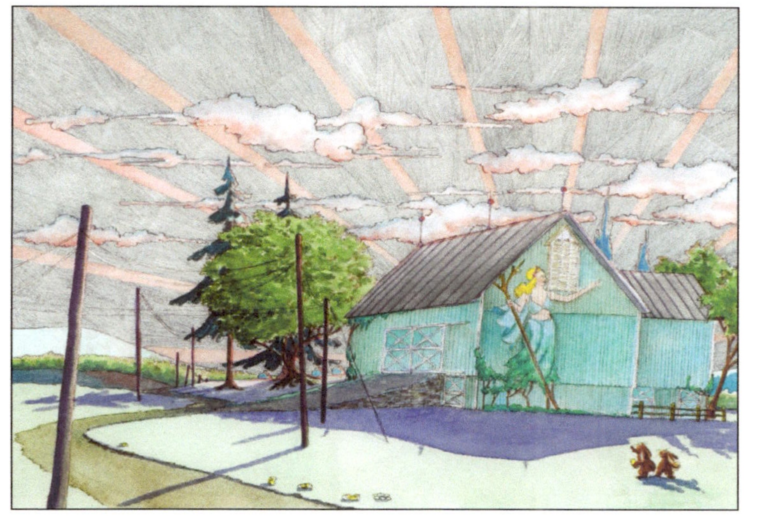

Mother Nature

Mother Nature turned away from the litter and greeted the dawn while the little rabbits puzzled, "Why have the humans left such a strange offering?"

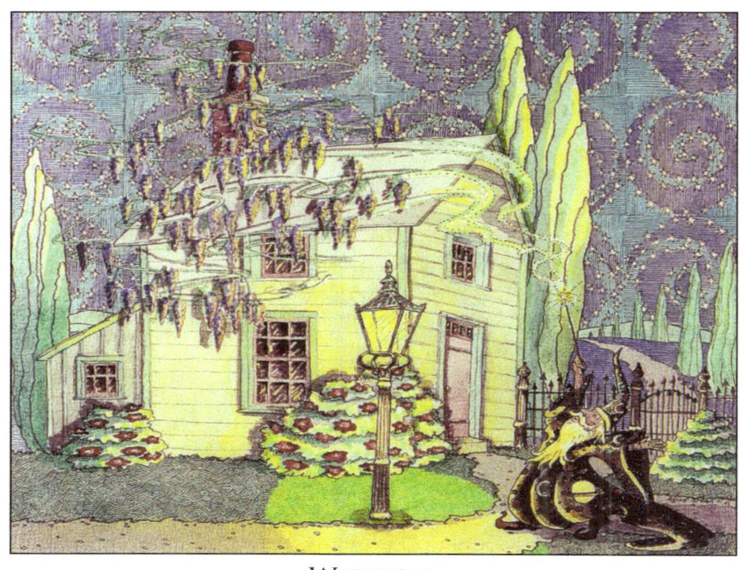

Wisteria

He had retired nearly 15 years ago when the golf and the books lost their luster. He went out at night to work in the old gardener's cottage. While others slept he tried on his ensemble and cranked up the star stick. The wisteria spiraled around the cottage at his command. Oh rapture!

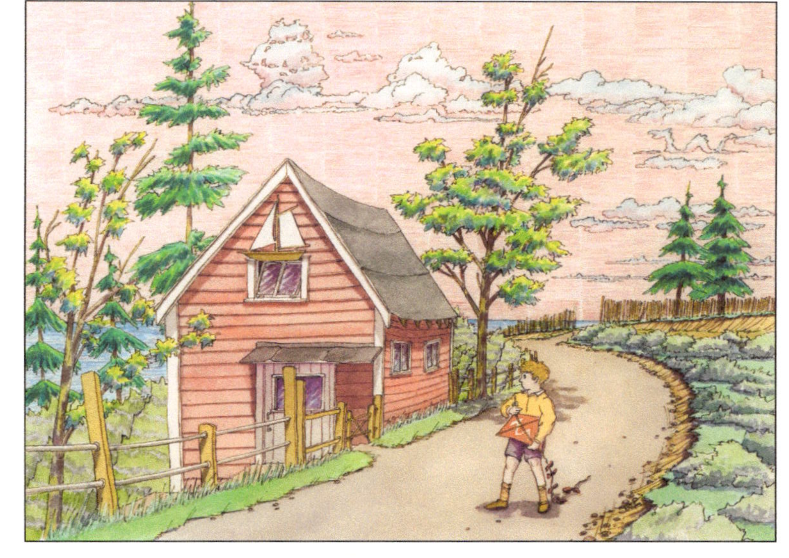

In The Clouds

Breeze up to the sky on dreams or kites. Ride the wind on sails or string. Chase the cloud dragon in your tall ship, free as a summer's day.

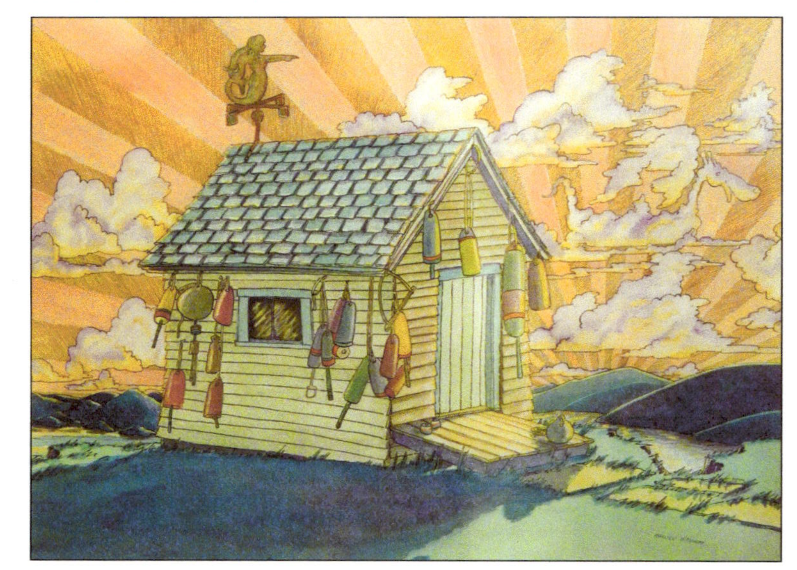

Mermaid

She was always there pointing the way and seeing what so many others missed. As the sun slid behind the hills, she alone heralded the magic in the sky.

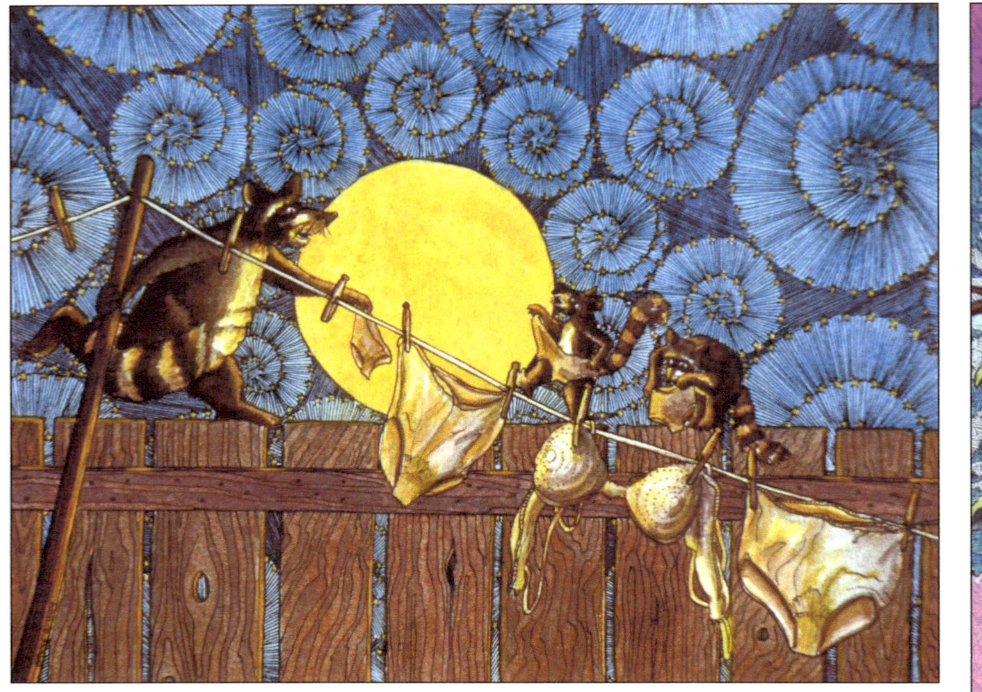

Tribute To Madonna

It seemed all the rage, so with the full moon as a spot light, the younguns' cavorted, and struck poses in the odd garments.

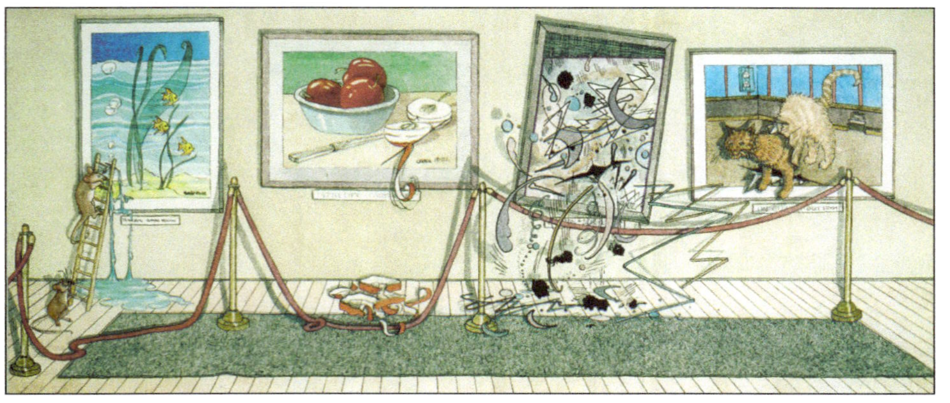

Gallery Mischief

That awful cat picture was too much so they slashed it--and really the action painting was horrid so they took some liberties--and suddenly the prank just sort of got the best of them. They were unware that their actions were producing quite unexpected results and that the mischief would be ending soon.

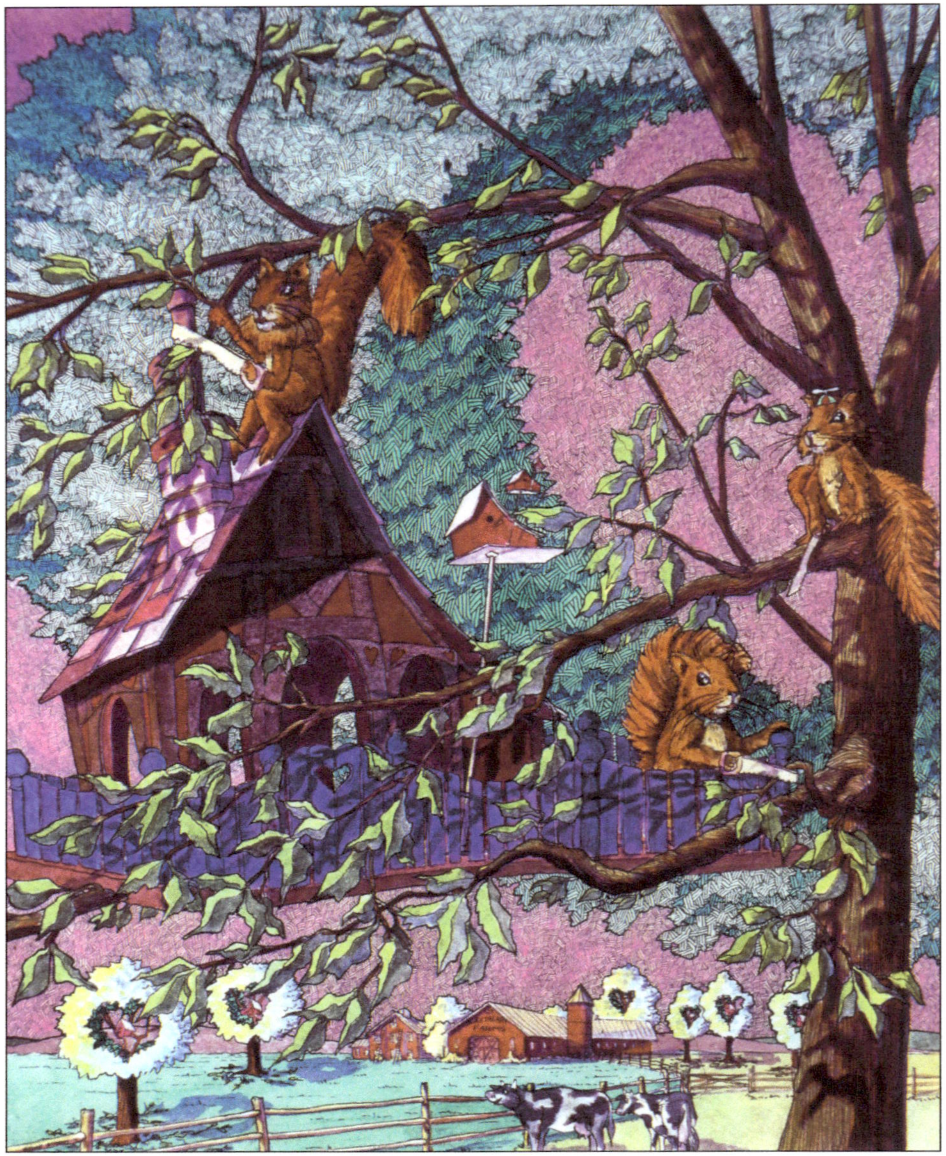

Sweet Heart Farms

The cows found it all quite amusing, "the squirrels' grand design." Nevertheless, in spite of the sawing and paint fumes, they couldn't deny it... there was romance in the air.

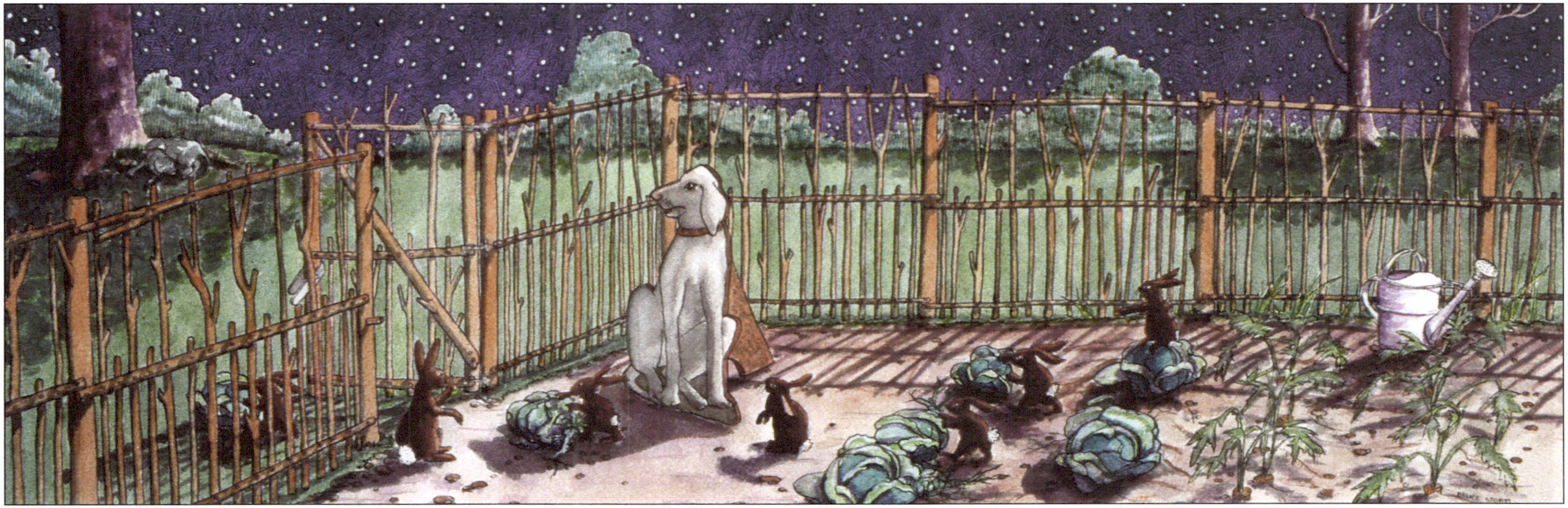

Faux Dog

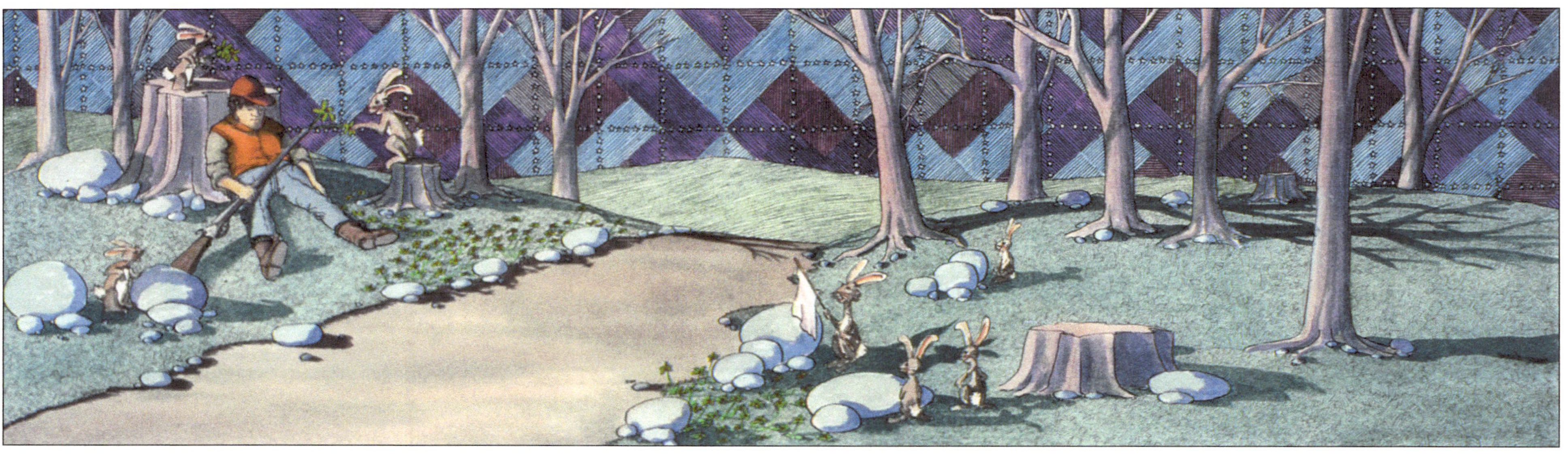

Truce

Jasper poked the heliopsis into the barrel and they'd leave Oscar's flag. Still they wondered...could he understand truce?

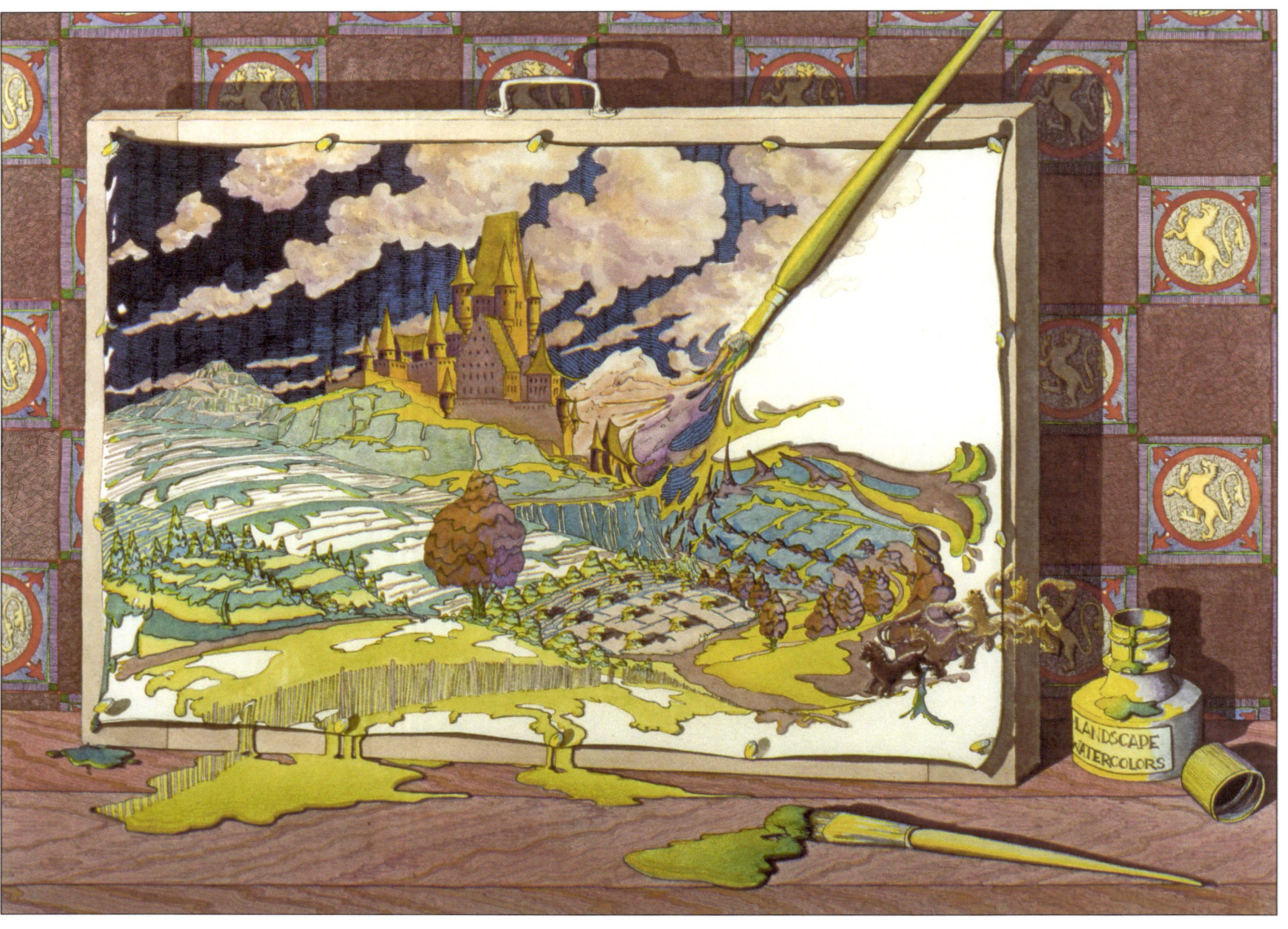

Landscape Watercolors

The artist had long dreamed of such a paint. He needed only to think the picture and move the brush. The images seemed to be spreading, he observed. Where would it end?

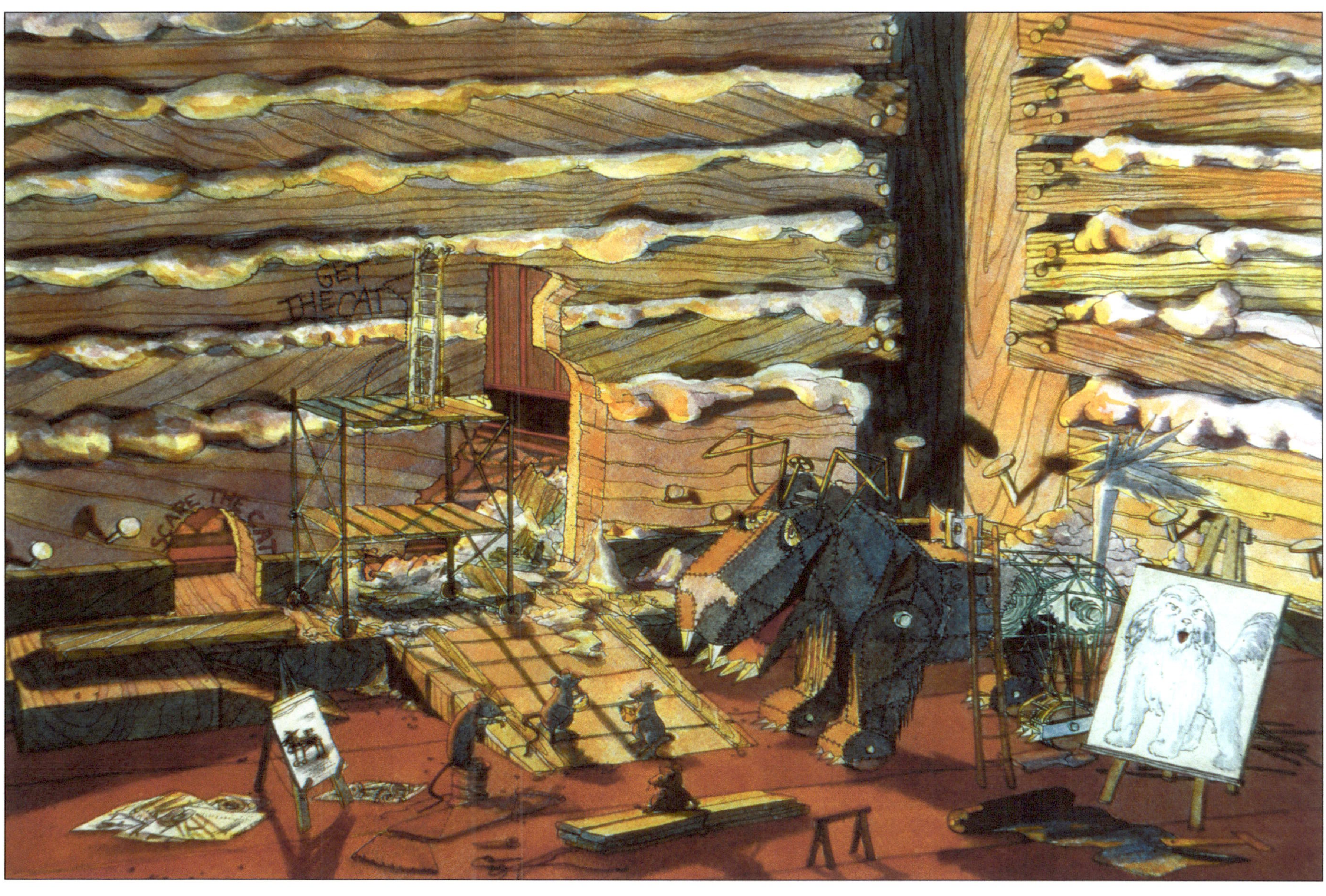

Trojan Dog

Relaxing after hours of work, he thought about how they had struck upon it quite by accident. Now it was nearing completion - the ultimate defense system-the Trojan dog.

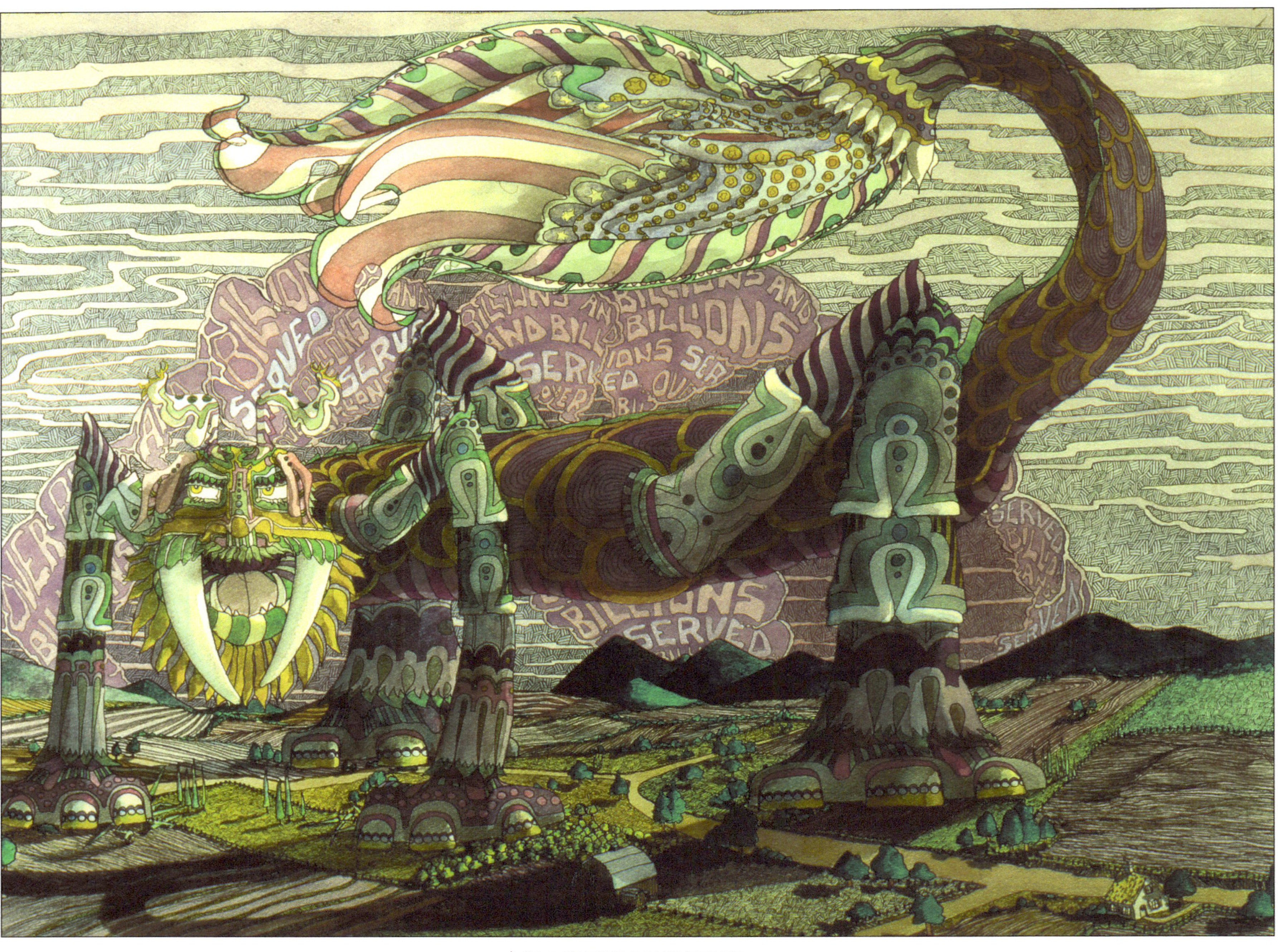

Across the Landscape

Across the sleeping country side the giant stomped. Flattening trees and fields oblivious to the destruction it created.

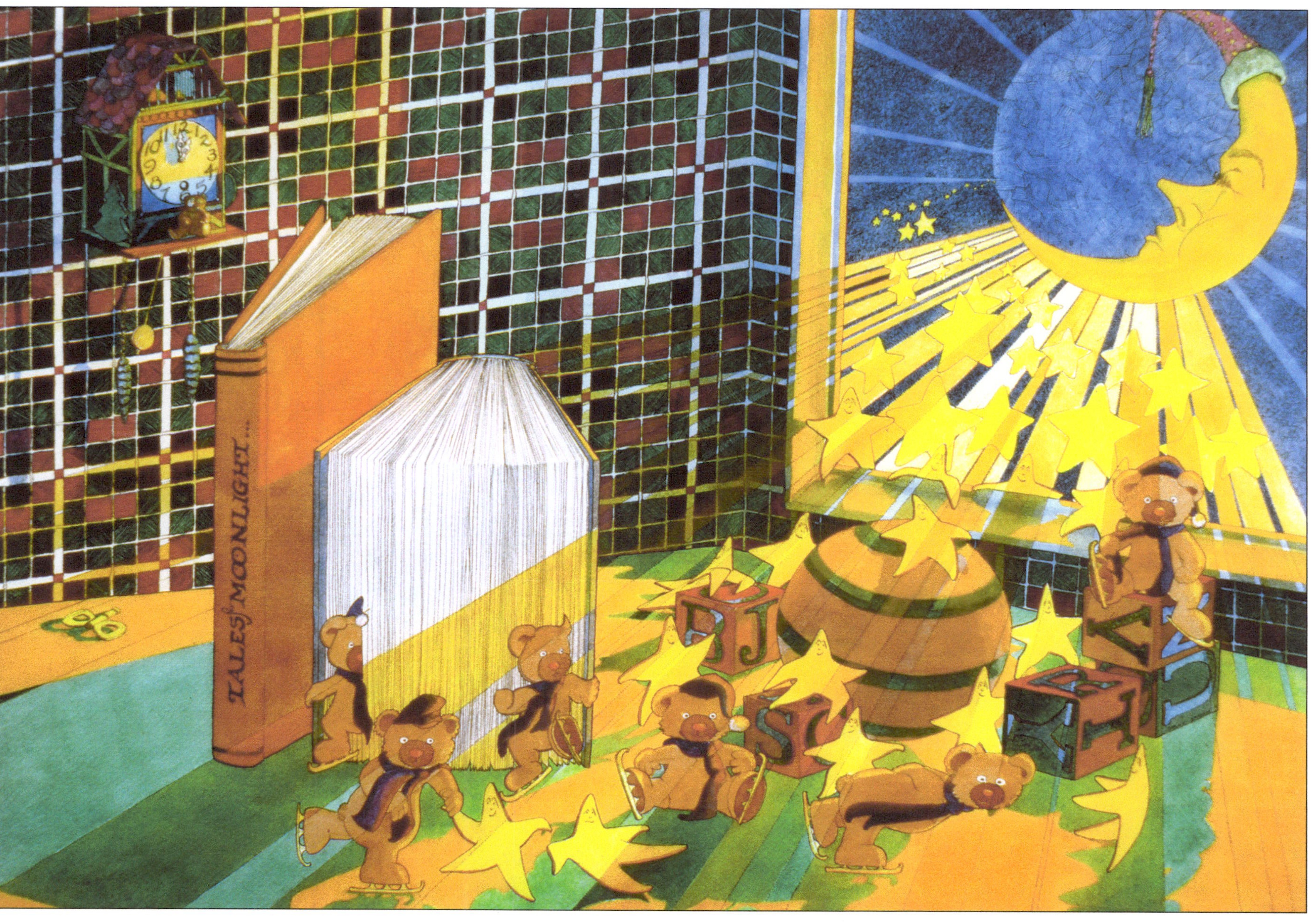

Tales of Moonlight

As the clock strikes the hour, the moon beams illuminate the old book, giving animation to the illustrated bears. They step into the light, which is as slippery as ice, and begin to skate about with the playful little stars who join them from the window.

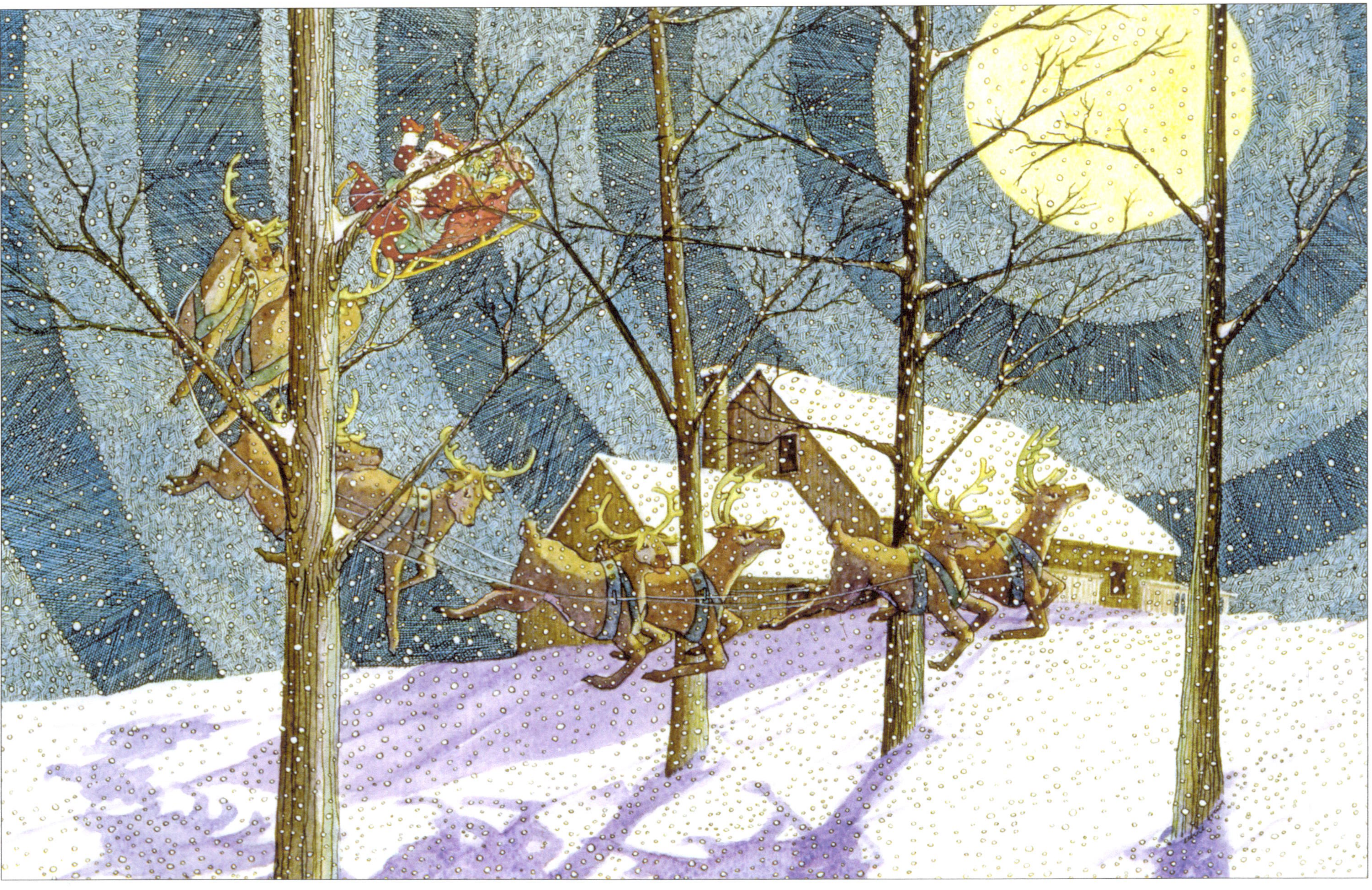

Santa Claus Visits the Mahonskis

The bag always felt much lighter after Santa visited the Mahonskis. Christopher, Loren and Jamie were sleeping when the reindeer bounded effortlessly into the sky and headed over the river to Williamsport.

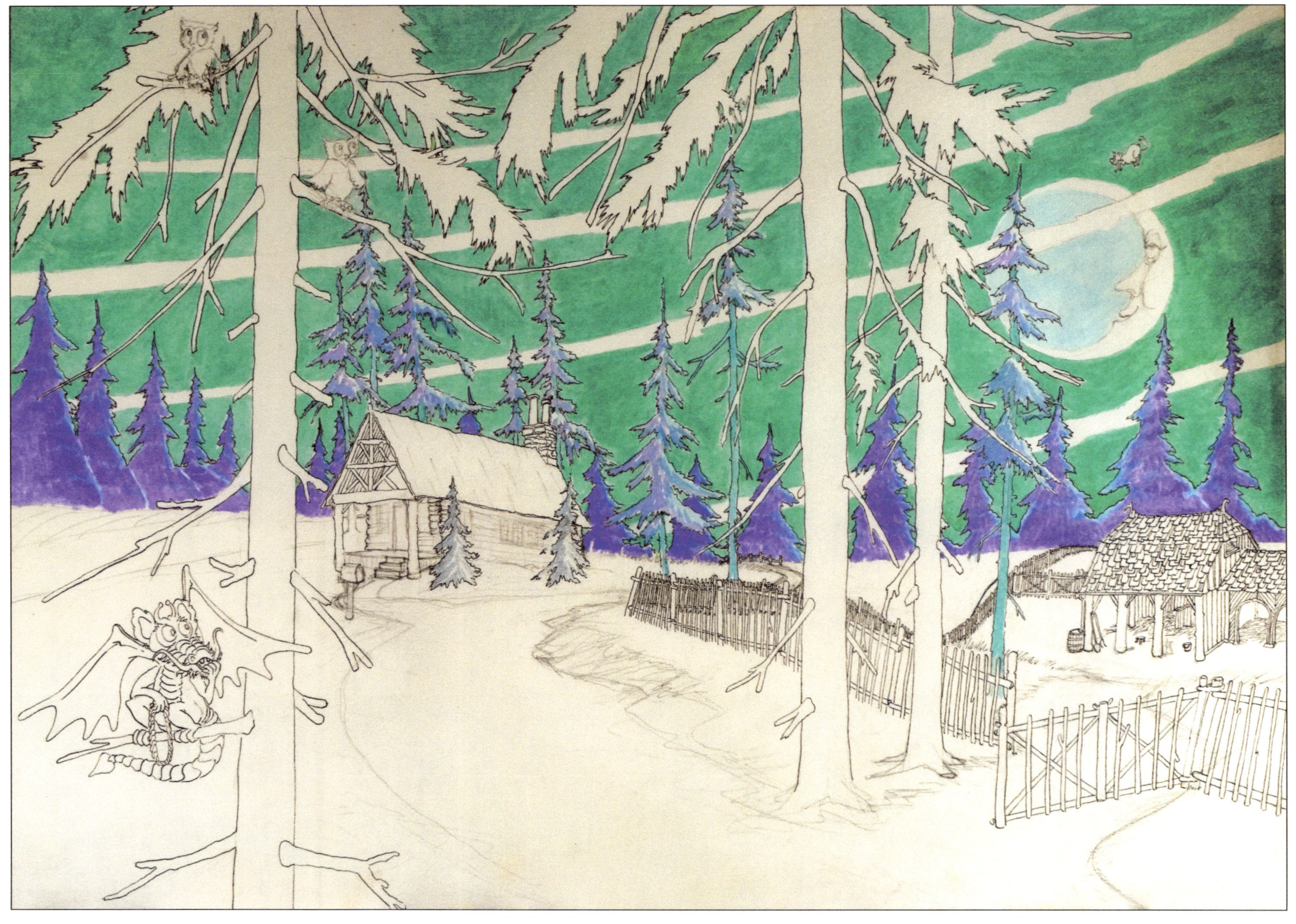

(Current work in progress)

Locations & Inspirations

Front Cover: Suppertime - Muncy Hills • German Castles • Artist's dogs called to their food bowls at suppertime

1 Preparing To Launch - French castles and landscapes

2 Love Letter - (dedication) from wife's art collection

3 Self Improvement - We are what we create; we make our art that shapes us

4 current work in progress

5 Night View - Pogodas in China • Rocks in West Quoddy Head State Park, Lubec, Maine • Mother's PA Dutch quilt sky

6 Dream Quilt - window at artist's brother Robert's home on Campobello Island, N.B., Canada • Muncy Hills • Father's barn • Mother's quilts

7 Sea Dragon - Toy Ships • European castles •Pallisade coast of Campobello Island, New Brunswick, Canada • What we do not see or recognize

8 Almost Enchanted - Frogs in artist's garden, North Main St., Muncy, PA • Muncy hills • Castle in France

9 Young Chris - Artist's dog Luna • Nephew Christopher

10 Jack Frost 2nd Observation - window at artist's brother Robert's home on Campobello Island, N.B., Canada

11 Narcissus - Artist's father's parrots • A huge night blooming Ceris plant that the Storm family had for many years • Egotists

12 North star - The oceans of Maine and Campobello Island, Canada • PA Dutch Quilts • Ship model that the artist restored • Animals to guide us • Hope

13 Misted Ship - The artist as the man in the moon (always) The moon sees, as artisits often do, what is ignored

14 Light Frost - St. Nizier d' Uriage Alps France • Love of the fall color • An appreciation for the masterful color change of the season • Artist's cat creature comforts

When Pigs Fly - Broadview Farm, New Hope Road, Pineville, PA • Artist's older brother Donald and younger brother Robert along with artist as the three pigs.

15 Fall News - The word news from North, East, West, South • The amazing fact that deer migrate into no hunting areas in the fall • The garden house at the famous secret garden in England

Alphabet Lesson - Artist's mother, father and sister Janell along with the artist as rabbits • Mother's quilts • Father's thirst for knowledge

16 Lost Coins - As children the artist and his siblings would rush to check for coins in sofas and chairs after guests had left • The sense that art is as real as any other reality • The artist recalls the figure in the painting from his early morning newspaper route

17 The Night Light - Artist's lighting collection • The power of creativity is extended far beyond our understanding • Books spark dreams • Mont-Saint-Michel, France

18 Sandman - The artist as the watchful moon • The winding roads of PA • Why do we sleep?

19 Night Sweats - Welshpool, Campobello Island, N.B., Canada • What happens to "our stuff" when we sleep? ...•(the critters that come in our gardens and play)

20 Acceptance - Self portrait

21 Love Spell - William and Selinda Kennedy's out building on North Market Street, Muncy, PA.

22 Rabbit Expose - Broadview Farm, New Hope Road, Pineville, PA

Playing Statue - Marlboro, England

23 Tale of a Dragon's Tail - Bay of Fundy region • St. Nizier d' Uriage (Alps) France • Nephew Christopher as guards

24 Jack's Back - Amersham, England, William Penn's hometown

25 Keeping Watch Over All - Road to Paradise, St. Nizier d' Uriage (Alps), France • European castles • Nephew Christopher as guards

26 Mice Craftsmen - Rick Mahonski family and Goldsmith Studio, South Williamsport, PA

Art Director - Artist's home on North Main Street, Muncy, PA • Combined with the Storm family farm, Pfeiffer's Corner, PA

27 Mouse House - Grampian Boulevard, Williamsport, PA.

Swiss Fantasy - Luggage used when artist went to Penn State Univeristy

28 Hi Ho Off We Go - Artist's dog Footsie • Welshpool, Campobello Island, N. B., Canada

29 Sure Signs of Fall - Water tower at the Algonquin Hotel, St. Andrews, New Brunswick, Canada • The castle is based on the sculpture that the artist made from 300 pounds of clay for his wife Nella

30 After Hours - A portion of the painting Young Chris is visible in this representation of a favorite nursery rhyme • Former B & S Gallery, Market Street, Willimasport, PA

31 Through Roesen Colored Glasses - Themed invitational art exhibit featuring the heritage of Williamsport, PA. Held at the B & S Gallery formerly at Market Street, Williamsport, PA

32 Faux Mailbox - Artist's dogs • Welshpool, Campobello Island, N.B., Canada

Sushi - Artist's family stories

33 For Sale - North Road house for sale, neglected and overgrown in Welshpool, Campobello Island, N.B., Canada: The artist returned a year later and surprisingly found that many of his imagined property changes had been accomplished

Smell of Home Cooking - Welshpool Campobello Island, N.B., Canada • Dragon pull toy artist's design

34 Sandman Country Town - Amersham, England, William Penn's hometown

35 Star Hanger - As seen from the artist's back garden

36 Night Light Adventure - Plymouth Auto dealership table lamp from the artist's lighting collection

37 Tractor Crossing - Broadview Farm, New Hope road, Pineville, PA • Pennsylvania Dept. of Transportation "ped-xing" highway signs

Gingerbread House - Artist's kitchen, North Main Street, Muncy, PA • Note "from" Nella

38 Roesen Still Life - Compote from artist's brother Robert's collection, Campobello Island, N.B., Canada • Niece Lindsey and nephew Christopher

39 Romance & Anniversary Toast - Artist's garden, North Main Street, Muncy, PA

Bedtime Froggy - Posed toy from artist's wife collection

Dance - Stories of the Storm family's numerous cats

40 Dragons Don't Tell - West Quoddy State Park, Lubec, Maine • German castles

41 Sandman City Scene - An alley off of the Strand in London, England

42 Love Bugs - Artist's garden, North Main Street, Muncy, PA

Novel Approach - Arts and crafts candle stick from the artist's lighting collection • Lead toys from the artist's toy collection

43 Artistic License - West Quoddy Head State Park, Lubec, Maine

Free Kittens - Storm family cat stories

Hollyhocks and Whipperwills - Artist's first home in Centerbridge, PA

44 Morning Cows - Milk bottle building in South Deerfield, Mass: since removed from the site

Night Cows - Lehigh Valley Dairy logo from artist's youth • Holstein cows of Lycoming County, PA

45 Dancing Down The Bunny Trail - Jaime Mahonski, South Williamsport, PA

46 Where Frogs Go in Winter - Frogs in artist's garden

Potholes - Eaglesmere, PA

47 Topiary Competition - Sibling rivalry

48 South Pasture - Dewart, PA farm: silo was recently demolished

Places Girls - Cinq Ports, England • Lycoming County, PA, cows

49 Cross Stitch - Muncy Hills, PA

50 Caution - Historic Deerfield, Mass. curtain rod decoration • Lamp from artist's childhood • Study in black and white by Whistler

51 Measuring-Up - Artist's desire to be as tall as his older brother Donald

Feeding Frenzy - Artist's terrace and garden

Taber's Christmas Card - Accompanied commission of the Tabers

Tabears - The Thomas T. Taber family, South Main Street, Muncy, PA

52 Congrats Jill Barto - A commission for an outstanding scholar and athlete from Hughesville High School, Hughesville, PA

53 Lunar Olympics - Grandview Lane, Welshpool, Campobello Island, N.B., Canada

54 Composing - Artist's self-portrait in answer to
55 the often asked question: where do you get your ideas? • Muncy Hills, PA

56 Checkerville - Traveling in the northern tier
57 of PA with cousin Barbara Baily McConnell trying to find the village of Checkerville - (never did), so the artist • created his own idyllic Checkerville based on Lycoming County, PA beautiful farms

58 That's My Wash - Broadview Farm, New Hope Road, Pineville, PA

Dutch Barn - Artist's 3 dogs: Luna, Wifee, McSnutter • PA German village and barn

59 Unsolved Mystery - Artist's brother Robert's nightlight • Niece Lindsey and nephew Christopher

Springmaid Dairy - Cross Keys Doylestown, PA, roadside advertising sign from the 1940's: now demolished • Lewisburg, PA, area landscape

60 Uninvited Guest - South Main Street, Muncy, PA

MOON JUMP - FROM A FAMILY STORY OF WHEN THE ARTIST'S UNCLE NAMED ONE OF HIS DAIRY COWS IN HONOR OF THE ARTIST'S MOTHER • SHE WASN'T THRILLED • MUNCY HILLS • MONT-SAINT-MICHEL, FRANCE

COLORING THE MACINTOSH - WENTZLER'S APPLE FARM, MUNCY, PA

61 JACK FROST RETURNS - BROADVIEW FARM, NEW HOPE ROAD, PINEVILLE, PA

GREAT RACE - RECALLING TIRE RACING WITH ARTIST'S BROTHER DONALD • THE FAMOUS LEHIGH VALLEY LOCOMOTIVE: THE BLACK DIAMOND

62 WITH RECKLESS ABANDON - LYCOMING COUNTY, PA., COVERED BRIDGES

SNOW BUNNY - ARTIST'S NEPHEW CHRISTOPHER AND HIS TOY RABBITS

63 SUPERGROW - ARTIST'S CHILDHOOD MEMORY OF ROADSIDE ADVERTISING

COOKIES DISCOVERY - RICK AND DIANE GLEN WRIGHT'S CATS OF QUARRY ROAD, MUNCY, PA

COMING YOUR WAY - FORMER B. & S. GALLERY, MARKET STREET, WILLIAMSPORT, PA • LITTLE LEAGUE WORLD SERIES

64 APPLE BRAND OUTDOOR PAINT - THE ARTIST'S STUDIO, NORTH MAIN STREET, MUNCY, PA • THE ARTIST HAS ALWAYS WANTED SUCH MAGICAL PAINT

FRESH MILK - ARTIST'S MOTHERS QUILT • CHILDHOOD TOYS • LEHIGH VALLEY DAIRY LOGO FROM ARTIST YOUTH

65 NEXT YEAR - GRANDVIEW LANE, CAMPOBELLO ISLAND, N.B., CANADA • THE DESIRE TO PAINT THE AURORA BOREALIS

GREATVIEW COTTAGE - GRAND VIEW LANE & NORTH ROAD, COMPOBELLO ISLAND, N.B., CANADA

66 CATASTROPHY - PINE TREES ON GRANDVIEW LANE, WELSHPOOL, CAMPOBELLO ISLAND, N.B., CANADA

67 TRACING YOUR ROOTS - ARTIST'S GERMAN COUSINS AND GERMAN CASTLES

TRYPTIC - BASED ON A NEW ENGLAND ANTIQUE WEATHERVANE COMMISSIONED BY DR. AND MRS. GORDON GODBEY

68 I'M NO ANGEL - ARTIST'S FATHER'S AQUARIUMS

69 THE BUGS WERE BAD THAT YEAR - EXPLORING THE BACK ROADS OF THE NOTHERN TIER PA. COUNTIES WITH COUSIN BARBARA BAILY MCCONNELL.

BROADVIEW FARMS - NEW HOPE ROAD, PINEVILLE, PA

70 ARCHITECTURAL IMPROVEMENTS - ARTIST'S CHILDHOOD MEMORY

71 CRIME WAVE - INSPIRED BY FELLOW TEACHERS AT HUGHESVILLE HIGH SCHOOL, HUGHESVILLE, PA

COWS AT PLAY - BARN OUTSIDE TURBOTVILLE, PA: SILO NOW DEMOLISHED

72 PLAIN SNAKE - ARTIST'S FATHER'S FARM WITH ARTIST'S FATHER FLYING KITE AT PHEIFERS CORNER, PA •FENCE LOCATED NEAR TURBOTVILLE, PA

73 TIME FOR BED - ARTIST'S YOUNGER BROTHER ROBERT • GRANDVIEW LANE, WELSHPOOL, CAMPOBELLO ISLAND, N.B., CANADA

74 JACK FROST - ARTIST'S GARDENS • YOUNGER BROTHER ROBERT AS JACK

75 HEAVY FROST - ROAD TO PARADISE ST. NIZIER D' URIAGE (ALPS) FRANCE • ARTIST'S CAT CREATURE COMFORTS

DRAGON DOG - • BAY OF FUNDY REGION • ARTIST'S DOGS

TRUTH IN ADVERTISING - KENT, ENGLAND

DANCE RENDEZVOUS - WELSHPOOL, CAMPOBELLO ISLAND, N.B., CANADA: BOTH FENCE AND GAZEBO HAVE SINCE BEEN DEMOLISHED

76 ONE MANS HOME - WELSHPOOL, CAMPOBELLO ISLAND, N.B., CANADA • ARTIST'S CAT CREATURE COMFORTS • LOIRE VALLEY CASTLES, FRANCE

77 MOTHER NATURE - BARN ON HEBERLING ROAD MUNCY, PA • ARTIST'S WIFE NELLA IS MOTHER NATURE

IN THE CLOUDS - BACK LANE, WELSHPOOL , CAMPOBELLO ISLAND, N.B., CANADA

MERMAID - BUILDING IN WELSHPOOL, CAMPOBELLO ISLAND, N.B., CANADA • ARTIST'S WIFE NELLA IS THE MERMAID

WISTERIA - ARTIST'S GARDENER'S COTTAGE, NORTH MAIN ST., MUNCY, PA.

78 TRIBUTE TO MADONNA - BROADVIEW FARM, NEW HOPE ROAD, PINEVILLE, PA • POP STAR MADONNAS' FASHIONS

GALLERY MISCHIEF - FORMER B & S GALLERY, MARKET STREET, WILLIAMSPORT, PA.

SWEETHEART FARMS - SQUIRRELS IN THE ARTIST 'S GARDENS • RURAL ROADS AND FARMS OF MAHONING VALLEY, PA

79 FAUX DOG - THE STICK FENCES OF CAMPOBELLO ISLAND, N.B., CANADA

TRUCE - THE ARTIST WANTED THE CHALLENGE OF CREATING A LONG HORIZONTAL PAINTING • THE GAME LANDS NEAR ELIMSPORT, PA

80 LANDSCAPE WATERCOLORS - THE ARTIST HAS ALWAYS WANTED SUCH MAGICAL PAINT • ARTIST'S STUDIO, NORTH MAIN STREET, MUNCY, PA • CASTLE FROM COCHEM, GERMANY

81 TROJAN DOG - ARTIST'S DOG MCSNUTTER

82 ACROSS THE LANDSCAPE - ARTIST'S REACTION TO OUT OF CONTROL SUBURBAN SPRAWL

83 TALES OF MOONLIGHT - ARTIST'S STUDIO MAGIC

84 SANTA CLAUS VISITS THE MAHONSKIS - CLINTON AVENUE, SOUTH WILLIAMSPORT, PA

85 **CURRENT WORK IN PROGRESS - BACK LANE COMPOBELLO ISLAND, N.B. CANADA**

BACK COVER: 'MISTED' OPPORTUNITY - ARTIST'S CAT CREATURE COMFORTS • THE BUILDING IS IN WELSHPOOL, CAMPOBELLO ISLAND, N.B., CANADA

MISTED OPPORTUNITY - THEY GLIDE BY THOSE TWO SHIPS IN THE MOON MIST. TURN YOUR HEAD. GLANCE AWAY AND MISS THE LOVE OF YOUR LIFE OR THE CAT OF THE NIGHT.

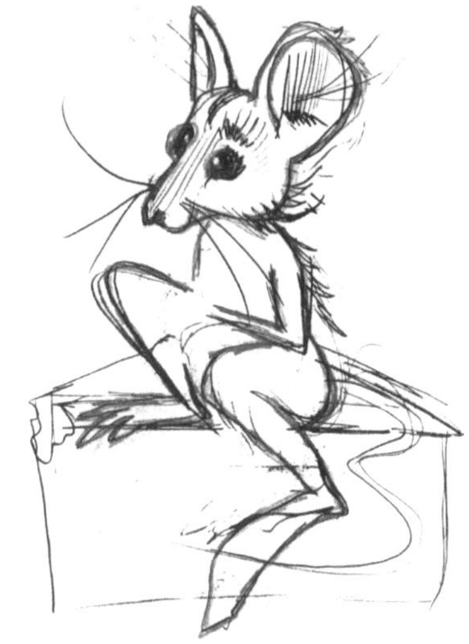

IF YOU OWN OR SUSPECT YOU HAVE A BRUCE STORM ORIGINAL PAINTING THAT IS NOT PICTURED IN THIS PUBLICATION, PLEASE CONTACT:

BRUCE STORM
114 SOUTH MAIN STREET
MUNCY, PA. 17756

FOR POSSIBLE INCLUSION IN FUTURE PROJECTS.

BOOK DESIGN
LAYOUT
&
PHOTGRAPHY
BY

' FREDERICK S. EATON '

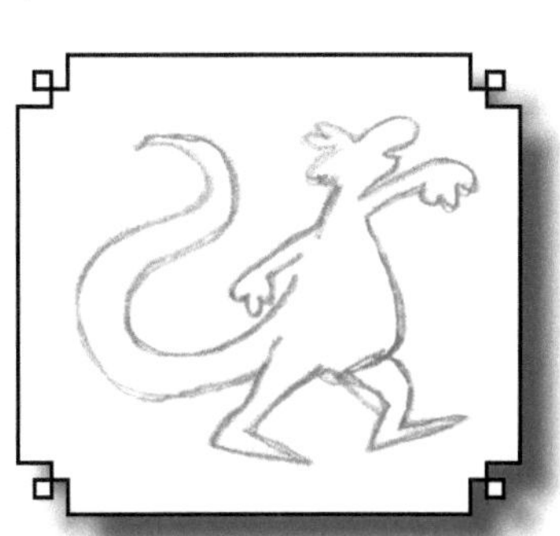

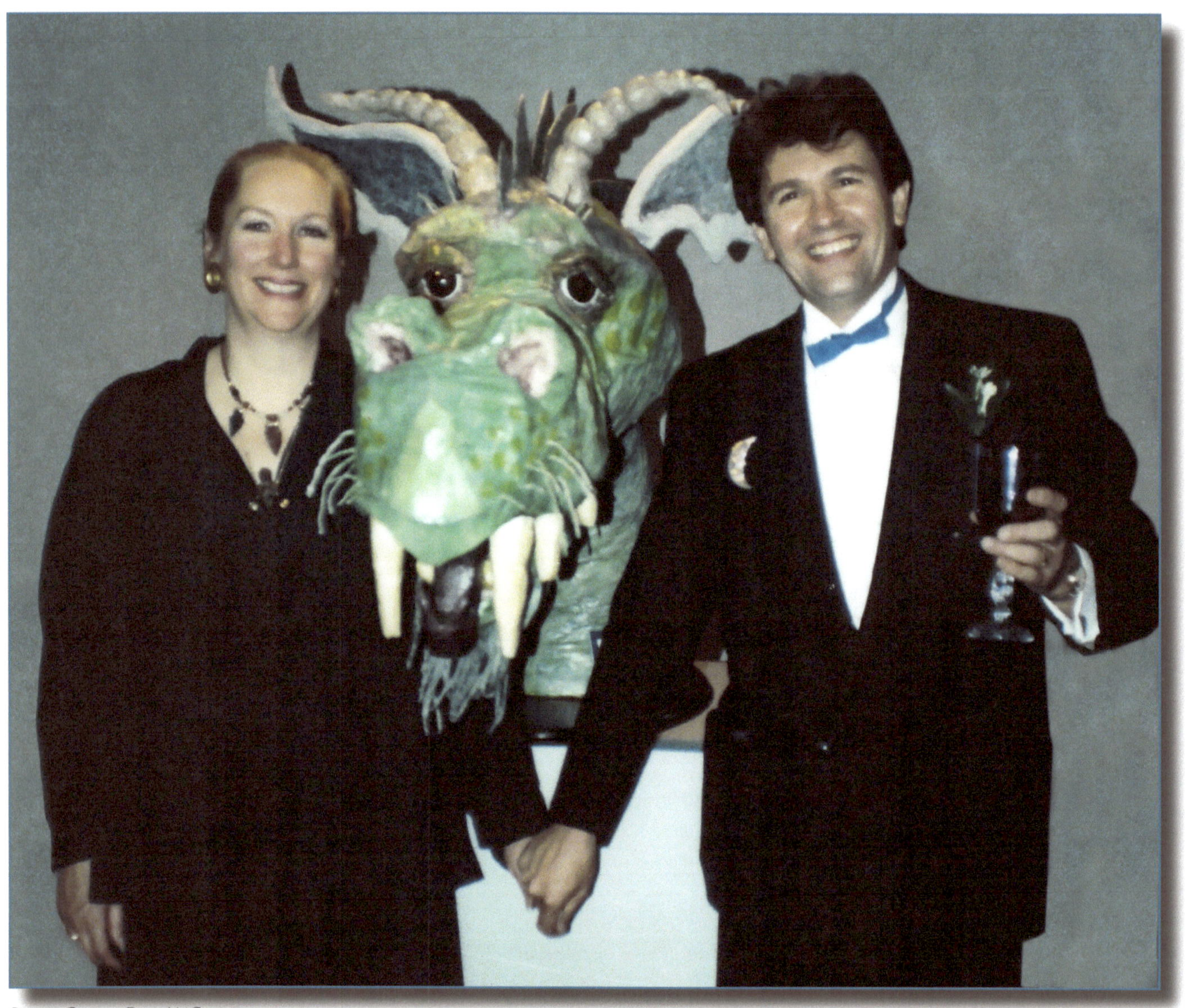

Photo Credit: Dave McGarvey

Frequently working en plein'air', storm concocts locales with architecture from different environs, thus a French Loire castle or a German one lands in his beloved Muncy Hills. Lanterns from along the strand plunk down in paintings of the artist's garden. Each piece is completely seen in the artist's mind before he begins working. Often the dragons, rabbits, mice, dogs, cats and other symbolic animals and heroes are developed in the artist's studio. These alter-egos add the humor, Poignancy, and philosophy that hallmarks storm's work. When a piece is completed he spends days studying it to live with his creation. Discussing it at length with his wife, Nella, it is then that she writes the saga which serves as the key to unlock the numerous layers of meaning in each painting. After the saga is written it is fine tuned by the artist. never does the saga develop prior to the painting.

www.ingramcontent.com/pod-product-compliance
Lightning Source LLC
LaVergne TN
LVHW070137110826
845147LV00002B/271

9780615184074